How to Use This Guide

This revision guide has been written and developed to help you get the most out of your revision.

This guide covers both Foundation and Higher Tier content.

HT Content that will only be tested on the Higher Tier papers appears in a pale yellow tinted box labelled with the HT symbol.

- The **coloured page headers** clearly identify the separate units, so that you can revise for each exam separately: Biology is red, Chemistry is purple, and Physics is blue.
- There are **practice questions** at the end of each unit so you can test yourself on what you've just learned. (The answers are given on pages 118–119 so you can mark your own answers.)
- You'll find **key v** [illegible] two-page sprea [illegible] colour within the text; higher tier key words are highlighted in orange. Make sure you know and understand all these words before moving on!
- There's a **glossary** at the back of the book. It contains all the key words from throughout the book so you can check any definitions you're not sure about.
- The **tick boxes** on the contents page let you track your revision progress: simply put a tick in the box next to each topic when you're confident that you know it.
- Don't just read the guide, **learn actively**! Constantly test yourself without looking at the text.

Good luck with your exams!

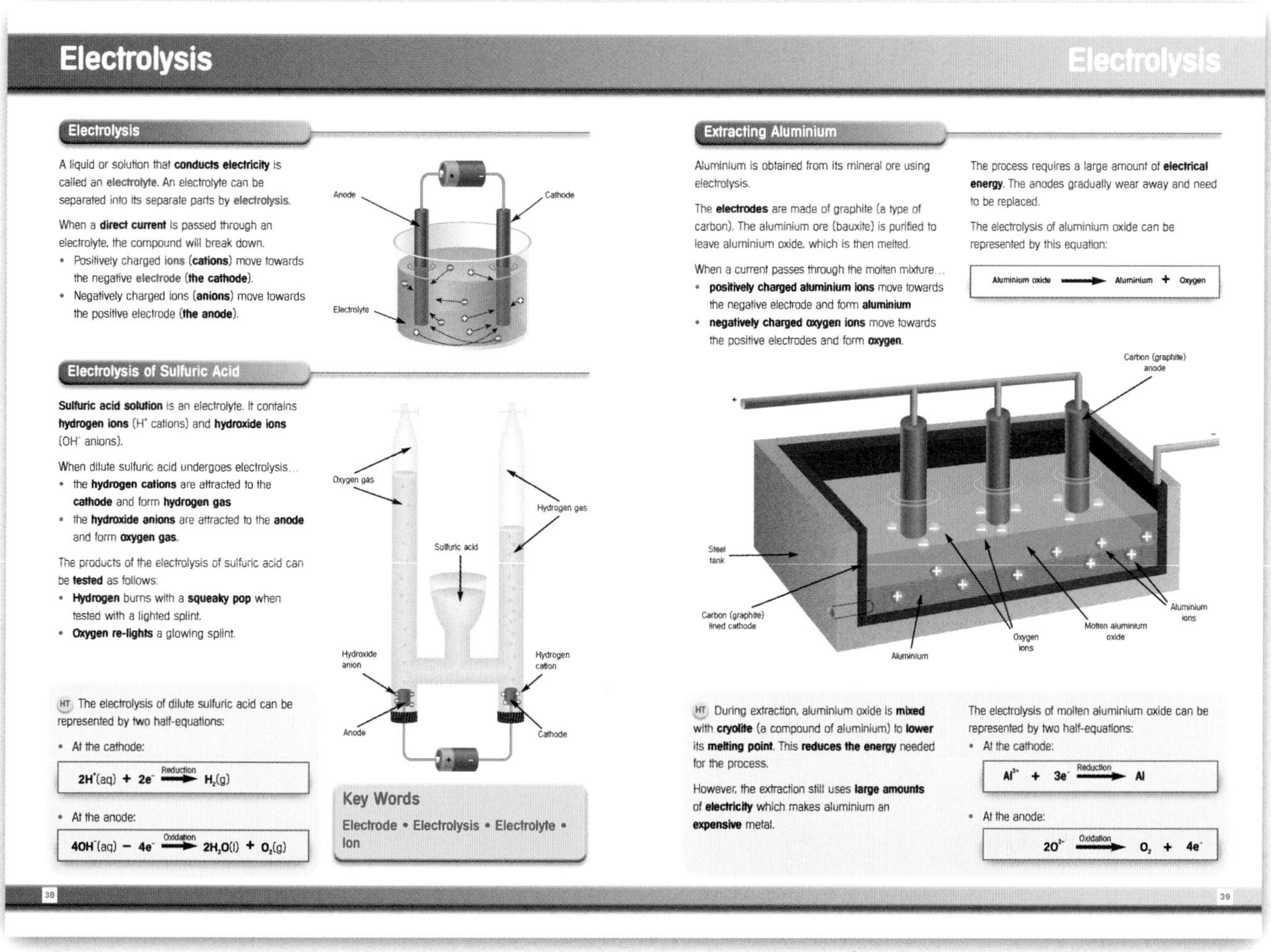

Electrolysis

Electrolysis

A liquid or solution that **conducts electricity** is called an **electrolyte**. An electrolyte can be separated into its separate parts by **electrolysis**.

When a **direct current** is passed through an electrolyte, the compound will break down.

- Positively charged **ions** (**cations**) move towards the negative **electrode** (**the cathode**).
- Negatively charged ions (**anions**) move towards the positive electrode (**the anode**).

Anode
Cathode
Electrolyte

Electrolysis of Sulfuric Acid

Sulfuric acid solution is an electrolyte. It contains **hydrogen ions** (H^+ cations) and **hydroxide ions** (OH^- anions).

When dilute sulfuric acid undergoes electrolysis...

- the **hydrogen cations** are attracted to the **cathode** and form **hydrogen gas**
- the **hydroxide anions** are attracted to the **anode** and form **oxygen gas**.

The products of the electrolysis of sulfuric acid can be **tested** as follows:

- **Hydrogen** burns with a **squeaky pop** when tested with a lighted splint.
- **Oxygen re-lights** a glowing splint.

Oxygen gas
Hydrogen gas
Sulfuric acid
Hydroxide anion
Hydrogen cation
Anode
Cathode

HT The electrolysis of dilute sulfuric acid can be represented by two half-equations:

- At the cathode:

$$2H^+(aq) + 2e^- \xrightarrow{\text{Reduction}} H_2(g)$$

- At the anode:

$$4OH^-(aq) - 4e^- \xrightarrow{\text{Oxidation}} 2H_2O(l) + O_2(g)$$

Key Words

Electrode • Electrolysis • Electrolyte • Ion

38

Extracting Aluminium

Aluminium is obtained from its mineral ore using electrolysis.

The **electrodes** are made of graphite (a type of carbon). The aluminium ore (bauxite) is purified to leave aluminium oxide, which is then melted.

When a current passes through the molten mixture...

- **positively charged aluminium ions** move towards the negative electrode and form **aluminium**
- **negatively charged oxygen ions** move towards the positive electrodes and form **oxygen**.

The process requires a large amount of **electrical energy**. The anodes gradually wear away and need to be replaced.

The electrolysis of aluminium oxide can be represented by this equation:

Aluminium oxide ⟶ Aluminium + Oxygen

Carbon (graphite) anode
Steel tank
Carbon (graphite) lined cathode
Aluminium
Oxygen ions
Molten aluminium oxide
Aluminium ions

HT During extraction, aluminium oxide is **mixed** with **cryolite** (a compound of aluminium) to **lower** its **melting point**. This **reduces the energy** needed for the process.

However, the extraction still uses **large amounts** of **electricity** which makes aluminium an **expensive** metal.

The electrolysis of molten aluminium oxide can be represented by two half-equations:

- At the cathode:

$$Al^{3+} + 3e^- \xrightarrow{\text{Reduction}} Al$$

- At the anode:

$$2O^{2-} \xrightarrow{\text{Oxidation}} O_2 + 4e^-$$

39

Contents

Contents

Molecules of Life

Cells

Fundamental processes of life take place inside cells. All cells contain the following:

- **Cytoplasm,** where many chemical reactions take place.
- A **cell membrane**, which controls movement in and out of the cell.
- A **nucleus,** which contains the genetic information and controls what the cell does.
- **Mitochondria** – **respiration** takes place inside mitochondria, supplying energy for the cell.

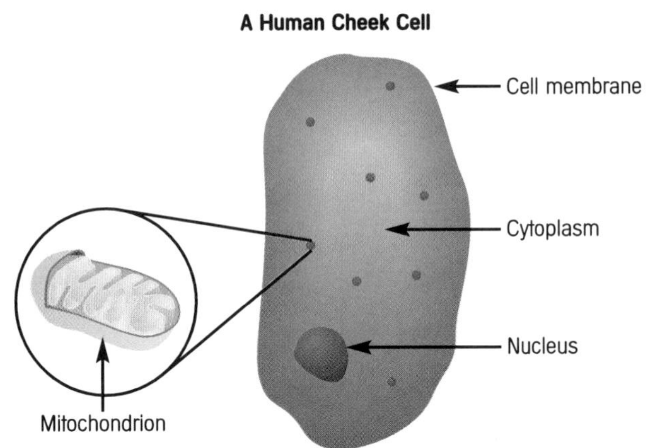

DNA

The **nucleus** of each cell contains a complete set of **genetic instructions**. The instructions are carried by **genes** on **chromosomes**. Genes are made from a chemical called **DNA** (deoxyribonucleic acid).

A DNA molecule is made of two strands coiled around each other in a **double helix** (spiral). The genetic instructions are in the form of a chemical code made up of four **bases** (A, T, C and G). These **bases** bond together in pairs, forming the cross-links.

Before a cell divides, it **copies** its DNA (**DNA replication**). So, each new cell contains a complete set of **genetic information** which it can pass on.

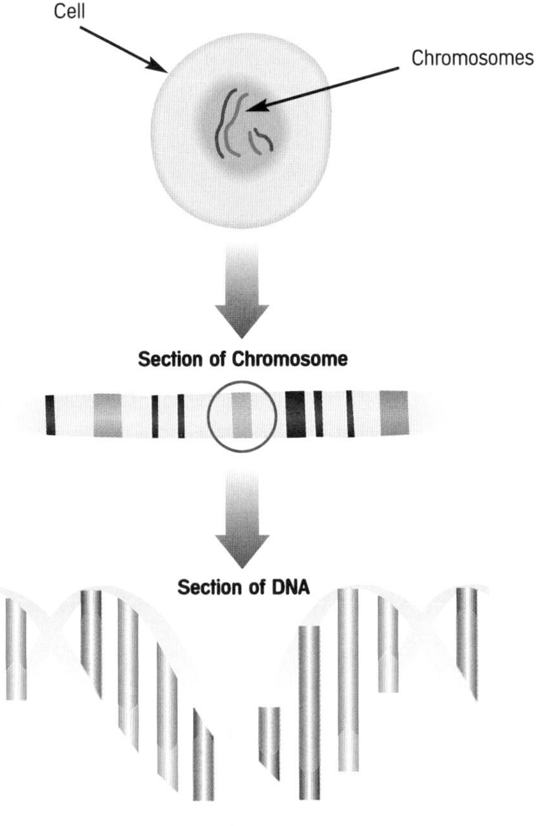

Key Words

Chromosome • Cytoplasm • DNA • DNA fingerprinting • Gene • Mitochondria • Nucleus • Protein • Respiration

HT The four bases in DNA are **A** (adenine), **C** (cytosine), **G** (guanine) and **T** (thymine).

On opposite strands of the DNA molecule…

- A always bonds with T
- C always bonds with G.

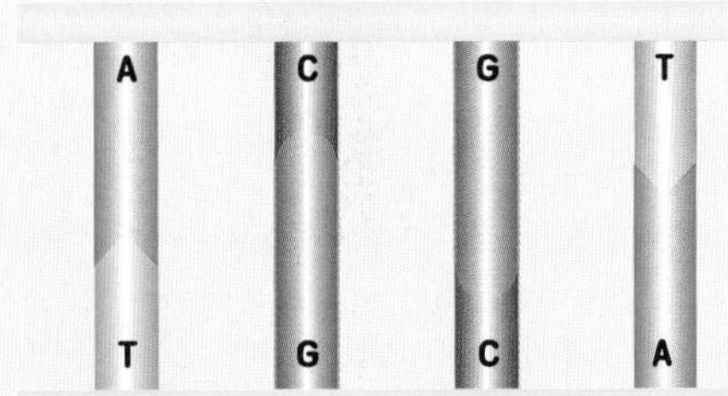

HT DNA Replication

A cell can make an exact copy of its DNA molecule in the following way:

1. The double helix 'unzips'.
2. New bases pair up with the exposed bases on each strand.
3. An enzyme bonds the new bases together to form complementary strands.
4. Two identical pieces of DNA are formed. Strand A has made a copy of strand B, and strand B has made a copy of strand A.

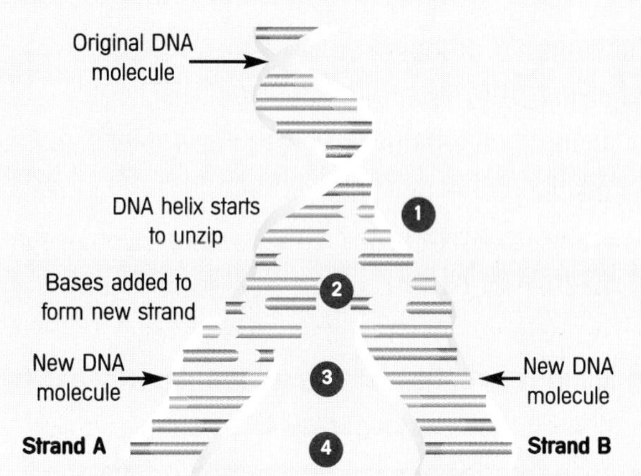

Protein Synthesis

DNA controls which **proteins** a cell synthesises (makes). Each **gene** codes for a **particular protein**.

Proteins are made up of **chains** of **amino acids**. The cell uses the amino acids that you get from your diet to make proteins.

Proteins are essential for the growth and repair of cells.

HT The **sequence of bases** in a gene represents the order in which the cell should assemble amino acids to make the protein. A group of **three bases** represents **one amino acid** in a protein chain. Each protein has a different function.

Your liver changes some amino acids into other amino acids in a process called **transamination**. Essential amino acids are the ones you must get from your diet because your body can't make them.

DNA Fingerprinting

Each person's DNA is **unique**, so it can be used for **identification** in a technique called **DNA fingerprinting**. For example, blood found at a crime scene can be compared with samples of suspects' DNA.

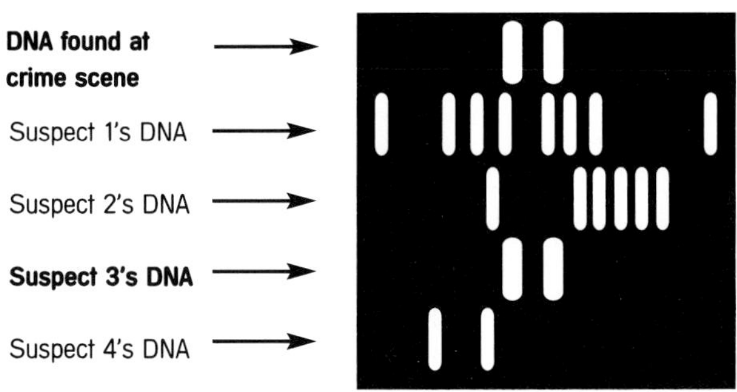

You can see that the unique DNA fingerprint from the blood sample found at the crime scene matches exactly with the DNA fingerprint of Suspect 3.

HT To make a DNA fingerprint, a sample of DNA is needed. DNA fingerprinting is carried out in four stages:

1. **Isolation** – DNA is extracted from blood, hair follicles or semen.
2. **Fragmentation** – the DNA is cut into fragments using **restriction** enzymes.
3. **Separation** – the DNA sections are separated using a technique called **electrophoresis**.
4. **Comparison** – the DNA fingerprint is analysed by comparing it with a reference sample, e.g. blood taken from the crime scene.

Molecules of Life

Enzymes

Enzymes are **proteins** which act as biological **catalysts**. They speed up chemical reactions, including those that take place in living cells, e.g. respiration, photosynthesis and protein synthesis.

Enzymes are highly specific. Each one will only speed up a **particular** reaction.

Enzyme activity, and therefore the rate of a reaction, can be affected by changes in **temperature** or **pH level**.

Enzyme Activity

A rise in temperature increases the enzyme activity until the **optimum temperature** is reached. Temperatures **above the optimum** permanently **damage** or **denature** the enzyme molecules, decreasing or stopping enzyme activity.

Different enzymes have different optimum temperatures. Enzymes in your body work best at about 37°C.

There is an **optimum pH** at which an enzyme works best. As the pH increases or decreases, the enzyme becomes less and less effective.

The optimum pH of different enzymes can vary considerably.

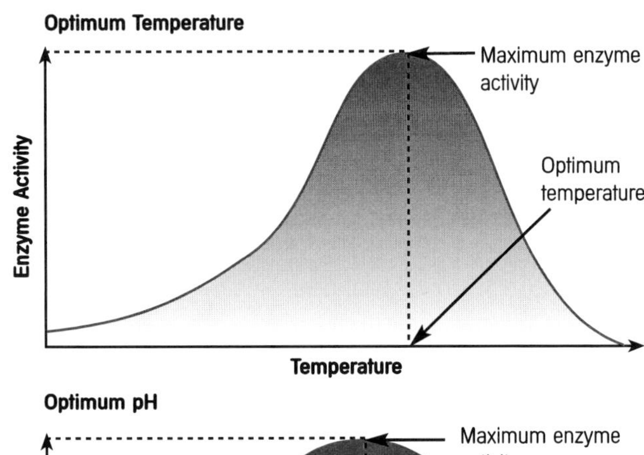

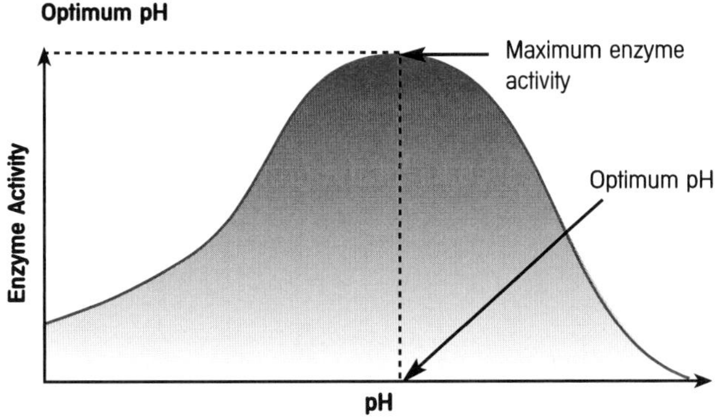

HT The Lock and Key Mechanism

Each **enzyme** has a different number and sequence of **amino acids**. This results in different shaped molecules which have different functions.

Each enzyme has an **active site** that only a specific reactant can fit into (like a key in a lock).

When enzyme molecules are exposed to high temperatures or extreme pH, the following occurs:

1. The bonds holding the shape of the protein break.
2. The shape of the enzyme's active site is **denatured** (changed irreversibly).
3. The 'lock and key' mechanism no longer works.

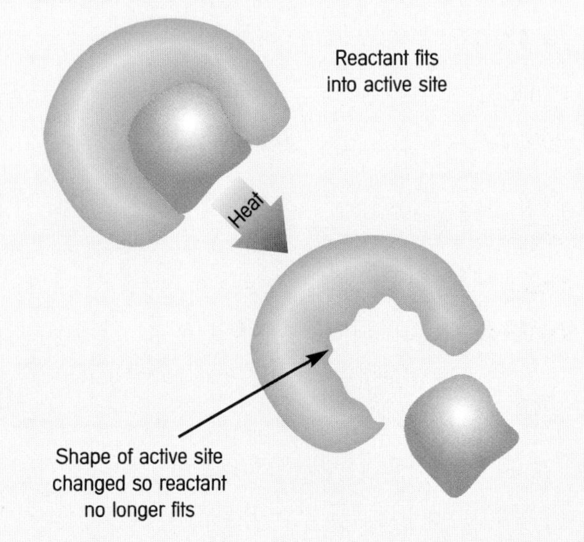

Diffusion

Living cells have to...

- obtain oxygen, glucose, water and minerals from their surroundings
- get rid of waste products, such as carbon dioxide.

These substances pass through the cell membrane by **diffusion**.

Diffusion is the movement of a substance from a region of **high concentration** to a region **of low concentration**.

A cell has...

- a low concentration of oxygen **inside** the cell (supplies are constantly being used up in respiration)
- a high concentration **outside** the cell (oxygen is constantly being replaced).

HT Particles move about in lots of different directions. This is called **random movement**. Diffusion is the **net (overall) movement** of particles from an area of high concentration to an area of low concentration.

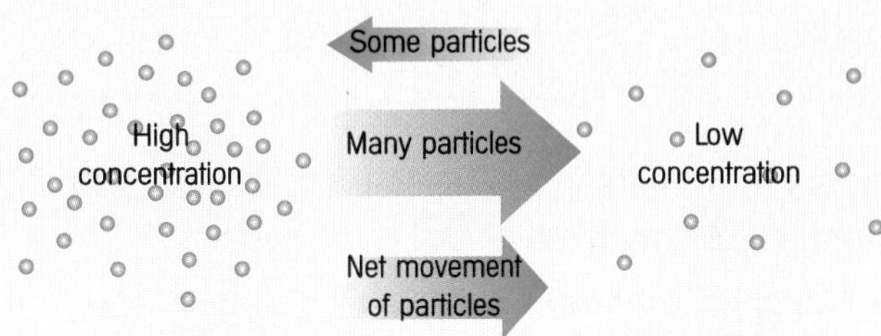

The **rate** of **diffusion** is increased when...

- there's a greater surface area of the cell membrane
- there's a greater difference between concentrations (a steeper gradient)
- the particles have a shorter distance to travel.

Diffusion in Plants

Carbon dioxide (CO_2) and oxygen (O_2) move in and out of plants through their leaves. During the day...

- **carbon dioxide** is used up in **photosynthesis**. The concentration inside the leaves is lower than the concentration outside the leaves.
- carbon dioxide diffuses into plants through the stomata (tiny pores) on the bottom of their leaves
- oxygen, a product of photosynthesis, diffuses from the plant into the atmosphere.

At **night**, photosynthesis stops. Oxygen diffuses into leaf cells and carbon dioxide diffuses out of leaf cells.

Water is lost from plant leaves by **evaporation**. Water **diffuses** out of cells into spaces in the spongy **mesophyll layer**. It then passes out of the leaf and **evaporates** into the atmosphere.

Magnified Cross-section of Leaf

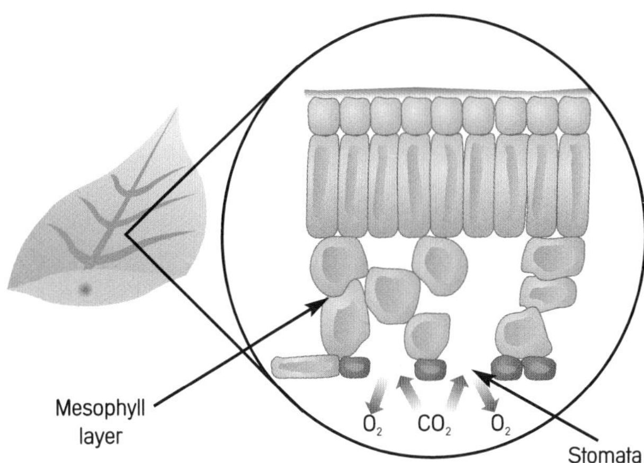

HT The **stomata** on the underside of leaves are specially adapted to...

- **open** – to help increase the rate of diffusion of carbon dioxide and oxygen
- **close** – to prevent excessive water loss in drought conditions.

Key Words

Enzyme • Catalyst • Denatured • Diffusion • Photosynthesis • Protein

Diffusion

Gaseous Exchange

In animals…

- **oxygen** enters the blood in the **lungs**, and **leaves** the blood in **body tissues**
- **carbon dioxide** enters the blood in body tissues, and **leaves** the blood in the **lungs**.

In the lungs…

- carbon dioxide **diffuses** from the blood into alveoli
- oxygen (from the air) diffuses from the alveoli into the blood.

This process is called **gaseous exchange**.

HT The alveoli are specially adapted for efficient gaseous exchange. They have a…

- huge surface area as there are so many of them
- moist permeable surface only one cell thick
- very good blood supply.

A Single Alveolus and a Capillary

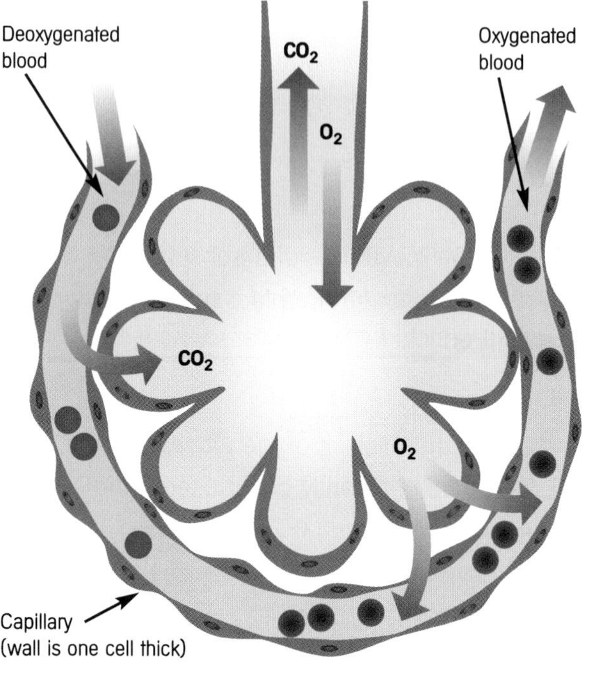

Exchange Surfaces

Food enters the body in the **small intestine**. The large and insoluble food molecules are **digested** into smaller, soluble molecules (glucose, amino acids, fatty acids and glycerol). The molecules **diffuse** into the **blood** and are carried to the body tissues where they **diffuse into cells**.

A **growing foetus** inside the uterus has no direct access to food or oxygen. So, the foetus…

- **receives** oxygen, food and water from the mother's blood, via the placenta
- **excretes** carbon dioxide and other waste products (urea) by diffusion through the placenta into the mother's blood.

HT Exchange surfaces are adapted for **efficient diffusion**.

- They have a **large surface area**:
  - intestine is folded into **villi** covered in **microvilli** (tiny extension of cells of villi)
  - placenta is folded to create large surface area
- They have a **good blood supply** so are able to remove substances quickly.

HT Transmitter Substances

Neurones (nerve cells) have very small gaps between them, called **synapses**. In order to carry signals from one neurone to the next, an electrical nerve impulse has to cross the synapse.

When an impulse reaches the **synapse**:

1. A chemical transmitter is released.
2. The transmitter crosses the synapse by diffusion.
3. The nerve impulse is carried across.

The Blood

Blood has **four** components – platelets, plasma, white blood cells and red blood cells.

Platelets clump together when a blood vessel becomes damaged in order to produce a **clot**.

Plasma transports several substances around the body including...

- carbon dioxide from the cells to the lungs
- glucose from the small intestine to the cells
- waste products from the liver to the kidneys
- hormones to the target organs
- antibodies to fight disease.

White blood cells protect the body against disease. Some have a flexible shape which allows them to engulf disease-causing microorganisms.

Red blood cells transport oxygen from the lungs to the tissues. They...

- are small and flexible, so they can pass through narrow blood vessels
- don't have a nucleus, so they can be packed with **haemoglobin**.

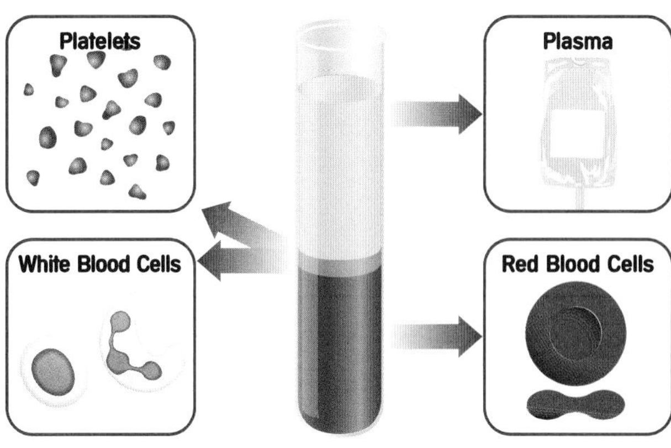

HT The small size and biconcave shape of red blood cells gives them a **large** **surface area : volume ratio** for transferring oxygen. When the cells reach the lungs, oxygen diffuses from the lungs into the blood.

The haemoglobin molecules in the red blood cells bind with the oxygen to form **oxyhaemoglobin**.

The blood is then pumped around the body to the tissues, where the reverse reaction takes place. Oxygen is released which diffuses into cells.

The Circulatory System

The different parts of the circulatory system work together to transport substances around the body.

Blood moves around the body in **arteries**, **veins** and **capillaries**:

- **Arteries** transport blood **away** from the **heart.**
- **Veins** transport **blood** towards the **heart.**
- **Capillaries** exchange materials with tissues.

The heart pumps blood around the body:

- The **right hand side** of the heart pumps blood **to the lungs**.
- The **left hand side** of the heart pumps blood to the rest of **the body**.
- Blood pumped into the arteries is under much higher pressure than the blood in the veins.

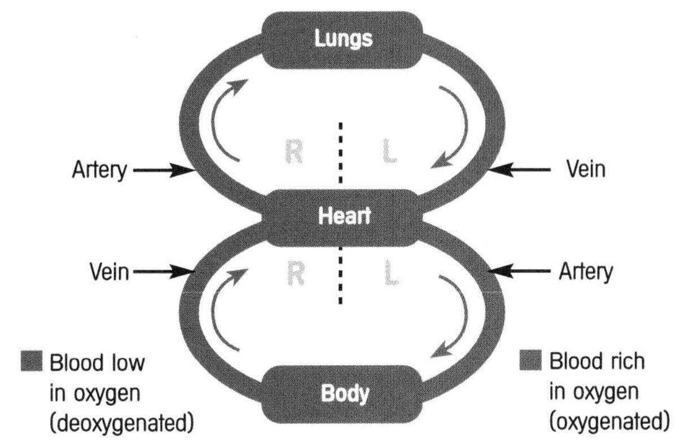

Key Words

Artery • Capillary • Diffusion • Haemoglobin • Oxyhaemoglobin • Surface area : volume ratio • Synapse • Vein

Keep it Moving

HT More on the Circulatory System

Mammals have a **double circulatory system**, i.e. it consists of two loops. The advantage of this is that blood is pumped to the body at a higher pressure than it is pumped to the lungs. This provides a much greater rate of flow to the body tissues.

Arteries, veins and capillaries have special adaptations to help with their function:

- **Arteries** have to cope with a high pressure of blood so they have a **thick wall** made of **elastic muscle fibres**.
- **Veins** have a **lumen** which is much bigger compared to the thickness of the walls. They have **valves** to prevent the backflow of blood.
- **Capillaries** are the only blood vessels that have **thin permeable** walls, to allow the **exchange of substances** between cells and the blood.

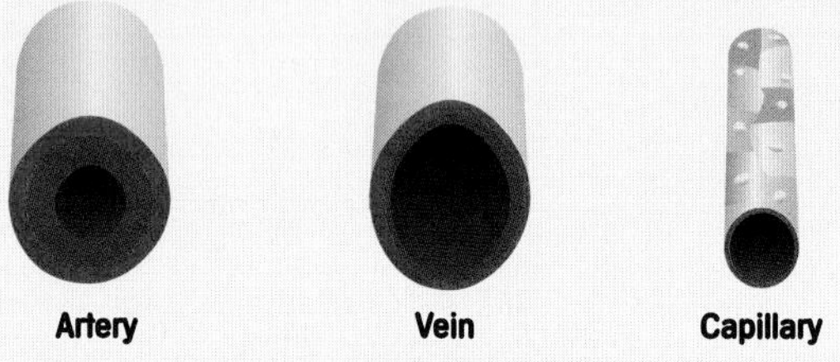

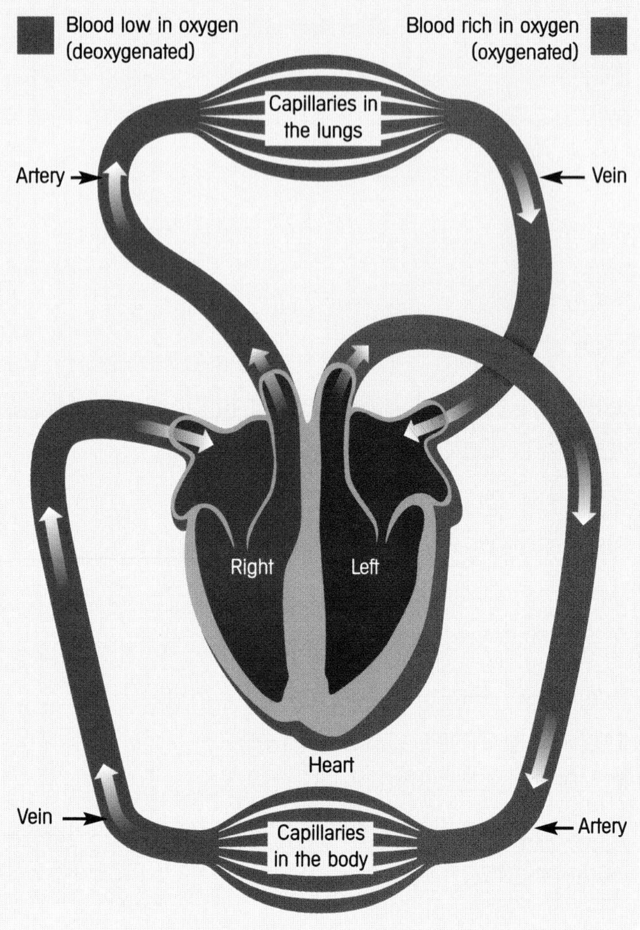

The Heart

Most of the wall of the heart is made of muscle. There are four main chambers:

- left and right **ventricles**
- left and right **atria**.

Ventricles contract to pump blood out of the heart. The right ventricle pumps blood a short distance to the lungs. The left ventricle is **more muscular** because it pumps blood under **higher pressure** around the whole body.

Atria receive blood coming back to the heart through the veins.

Semilunar, tricuspid and bicuspid **valves** make sure that the blood flows in the right direction (i.e. not backwards).

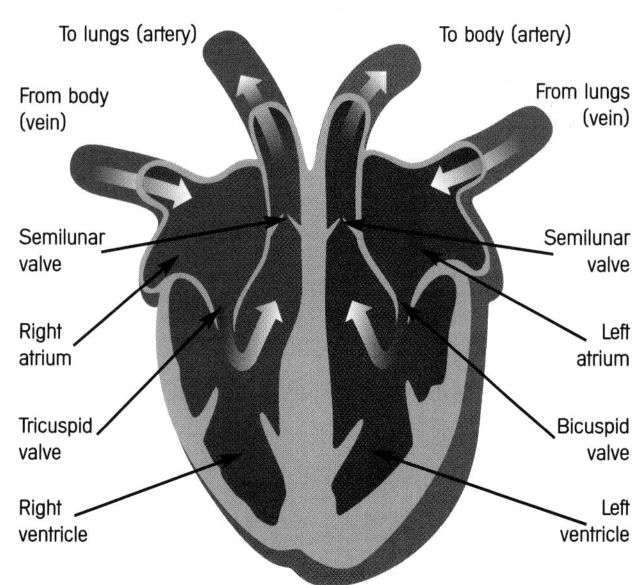

Coronary Heart Disease

Eating foods high in **saturated fat** and **cholesterol** can increase the amount of cholesterol in your arteries. A build up of cholesterol in arteries can restrict or stop blood flow.

The coronary artery supplies essential glucose and oxygen to the heart muscle. If it becomes blocked the heart muscle around it can die, causing a heart attack.

HT A build up of cholesterol can cause a hard plaque to form in the wall of the artery. This plaque bulges into the lumen, restricting or blocking blood flow through the artery.

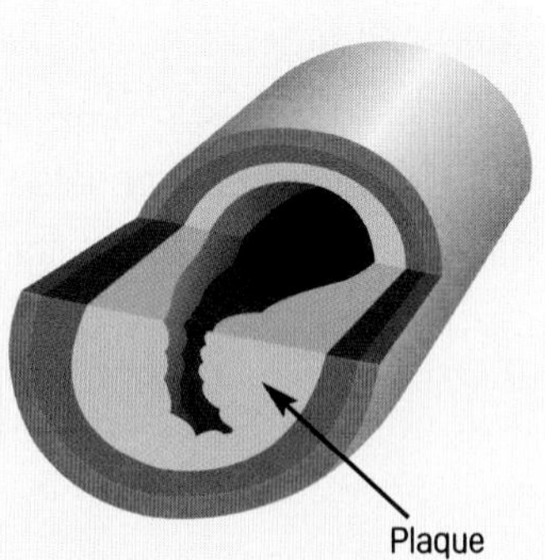

Mending the Heart

A diseased / damaged heart, or parts of a heart, can be replaced **mechanically** or **biologically**.

A pacemaker is a **mechanical** device implanted into the chest that stimulates the heart so that it beats in a regular rhythm. Pacemakers are powered by small batteries, which need to be replaced every two years, requiring a small operation.

Heart valves can be replaced with **mechanical** or **biological** valves if they become weak. Mechanical valves are more durable, but...

- they can cause blood clots, so the patient must take **anticoagulants** (blood thinning drugs) for the rest of their life
- the body's immune system can reject implants and surrounding tissues may die.

Heart Transplants

A severely diseased heart can be replaced in a **heart transplant**.

Some **problems** with heart transplants include:

- There's a shortage of donor hearts.
- The donor heart has to be the right size and age for the patient.
- The donor and the patient must have the same **blood type and tissue type** to avoid rejection.
- The patient has to take immunosuppressant drugs for the rest of their life to prevent their immune system from rejecting the new heart.

HT Many factors need to be considered when deciding whether a patient needs a heart transplant, pacemaker, or replacement valves fitted.

Heart pacemaker and valve replacement:

- Relatively minor operations.
- Pacemakers and valves can be mechanical, so a human donor isn't needed.
- Shorter waiting time than for a donor heart.
- Patient needs to take anticoagulants for rest of life.

Heart Transplant:

- Major, expensive operation.
- Replacement heart must come from a dead donor.
- Long waiting time for suitable donor (must be right age, size, etc.).
- Patient needs to take immunosuppressants for the rest of their life.
- Transplanted organ will last for the lifetime of the patient so it will not need to be replaced.

Key Words

Cholesterol • Saturated fat

Divide and Rule

Multi-Cell Organisms

Multi-cell organisms (e.g. animals and humans) are **large** and **complex**. They have **specialised** organs which contain differentiated cells to carry out functions like gas exchange and digestion.

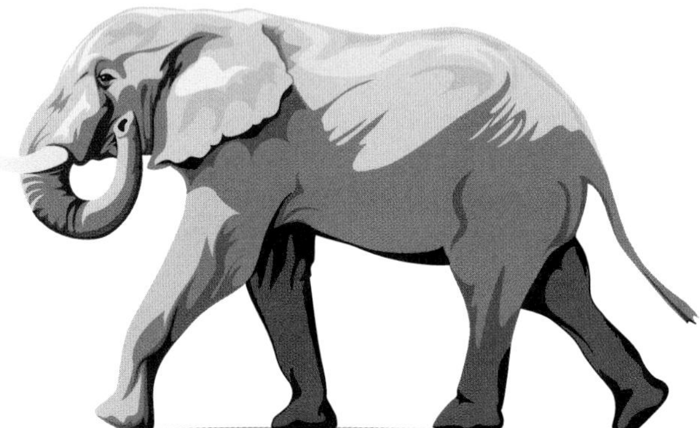

HT The advantage of being multi-cellular is that many smaller cells have a **larger** **surface area: volume ratio** than a single large one.

Diffusion of substances in and out of several smaller cells will therefore be much faster and more efficient.

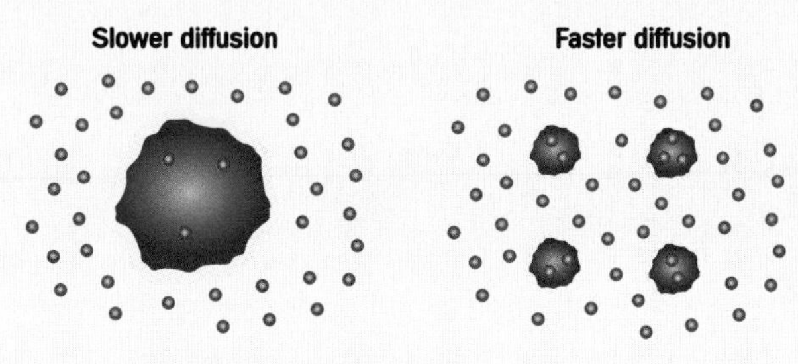

Cells and Gametes

In mammals, most body cells are **diploid** which means that they contain two sets of chromosomes. But, some cells can be **haploid** which means they contain only one set of chromosomes.

Gametes are sex cells (eggs and sperm). They are specialised **haploid** cells.

An **ovum** (egg cell) is a large cell because it needs to contain massive food reserves for the developing embryo. The nucleus contains one set of chromosomes from the **mother**.

A **sperm** is a tiny cell with a tail which makes it very mobile. It contains many mitochondria to supply the energy needed for swimming.

On contact with the ovum, its **acrosome** (cap-like structure on its 'head') bursts. This releases enzymes that digest the egg cell's membrane, allowing the sperm nucleus, containing one set of chromosomes from the **father**, to enter.

Sperm are produced and released in vast numbers to increase the chance of fertilisation occurring.

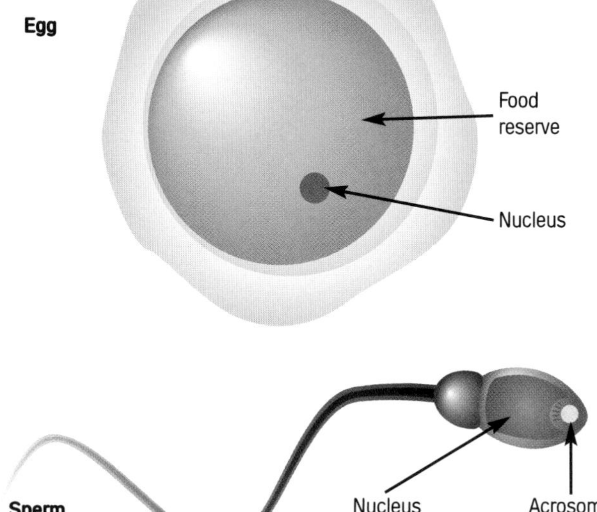

N.B. These egg and sperm images are not to scale.

Key Words

Diploid • Fertilisation • Gamete • Haploid • Meiosis • Mitosis • Specialised • Surface area : volume ratio • Zygote

Mitosis

Mitosis is the process by which a diploid cell **divides** to produce two more diploid cells. It produces new cells...

- for growth
- to repair damaged tissue
- to replace old cells.

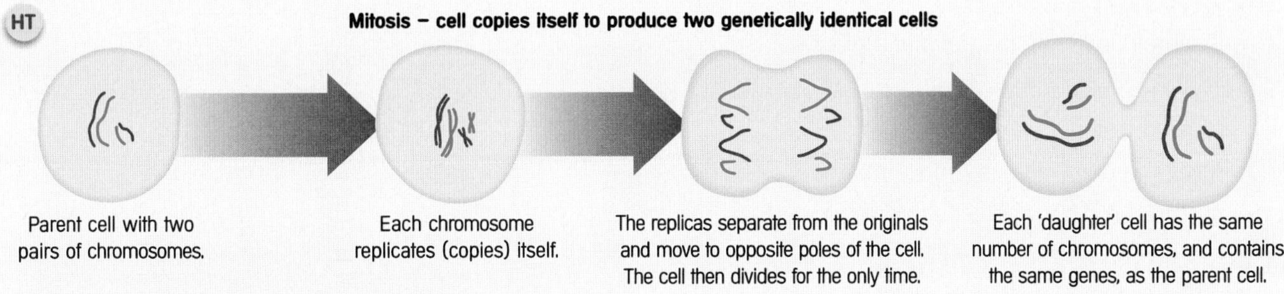

Meiosis

Meiosis is a type of cell division which occurs in the testes and ovaries. The cells in these organs divide to produce **gametes** for sexual reproduction. Meiosis introduces **variation**.

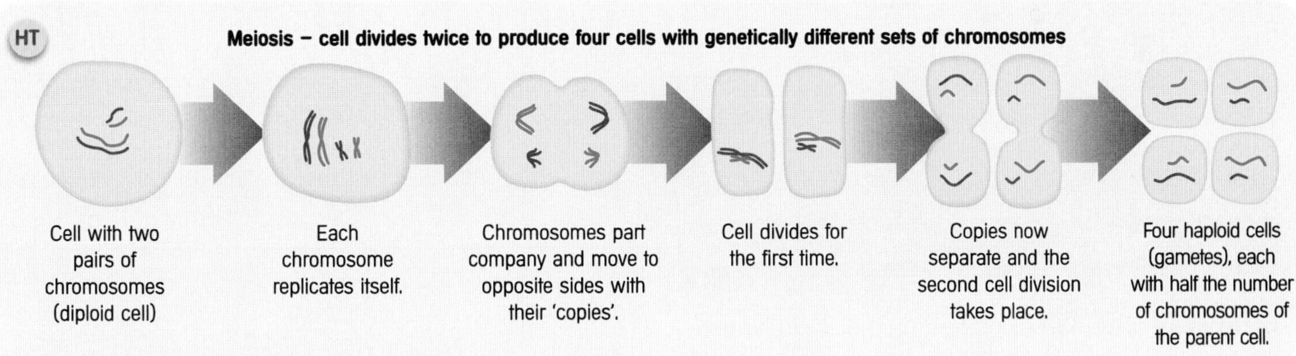

Fertilisation

Fertilisation occurs during sexual reproduction. Two gametes (egg and sperm) fuse together to form a **diploid zygote** (fertilised egg). The diploid zygote has **two sets** of chromosomes.

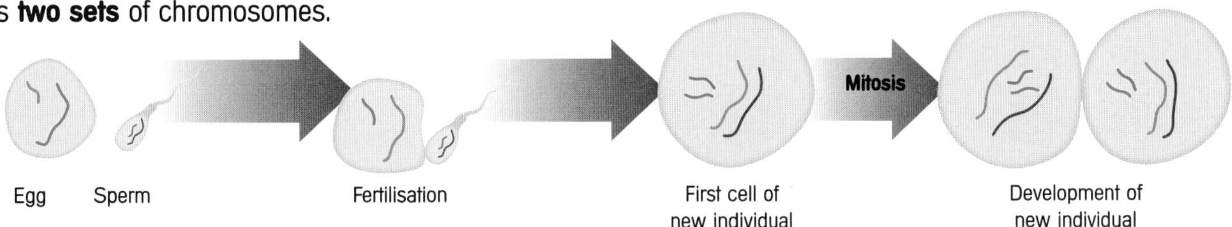

Growing Up

Plant Cells

Plant and animal cells contain a nucleus, cell membrane, and cytoplasm. Plant cells also contain...

- **chloroplasts**
- a **cellulose cell wall** to provide support
- a **vacuole** which contains cell sap and helps to provide support.

Use this method to see the parts of a plant cell:

1. Use tweezers to peel a thin layer of skin tissue from an onion.
2. Place the onion tissue onto a microscope slide on top of a drop of distilled water.
3. Add a drop of distilled water and a drop of iodine to the tissue and carefully cover the slide.
4. Look at the onion cell through the microscope at x100 magnification.

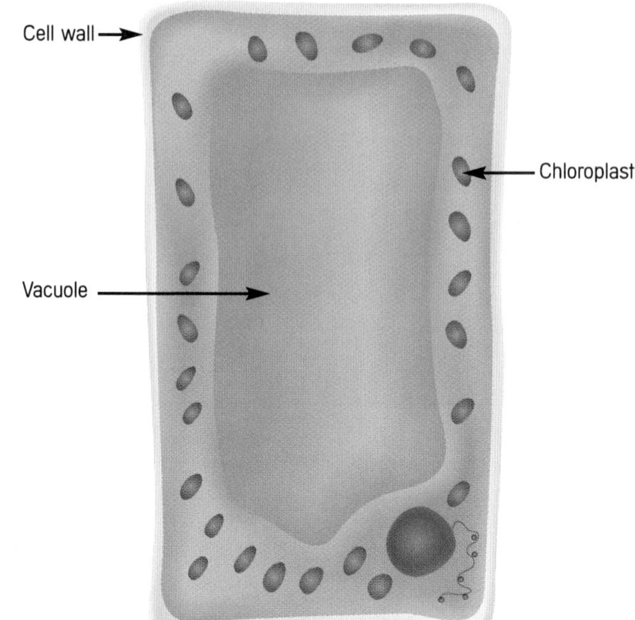

Growth

Growth involves both **cell division** and **cell differentiation**. Animals grow by increasing the number of cells. The cells **specialise** or **differentiate** into different types of cell at an early stage to form tissues and organs.

An animal will eventually stop growing. But, given the right conditions, many plants can grow continuously.

HT **Cell enlargement** is the main method by which plants gain height.

Cell division is mainly restricted to the tips of the roots and shoots.

Unlike animal cells, plant cells retain the ability to differentiate or specialise throughout their lives.

Stem Cells

Stem cells are undifferentiated animal cells, which can specialise and develop into different types of cells, tissues and organs.

HT There are a lot of potential uses for stem cells. Scientists believe that stem cells could potentially be used in many ways including for research, drug testing and transplants.

For research, scientists need to obtain large numbers of embryos to grow the stem cells in the laboratory. At present, unused embryos from IVF (*in vitro* fertilisation) treatments are used.

There are opposing views about obtaining embryos for stem cell research.

For – Embryos left over from an IVF treatment would otherwise be destroyed, so it's a good use for them.

Against – It's wrong to experiment on embryos because they have the potential to become a human being.

Gestation and Growth

The larger and more complex an organism is, the longer the **gestation period** (pregnancy) will be. For example, the average gestation period for a...

- mouse is 19 days
- human is 266 days

A human foetus grows very quickly in the uterus. Different body parts develop at different rates.

The head and brain grow rapidly at first to coordinate the complex growth of the rest of the body.

The five main stages to human growth are **infancy**, **childhood**, **adolescence** (puberty), **maturity** (adulthood) and **old age**.

The Five Main Stages of Human Growth

Baby Growth

A human baby's weight and growth are carefully monitored for the first few years to ensure that measurements are normal for a child of that age.

Example

The **weight** and **head circumference** of a baby were measured once a month for a year. The measurements are plotted on the graphs.

By comparing the baby's measurements to the normal range, you can see that the baby's measurements were towards the lower end of healthy weight and head circumference.

HT **Head circumference** is an indication of whether the brain is growing normally. Weight (proportional to length) reveals if the baby is getting enough food to grow healthily.

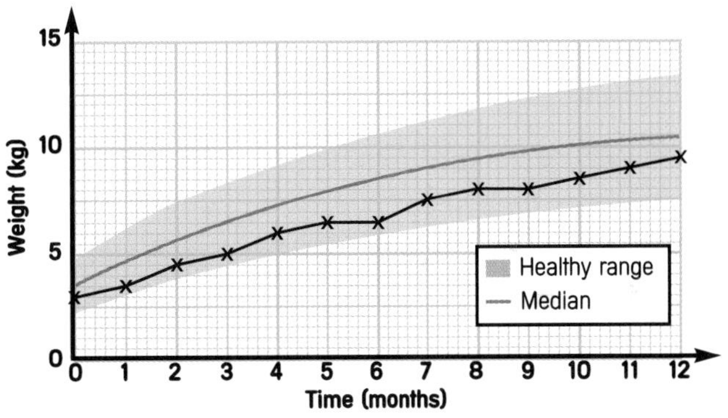

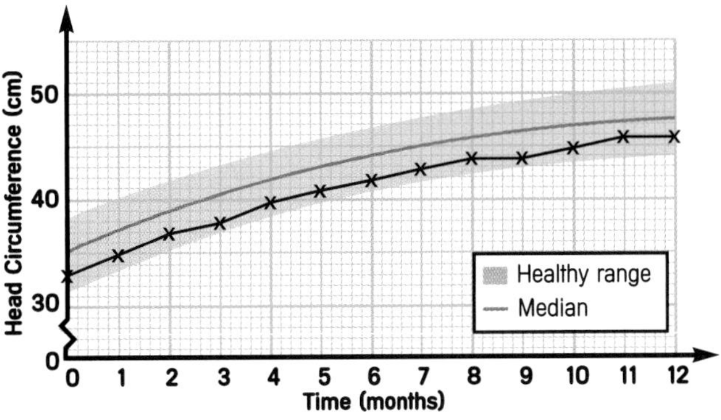

Childhood and Adolescent Growth

Your body grows fastest during infancy and early childhood, with another growth spurt in adolescence during puberty. As an adult (18 and over) you will grow very little, if at all.

Key Words

Differentiation • Stem cells

Controlling Plant Growth

Plant Hormones

Plant **hormones (auxins)** are chemicals that control...

- the growth of shoots and roots
- flowering
- the ripening of fruits.

The hormones move through the plant in solution. They affect its growth by responding to **gravity** (**geotropism**) and **light** (**phototropism**).

Shoots grow...

- towards light (positive phototropism)
- against gravity (negative geotropism).

Roots grow...

- away from light (negative phototropism)
- downwards in the direction of gravity (positive geotropism).

Experiment to show that shoots grow towards light.

1. Cut a hole in the side of a box. Put three cuttings into the box. The cuttings detect light coming from the side, and will grow towards it.
2. Cut a hole in the side of another box. Put three cuttings with foil-covered tips in the box. These shoots can't detect the light so they grow straight up.

Hole

Plant cuttings

Hole

Tin foil

HT **Auxin** is made in the shoot **tip**. Its distribution through the plant is determined by light, and can, therefore, be unequal. This is what happens when light shines on a shoot:

1. The hormones in direct sunlight are destroyed.
2. The hormones on the shaded side continue to function, causing the cells to elongate (lengthen).
3. The shoot bends towards the light.

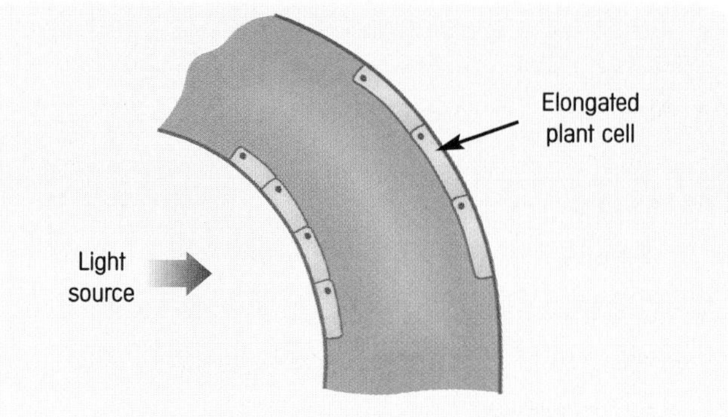

Commercial Uses of Hormones

Plant hormones can be used in agriculture to speed up or slow down plant growth:

- **Rooting powder** – a hormone which encourages the growth of roots in stem cuttings, so many plants can be obtained from one plant.
- **Fruit-ripening hormone** – causes fruit to ripen. Ripening can be accelerated or delayed if required for transportation or storage.
- **Selective weedkillers** – hormones in the weedkiller disrupt the growth patterns of their target plants without harming other plants.
- **Control of dormancy** – hormones can be used to speed up or slow down plant growth and bud development.

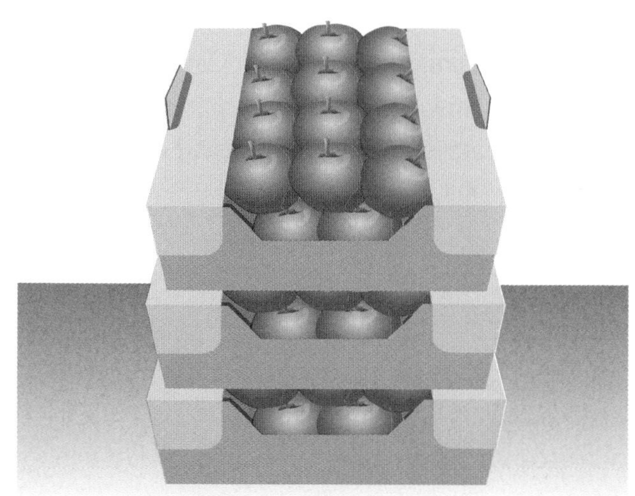

Mutations

Gene **mutations** are changes to **genes**. These changes can be spontaneous, but the rate can be increased by environmental factors such as radiation or chemicals. **Most** mutations are **harmful** although **occasionally** a **beneficial mutation** occurs.

HT Mutations change the base sequence of **DNA**. This alters or prevents the production of the protein that the gene normally codes for.

Selective Breeding

Selective breeding can be used in the development of plants and animals.

Animals or plants with favourable characteristics are **selected** and **deliberately crossbred** to produce offspring with the desired characteristics. These offspring can then also be selected and bred until the desired result is achieved. But, it can take many, many generations to get the desired results.

Selective breeding can contribute to **improved agricultural** yields in animals and crops. For example:

- **Quantity of milk** – cows have been selectively bred to produce herds that produce **high volumes of milk** daily.
- **Quality of milk** – Jersey cows have been selectively bred to produce milk that is **rich** and **creamy**.
- **Beef production** – Some cattle have been selectively bred for characteristics such as hardiness, early maturity and high numbers of offspring.

HT There are risks and disadvantages to selective breeding. Intensive selective breeding reduces the gene pool, and the number of different **alleles** in the population decreases so there is **less variation**.

Lack of variation…

- reduces the species' ability to respond to environmental change
- limits the opportunities for further selective breeding
- can lead to an accumulation of harmful recessive characteristics (in-breeding).

Example of Selective Breeding

Choose the spottiest two to breed...

... and then the spottiest of their offspring...

... to eventually get Dalmatians.

Key Words

Auxin • Gene • Gravity • Hormone • Mutation • Selective breeding

New Genes for Old

Genetic Engineering

All living organisms use the same basic genetic code (**DNA**), so, genes can be transferred from one organism to another. This process is called **genetic engineering** or **genetic modification** (**GM**).

Altering the genetic make-up of an organism can be done for many reasons:

- **To improve crop resistance** to frost damage, disease or herbicides, e.g. soya plants are genetically modified by inserting a gene that makes them resistant to a herbicide, so the plants can grow better without competition from weeds.
- **To improve the quality of food**, e.g. people who eat a diet mainly of rice may become deficient in Vitamin A. The genes responsible for producing beta-carotene (which the body converts into vitamin A) can be transferred from carrots to rice plants, so people can get beta-carotene from the genetically modified rice.
- **To produce a required substance**, e.g. the gene for human **insulin** can be inserted into bacteria to make insulin on a large scale to treat diabetes.

Genetic engineering...

- allows organisms with new features to be produced
- can be used to make biochemical processes cheaper and more efficient.

However, the inserted genes may have **unexpected harmful effects**.

HT Production of Insulin

This example of producing insulin outlines the principles of genetic engineering:

1. The human gene for insulin production is **selected**.
2. The gene is **isolated** and removed using an enzyme which cuts through the DNA strands in precise places.
3. A ring of bacterial DNA (a plasmid) is cut open using an enzyme. The section of human DNA is **inserted** into the plasmid.
4. The plasmid is reinserted into a bacterium. It starts to **divide** rapidly, replicating the plasmid.
5. The bacteria are cultivated on a large scale to make insulin.

Ethical Considerations

Benefits of genetic engineering include...

- producing disease-resistant crops and higher yields
- potentially replacing faulty genes to reduce certain diseases.

But, there are concerns that...

- genetically modified plants may cross-breed with wild plants and release their new genes into the environment
- GM foods may not be safe to eat in the long term
- the genetic make-up of children could be modified or engineered ('designer babies')
- unborn babies with genetic faults could be aborted
- insurance companies could genetically screen applicants and refuse to insure people who have an increased risk of illness.

More of the Same

Asexual Reproduction in Plants

Plants can reproduce asexually (i.e. without a partner). A cell divides by **mitosis** to produce two **clones** (identical cells). Each new cell continues to divide and develop to produce genetically identical individuals.

Spider plants, strawberry plants and potato plants all reproduce in this way.

Spider Plant Stolons

Stolon – a rooting side branch

New individual established

New individual now independent

Taking Cuttings

If a plant has desirable characteristics, it can be reproduced by taking stem, leaf or root cuttings.

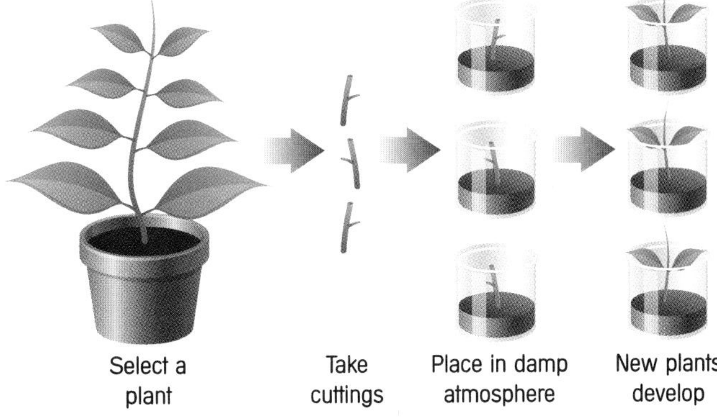

Key Words

Clone • DNA • Genetic engineering • Mitosis

Commercial Cloning of Plants

Plants can be cloned to be sold commercially.

Advantages include:

- The cloned plants will be genetically identical to the parent, so all the characteristics will be known.
- It is possible to mass-produce plants that may be difficult to grow from seeds.

Disadvantages include:

- Any susceptibility to disease, or sensitivity to environmental conditions will affect all the plants.
- The reduction in **genetic variation** reduces the potential for further selective breeding.

HT Cloning by Tissue Culture

Cloned plants can be produced by the following method:

1. Select a parent plant with desired characteristics.
2. Scrape off a lot of small pieces of tissue into beakers containing nutrients and hormones. Make sure that this process is done **aseptically** (without the presence of bacteria) to avoid the new plants rotting.
3. Lots of genetically identical plantlets will then grow (these can also be cloned).

Many older **plants** are still able to **differentiate** or **specialise**, whereas animal cells lose this ability. So, cloning plants is easier than cloning animals.

More of the Same

Cloning Animals

Cloning is an example of asexual reproduction which produces genetically identical copies. Identical twins are **naturally occurring** clones.

Animals can be **cloned artificially**. The most famous example is Dolly the sheep. Dolly was the first mammal to be successfully cloned from an adult body cell.

A cloning technique called **embryo transplantation** is now commonly used in cattle breeding.

Embryo Transplantation

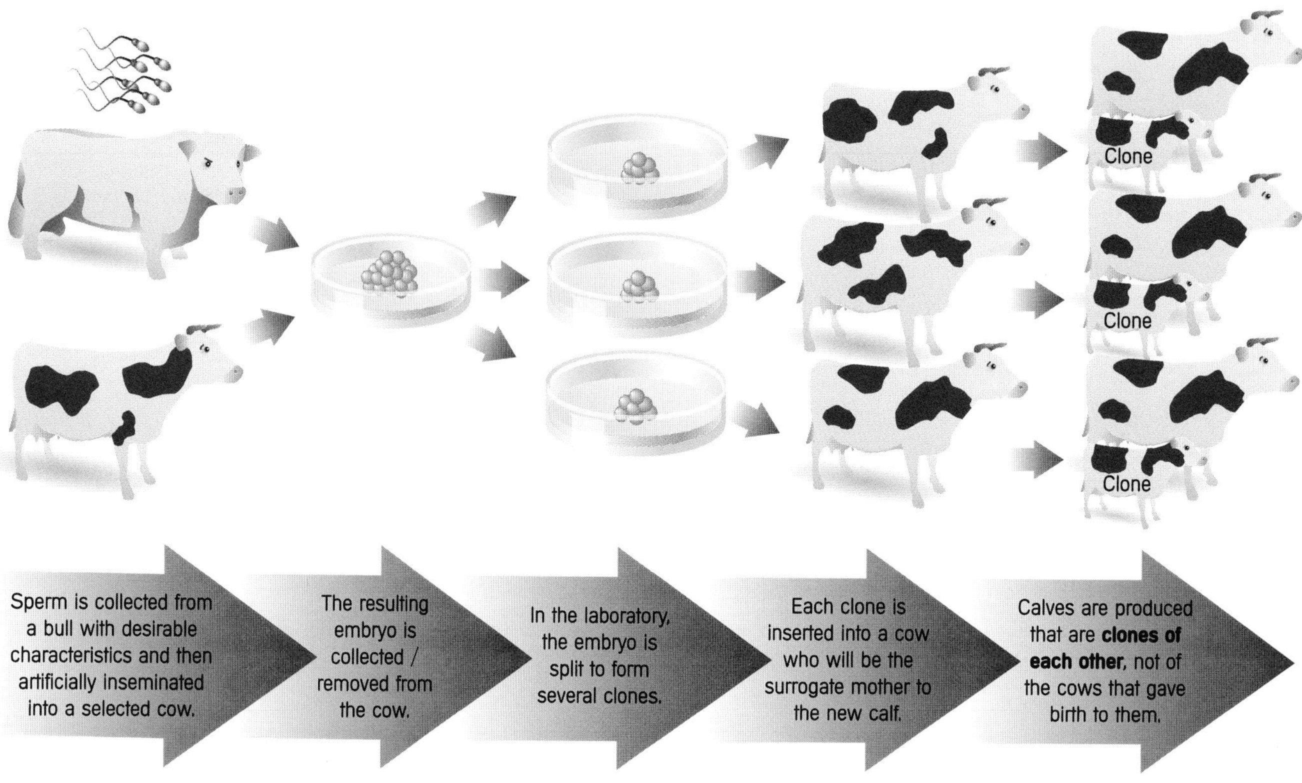

Animal Organ Donors

There is a **shortage** of **human organ donors** for **transplants**. One possible solution would be to **genetically engineer** an **animal organ** so it wouldn't be rejected by the human body. The organ could then be **cloned** to produce a ready supply of identical donor organs.

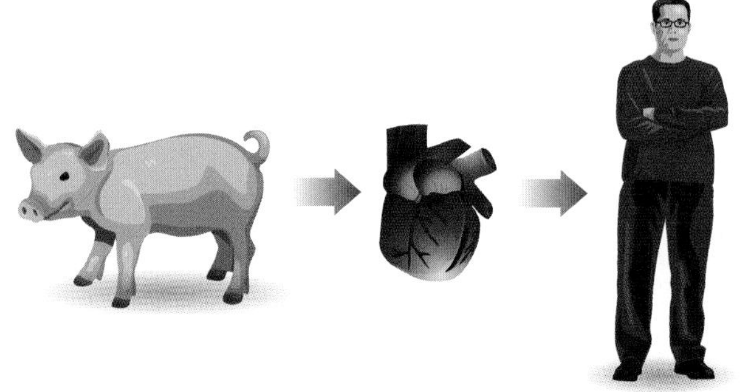

HT Animal organ donors could solve the problem of waiting lists for human transplants. But, there are...

- concerns that infections might be passed from animals to humans
- ethical issues concerning animal welfare and rights.

Key Words

Clone • Genetic engineering • Stem cells

More of the Same

Human Cloning

It's possible to clone human embryos in the same way that animals are cloned. This technique could be used to provide **stem cells** for medical purposes.

But, there are **ethical dilemmas** because if the embryos were allowed to develop they would produce **human clones**. This type of research is **currently illegal**.

HT There are major ethical dilemmas about cloning humans:

- The cloning process is very unreliable – the majority of cloned embryos don't survive.
- Cloned animals seem to have a limited life span and die early.
- The effect of cloning on a human's mental and emotional development isn't known.

HT Adult Cell Cloning

The following method was used to produce a cloned sheep (i.e. Dolly):

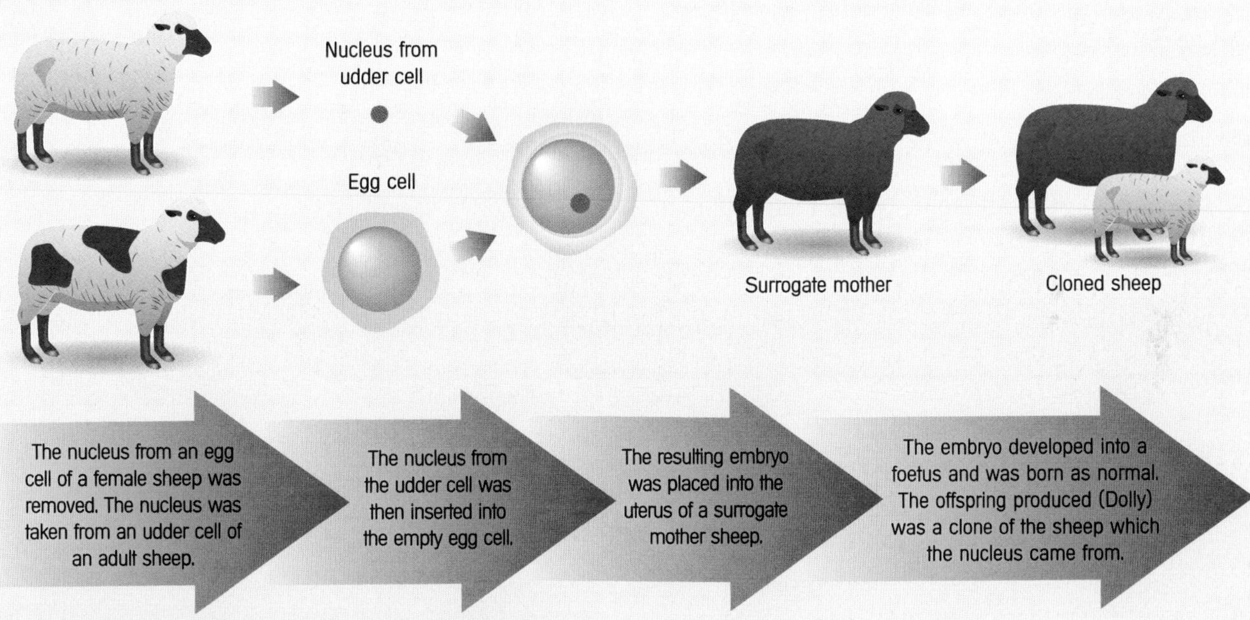

Benefits and Risks of Cloning

There are benefits and risks associated with cloning technology. **Benefits** include:

- Genetically identical cloned animals will all have the same characteristics.
- The sex of an animal and timing of birth can be controlled.
- Top-quality bulls and cows can be kept for egg and sperm donation, whilst other animals can be used to carry and give birth to the young.

Risks include:

- Cloning reduces genetic variation.
- Animals are in-bred so there is the potential for accumulating inherited diseases.
- Welfare concerns – cloned animals may not be as healthy or live as long as 'normal' animals.

Module B3 Practice Questions

1. Link each part of an animal cell with its correct function.

Mitochondrion	Where chemical reactions happen in the cell
Nucleus	Controls the movement of substances in and out of the cell
Cell membrane	Releases energy from food through respiration
Cytoplasm	Contains DNA (the genetic information)

2. Are the following statements about DNA **true** or **false**?

a) The shape of a DNA molecule is a double helix. ....

b) DNA is made from a chain of amino acids. ....

c) A gene is made from protein. ....

d) A gene codes for a particular protein. ....

HT 3. Why is the sequence of the bases important in a DNA molecule?

....

4. **a)** What effect do enzymes have on reaction rates? ....

b) Give two factors that can affect the rate of enzyme activity.

i) .... **ii)** ....

c) Explain what is meant by **the optimum temperature** for an enzyme.

....

d) What would happen to an enzyme, and the reaction, if the temperature rises too high?

....

....

5. **a)** What is diffusion?

....

HT **b)** Give two factors which will increase the rate of diffusion of substances in and out of cells.

i) ....

ii) ....

6. Explain how the lungs are adapted for rapid diffusion.

....

7 List the four components of the blood.

i) .... ii) .... iii) .... iv) ....

8 **a)** Which blood vessels transport blood away from the heart?

....

b) Why is the wall of an artery much thicker than the wall of a vein?

....

HT 9 Give two problems involved with heart transplants.

i) ....

ii) ....

10 Explain what advantage there is to being a large, multi-cellular organism compared to a single-celled organism, in terms of diffusion.

....

....

11 Briefly explain what mitosis is.

....

....

12 *All gene mutations are beneficial and harmless.* Is this statement **true** or **false**? ....

13 Crops can be genetically engineered to produce disease-resistant crops and higher yields. Give two disadvantages of genetically engineering crops.

i) ....

ii) ....

14 Explain, in as much detail as you can, how an animal can be cloned using the technique of embryo transplantation.

....

....

....

Fundamental Chemical Concepts

Atoms

All substances are made up of **atoms**. Atoms contain **three types** of particles:

- **protons**
- **neutrons** (except hydrogen)
- **electrons**.

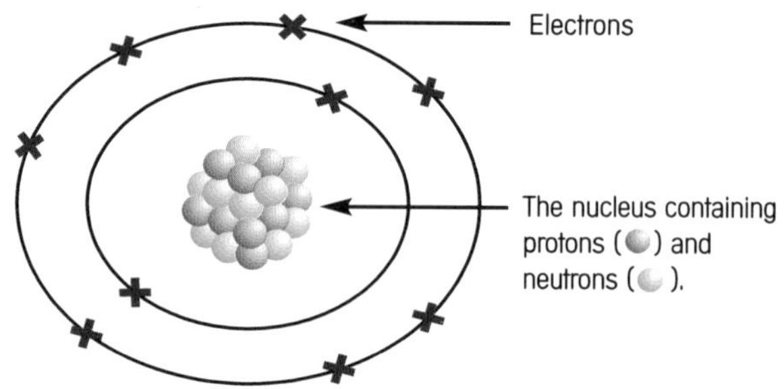

Elements and Compounds

Elements are substances made up of just **one type** of atom.

Compounds are substances formed from the atoms of two or more elements, which have been joined together by a **chemical bond**.

Compounds can join together in two ways:

- **covalent bonding** – two atoms **share** a pair of electrons
- **ionic bonding** – atoms become charged **ions** by **gaining or losing** electrons.

Chemical Symbols

Each element is represented by a different **chemical symbol**, for example...

- Fe represents iron
- Na represents sodium.

The symbols are arranged in **periods** (rows) and **groups** (columns) in the periodic table.

Key Words

Atom • Compound • Covalent bond • Electron • Element • Group • Ion • Ionic bond • Neutron • Period • Proton

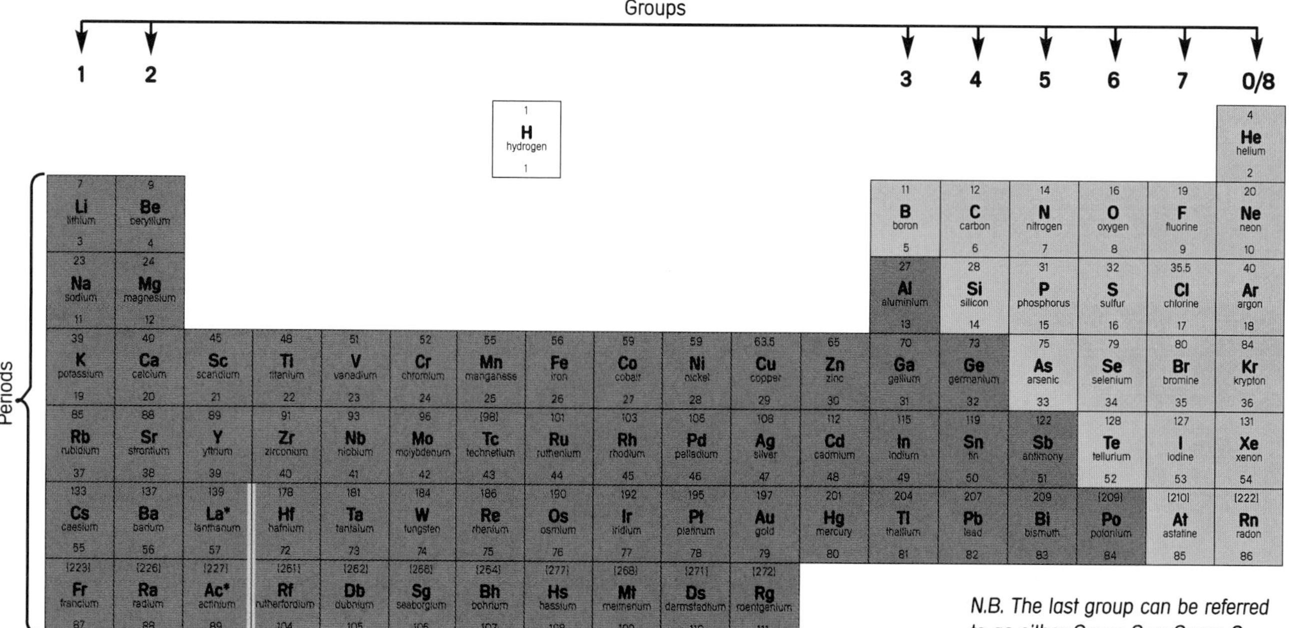

N.B. The last group can be referred to as either Group 8 or Group 0

Fundamental Chemical Concepts

Formulae

Numbers and chemical symbols are used to write formulae that represent molecules of compounds, e.g. …
- H_2O represents water
- CO_2 represents carbon dioxide
- NH_3 represents ammonia.

Formulae are used to show the…
- **different elements** in a compound
- **number of atoms** of each element in one molecule of the compound.

Brackets around part of the formula mean that everything **inside the brackets** is multiplied by the **number outside**.

1 Sulfuric Acid, H_2SO_4

Sulfuric acid contains…
- two hydrogen atoms
- one sulfur atom
- four oxygen atoms.

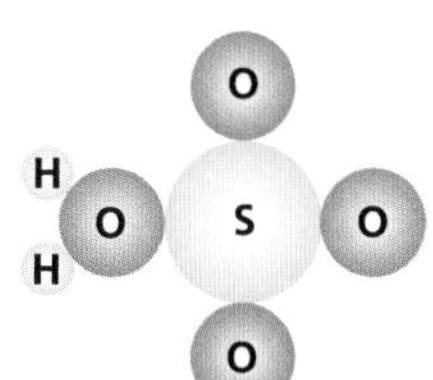

2 Calcium Nitrate, $2Ca(NO_3)_2$

The '2' means that there are two calcium nitrates.

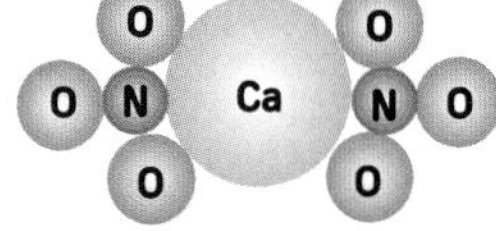

Each calcium nitrate contains…
- one calcium atom
- two nitrogen atoms
- six oxygen atoms.

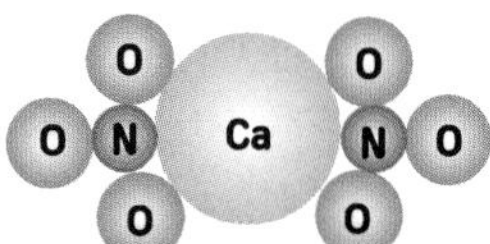

Displayed formula can also be used to show the composition of a molecule, e.g. **Ethanol, C_2H_5OH.**

```
    H   H
    |   |
H - C - C - O - H
    |   |
    H   H
```

This formula shows…
- the **different type** of atoms in the molecule – carbon, hydrogen and oxygen
- the number of **each type** of atom – one oxygen atom, two carbon atoms and six hydrogen atoms
- the covalent bonds between the atoms (–).

HT You need to know the formula for these compounds.

Carbonates	
Copper (II) carbonate	$CuCO_3$
Iron (II) carbonate	$FeCO_3$
Manganese carbonate	$MnCO_3$
Zinc carbonate	$ZnCO_3$
Chlorides	
Barium chloride	$BaCl_2$
Magnesium chloride	$MgCl_2$
Potassium chloride	KCl
Sodium chloride	NaCl
Hydroxides	
Copper (II) hydroxide	$Cu(OH)_2$
Iron (II) hydroxide	$Fe(OH)_2$
Iron (III) hydroxide	$Fe(OH)_3$
Lithium hydroxide	LiOH
Potassium hydroxide	KOH
Sodium hydroxide	NaOH
Oxides	
Aluminium oxide	Al_2O_3
Copper (II) oxide	CuO
Iron (II) oxide	FeO
Magnesium oxide	MgO
Manganese oxide	MnO
Sodium oxide	Na_2O
Zinc oxide	ZnO
Others	
Carbon dioxide	CO_2
Methane	CH_4
Silver nitrate	$AgNO_3$
Water	H_2O

Fundamental Chemical Concepts

Equations

Equations are used to show what happens during a **chemical reaction**. The **reactants** (starting substances) are on one side and the **products** (new substances formed) are on the other.

No **atoms** are lost or gained during a reaction, so the equation must be balanced. There must always be the same number of atoms of each element on both sides of the equation.

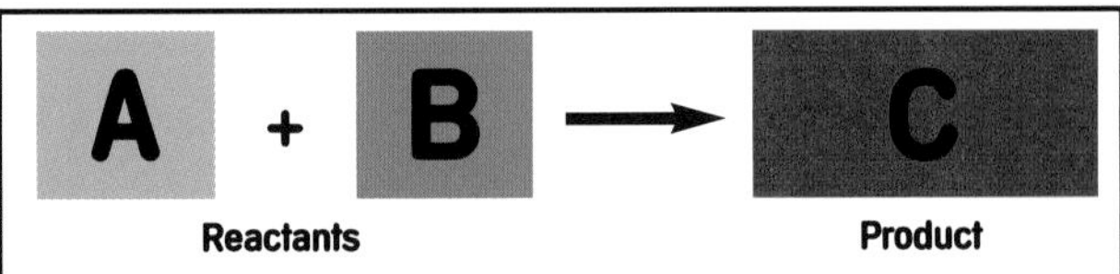

Balancing Equations

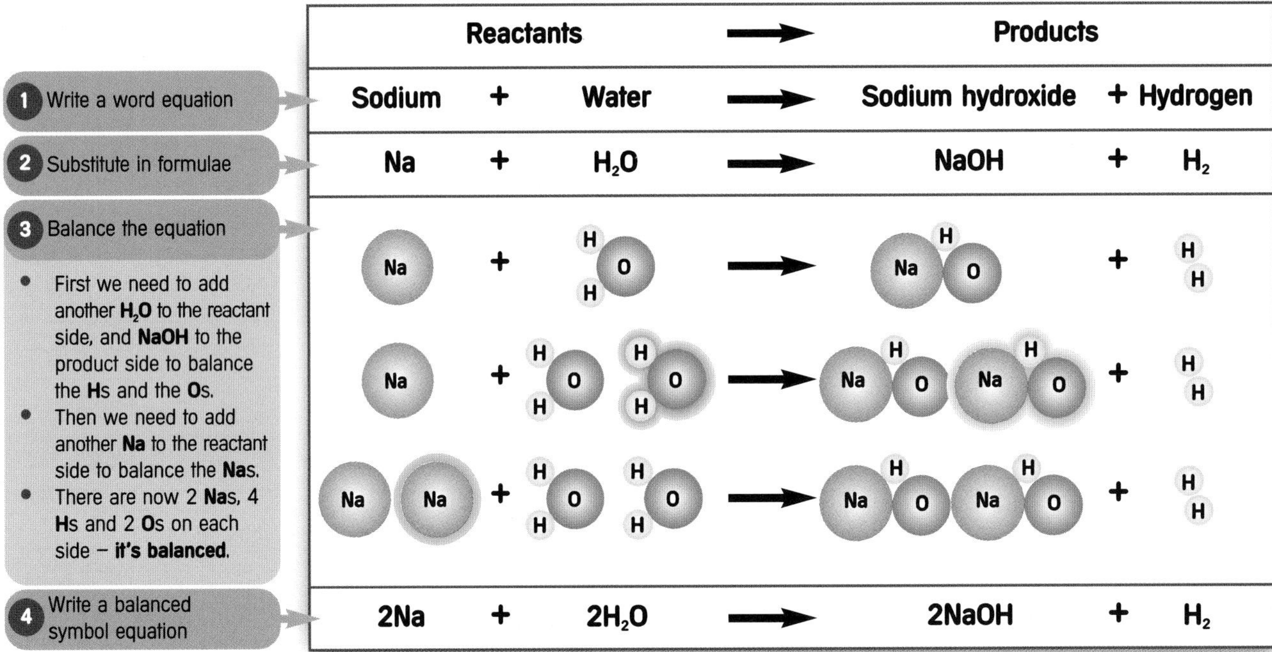

HT You should be able to balance equations by looking at the formulae (i.e. without drawing the atoms).

1 Write a word equation	Calcium carbonate	+	Nitric acid	→	Calcium nitrate	+	Carbon dioxide	+	Water
2 Substitute in formulae	$CaCO_3$	+	HNO_3	→	$Ca(NO_3)_2$	+	CO_2	+	H_2O
3 Balance the equation	$CaCO_3$	+	$2HNO_3$	→	$Ca(NO_3)_2$	+	CO_2	+	H_2O
4 Write a balanced symbol equation with state symbols	$CaCO_3(s)$	+	$2HNO_3(aq)$	→	$Ca(NO_3)_2(aq)$	+	$CO_2(g)$	+	$H_2O(l)$

Equations can also be written using displayed formulae. These must be balanced too.						
	Methane	+	Oxygen	→	Carbon dioxide +	Water
	H–C–H (with H above and below C)	+	O=O, O=O	→	O=C=O +	H–O–H, H–O–H

What are Atoms Like?

Structure of an Atom

An **atom** has a central **nucleus** surrounded by negatively charged **electrons**. The nucleus is made up of **protons** and **neutrons** and is **positively charged**. An atom has no overall charge.

HT An atom has no overall charge because it has the **same number** of **protons** and **electrons**. So, the charges **cancel** each other out.

Atomic Particle	Relative Charge	Relative Mass
Proton	+1	1
Neutron	0	1
Electron	-1	0.0005 (zero)

Elements and Compounds

An **element** contains one type of atom, and is a substance that can't be chemically broken down. There are over 100 elements.

A **compound** is a substance that contains at least two elements that are **chemically combined**. You can identify the elements in a compound from its formula, using the periodic table.

For example...

- the **compound** sodium chloride (NaCl) contains the **elements** sodium (Na) and chlorine (Cl)
- the **compound** potassium nitrate (KNO_3) contains the **elements** potassium (K), nitrogen (N) and oxygen (O).

Mass Number and Atomic Number

The **mass number** is the total number of **protons** and **neutrons** in an atom. The **atomic number** is the number of **protons** in an atom.

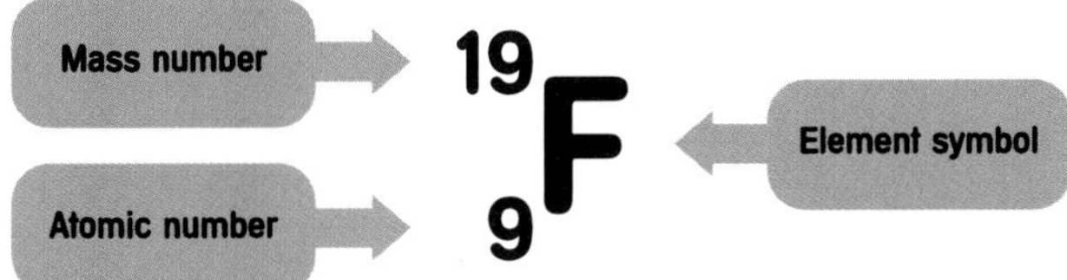

The elements in the periodic table are arranged in **increasing atomic number**. You can use the periodic table to find...

- an element from its atomic number
- the atomic number of an element.

Key Words

Atom • Atomic number • Compound • Electron • Element • Mass number • Neutron • Product • Proton • Reactant

HT You can work out the number of protons, electrons and neutrons in a particle if you know its atomic number, mass number and charge.

Name and Symbol	No. of Protons	No. of Electrons	No. of Neutrons
Hydrogen $^{1}_{1}H$	1	1	0 (1 − 1 = 0)
Helium $^{4}_{2}He$	2	2	2 (4 − 2 = 2)
Oxygen $^{16}_{8}O$	8	8	8 (16 − 8 = 8)
Sodium $^{23}_{11}Na$	11	11	12 (23 − 11 = 12)

What are Atoms Like?

Isotopes

Isotopes are **atoms** of the **same element** that have the **same atomic number** but a **different mass number**.

For example, chlorine has two isotopes:

$^{35}_{17}Cl$ Mass number = 35, Atomic number = 17

$^{37}_{17}Cl$ Mass number = 37, Atomic number = 17

HT You can identify isotopes from data about the number of electrons, protons and neutrons in particles. Each isotope has the **same number of protons** and **electrons**, but a **different number** of **neutrons**. For example, carbon has three main isotopes.

Isotope	Symbol	Mass Number	Atomic Number	Protons	Neutrons	Electrons
Carbon-12	$^{12}_{6}C$	12	6	6	6	6
Carbon-13	$^{13}_{6}C$	13	6	6	7	6
Carbon-14	$^{14}_{6}C$	14	6	6	8	6

Electron Configuration

Electron configuration tells you how the electrons are arranged around the nucleus in **shells (energy levels)**:

- The first shell can hold a maximum of two electrons.
- The shells after this can hold a maximum of eight electrons.

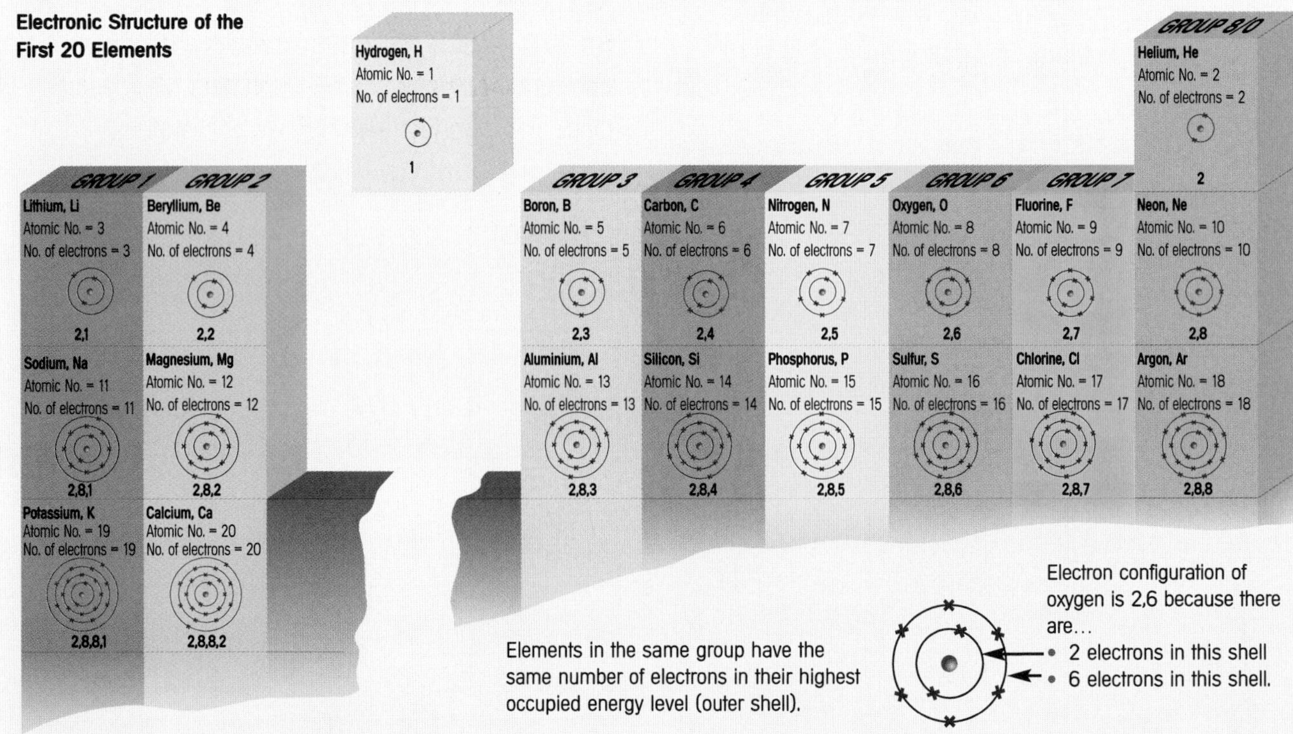

How Atoms Combine – Ionic Bonding

Ions, Atoms and Molecules

An **atom** is an element on its own, e.g. Na, Cl.

A **molecule** is two or more atoms bonded together, e.g. Cl_2, CO_2.

An **ion** is a **charged atom** or group of atoms, e.g. Na^+, Cl^-, NH_4^+, SO_4^{2-}.

Key Words

Atom • Atomic number • Element • Ion • Ionic bond • Isotopes • Mass number

Forming Ions

A **positive ion** is formed when an atom, or group of atoms, **loses** one or more electrons. For example, losing two electrons makes a 2^+ ion, e.g. Mg^{2+}.

Atom or group of atoms	− Electron(s)	→	Positive ion

A **negative ion** is formed when an atom, or group of atoms, **gains** one or more electrons. For example, gaining two electrons makes a 2^- ion, e.g. O^{2-}.

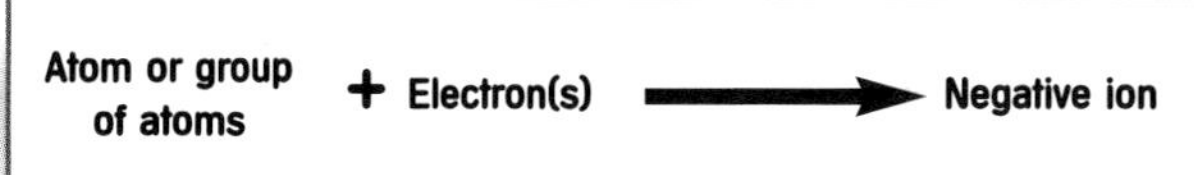

Ionic Bonding

In **ionic bonding**...

- the metal atoms **transfer electrons** to become **positive ions**
- the non-metal atoms **receive electrons** to become **negative ions**
- the positive and negative ions are attracted to each other.

Two ionically bonded compounds are **sodium chloride** and **magnesium oxide**:

- They have high melting points.
- They don't conduct electricity when solid.

Sodium chloride dissolves in water and **can conduct electricity** when **in solution**. Magnesium oxide **can conduct electricity** when **molten**.

HT Structure and Physical Properties

Sodium chloride (NaCl) and magnesium oxide (MgO) form **giant ionic lattices** in which positive and negative ions are **electrostatically attracted** to each other. This means that they...

- have high melting points
- can conduct electricity when molten or in solution because the charged ions are free to move about
- don't conduct electricity when solid, because the ions are held in place and can't move.

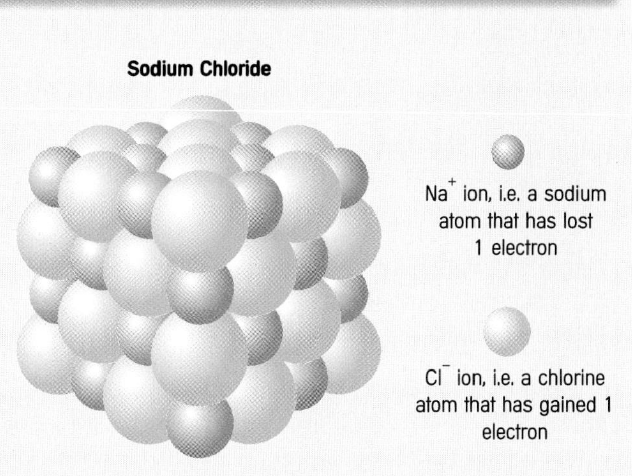

How Atoms Combine – Ionic Bonding

HT The Ionic Bond

When a metal and a non-metal combine, electrons are transferred from one **atom** to the other to form **ions**. Each ion will have a complete outer shell (**a stable octet**).

Example 1

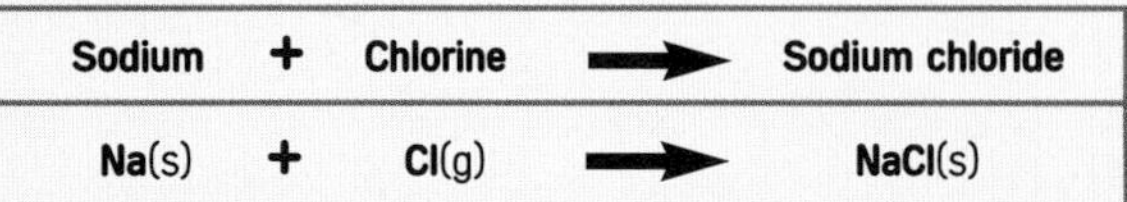

Sodium	+	**Chlorine**	→	**Sodium chloride**
Na(s)	+	**Cl**(g)	→	**NaCl**(s)

1. The sodium atom has 1 electron in its outer shell.
2. The electron is transferred to the chlorine atom. Both atoms now have 8 electrons in their outer shell.
3. The atoms become ions (Na^+ and Cl^-).
4. The compound formed is sodium chloride, NaCl.

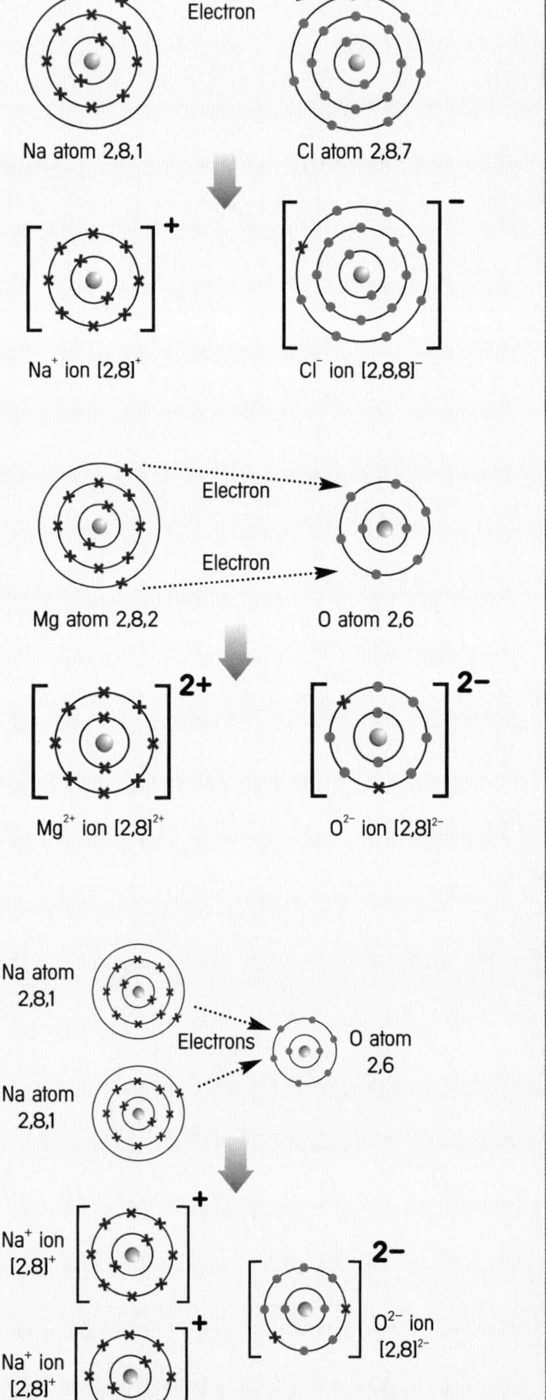

Example 2

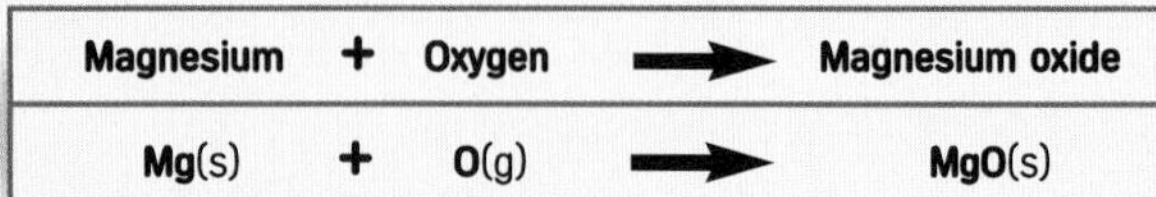

Magnesium	+	**Oxygen**	→	**Magnesium oxide**
Mg(s)	+	**O**(g)	→	**MgO**(s)

1. The magnesium atom has 2 electrons in its outer shell.
2. The 2 electrons are transferred to the oxygen atom. Both atoms now have 8 electrons in their outer shell.
3. The atoms become ions (Mg^{2+} and O^{2-}).
4. The compound formed is magnesium oxide, MgO.

Example 3

Sodium	+	**Oxygen**	→	**Sodium oxide**
2Na(s)	+	**O**(g)	→	**Na_2O**(s)

1. The sodium atom has 1 electron in its outer shell.
2. An oxygen atom needs 2 electrons, so 2 Na atoms are needed.
3. The atoms become ions (Na^+, Na^+ and O^{2-}).
4. The compound formed is sodium oxide, Na_2O.

How Atoms Combine – Ionic Bonding

HT The Ionic Bond (cont.)

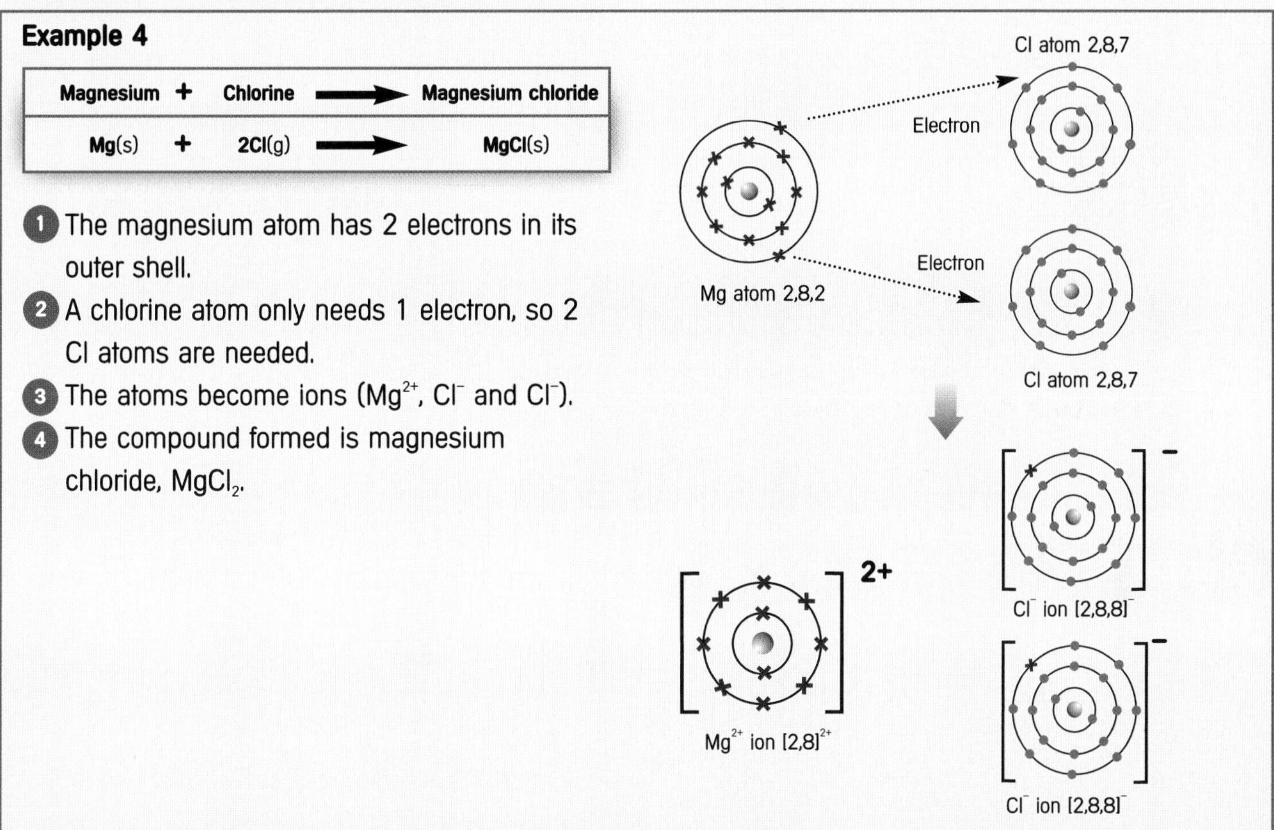

Example 4

Magnesium +	**Chlorine** →	**Magnesium chloride**
Mg(s) +	**2Cl**(g) →	**MgCl**(s)

1. The magnesium atom has 2 electrons in its outer shell.
2. A chlorine atom only needs 1 electron, so 2 Cl atoms are needed.
3. The atoms become ions (Mg^{2+}, Cl^- and Cl^-).
4. The compound formed is magnesium chloride, $MgCl_2$.

Formulae of Ionic Compounds

Ions with different charges combine to form **ionic compounds** which have **equal amounts** of **positive** and **negative** charge.

Positive Ions: 1+ e.g. K^+, Na^+		Positive Ions: 2+ e.g. Mg^{2+}, Cu^{2+}		Positive Ions: 3+ e.g. Al^{3+}, Fe^{3+}		Negative Ions
KCl 1+ 1−	$NaOH$ 1+ 1−	$MgCl_2$ 2+ 2 x 1− = 2−	$Cu(OH)_2$ 2+ 2 x 1− = 2−	$AlCl_3$ 3+ 3 x 1− = 3−	$Fe(OH)_3$ 3+ 3 x 1− = 3−	1− e.g. Cl^-, OH^-
K_2SO_4 2 x 1+ = 2+ 2−	Na_2O 2 x 1+ = 2+ 2−	$MgSO_4$ 2+ 2−	CuO 2+ 2−	$Al_2(SO_4)_3$ 2 x 3+ = 6+ 3 x 2− = 6−	Fe_2O_3 2 x 3+ = 6+ 3 x 2− = 6−	2− e.g. SO_4^{2-}, O^{2-}

Covalent Bonding and the Periodic Table

The Periodic Table

1	2											3	4	5	6	7	0/8
						1 **H** hydrogen 1											4 **He** helium 2
7 **Li** lithium 3	9 **Be** beryllium 4											11 **B** boron 5	12 **C** carbon 6	14 **N** nitrogen 7	16 **O** oxygen 8	19 **F** fluorine 9	20 **Ne** neon 10
23 **Na** sodium 11	24 **Mg** magnesium 12											27 **Al** aluminium 13	28 **Si** silicon 14	31 **P** phosphorus 15	32 **S** sulfur 16	35.5 **Cl** chlorine 17	40 **Ar** argon 18
39 **K** potassium 19	40 **Ca** calcium 20	45 **Sc** scandium 21	48 **Ti** titanium 22	51 **V** vanadium 23	52 **Cr** chromium 24	55 **Mn** manganese 25	56 **Fe** iron 26	59 **Co** cobalt 27	59 **Ni** nickel 28	63.5 **Cu** copper 29	65 **Zn** zinc 30	70 **Ga** gallium 31	73 **Ge** germanium 32	75 **As** arsenic 33	79 **Se** selenium 34	80 **Br** bromine 35	84 **Kr** krypton 36
85 **Rb** rubidium 37	88 **Sr** strontium 38	89 **Y** yttrium 39	91 **Zr** zirconium 40	93 **Nb** niobium 41	96 **Mo** molybdenum 42	[98] **Tc** technetium 43	101 **Ru** ruthenium 44	103 **Rh** rhodium 45	106 **Pd** palladium 46	108 **Ag** silver 47	112 **Cd** cadmium 48	115 **In** indium 49	119 **Sn** tin 50	122 **Sb** antimony 51	128 **Te** tellurium 52	127 **I** iodine 53	131 **Xe** xenon 54
133 **Cs** caesium 55	137 **Ba** barium 56	139 **La*** lanthanum 57	178 **Hf** hafnium 72	181 **Ta** tantalum 73	184 **W** tungsten 74	186 **Re** rhenium 75	190 **Os** osmium 76	192 **Ir** iridium 77	195 **Pt** platinum 78	197 **Au** gold 79	201 **Hg** mercury 80	204 **Tl** thallium 81	207 **Pb** lead 82	209 **Bi** bismuth 83	[209] **Po** polonium 84	[210] **At** astatine 85	[222] **Rn** radon 86
[223] **Fr** francium 87	[226] **Ra** radium 88	[227] **Ac*** actinium 89	[261] **Rf** rutherfordium 104	[262] **Db** dubnium 105	[266] **Sg** seaborgium 106	[264] **Bh** bohrium 107	[277] **Hs** hassium 108	[268] **Mt** meitnerium 109	[271] **Ds** darmstadtium 110	[272] **Rg** roentgenium 111							

Groups

A vertical column of **elements** in the periodic table is called a **group**. Lithium (Li), sodium (Na) and potassium (K) are elements in Group 1.

Elements in the same group have **similar chemical properties** because they have the **same number** of **electrons** in their **outer shell**. This outer number of electrons is the same as their group number.

For example...

- Group 1 elements have one electron in their outer shell
- Group 7 elements have seven electrons in their outer shell
- Group 8 elements have a full outer shell, i.e. eight electrons.

Periods

A **horizontal row** of elements in the periodic table is called a **period**. Lithium (Li), carbon (C) and neon (Ne) are elements in the second period.

The **period** for an element is related to the number of **occupied shells** it has. For example, sodium (Na), aluminium (Al) and chlorine (Cl) have three shells of electrons so they are in the third period.

HT Electronic Structure

There is a connection between the...

- **number of electrons** in an element's outer shell and its **group**
- **number of shells** of electrons an element has and its **period**.

So, if you are given an element's electronic structure, you can deduce its position in the periodic table.

For example, sulfur's electronic structure is 2,8,6 so it has...

- three electron shells, so it can be found in the **third period**
- six electrons in its outer shell, so it can be found in **Group 6**.

Covalent Bonding and the Periodic Table

Bonding

A molecule is two or more **atoms** bonded together. There are two types of bonding:

- **Ionic bonding**
- **Covalent bonding.**

Key Words

Atom • Covalent bond • Electron • Element • Group • Period

Covalent Bonding

Covalent bonding is when **non-metals** combine by **sharing pairs** of **electrons**. Water and carbon dioxide are covalently bonded molecules.

Water (H_2O)...

- is a liquid with a low melting point
- doesn't conduct electricity.

One molecule of water is made up of **one atom of oxygen** and **two atoms of hydrogen**.

Carbon dioxide (CO_2)...

- is a gas with a low melting point
- doesn't conduct electricity.

One molecule of carbon dioxide is made up of **one atom of carbon** and **two atoms of oxygen**.

HT Simple covalently bonded molecules have **weak intermolecular** forces of attraction.

So, they have low melting points, and don't conduct electricity because there aren't any free electrons.

Representing Atoms

You should be familiar with how simple covalently bonded molecules are formed.

Water (H_2O) – the outer shells of the hydrogen and oxygen atoms overlap. The oxygen atom shares a pair of electrons with each hydrogen atom to form a water molecule.

Hydrogen (H_2) – the two hydrogen atoms share a pair of electrons.

Methane (CH_4) – the carbon atom shares a pair of electrons with each hydrogen atom.

Chlorine (Cl_2) – the two chlorine atoms share a pair of electrons.

Carbon dioxide (CO_2) – the outer shells of the carbon and oxygen atoms overlap. The carbon atom shares two pairs of electrons with each oxygen atom to form a double covalently bonded molecule.

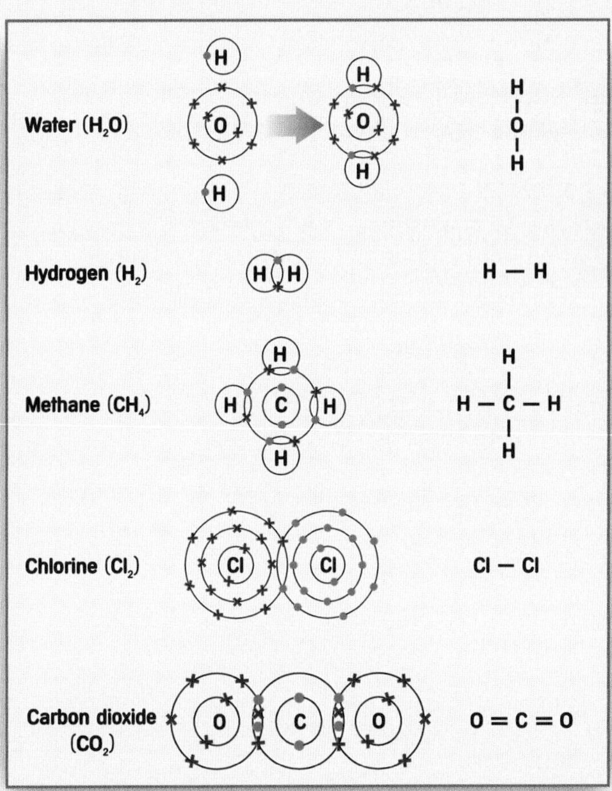

The Group 1 Elements

Group 1 – The Alkali Metals

The **alkali metals** occupy Group 1 of the periodic table. The first three elements in the group are lithium, sodium and potassium. They all have one electron in their outer shell so they have **similar properties**.

Alkali metals are stored **under oil** because they...
- react with air
- react vigorously with water.

Reactions with Water

Alkali metals react with water to produce **hydrogen** and a **hydroxide**. Alkali metal hydroxides are soluble and form alkaline solutions.

The alkali metals react more vigorously as you go down the group.
- Lithium reacts gently.
- Sodium reacts more aggressively than lithium.
- Potassium reacts more aggressively than sodium – it melts and burns with a lilac flame.

	Lithium + Water → Lithium hydroxide + Hydrogen
HT	$2Li(s) + 2H_2O(l) \rightarrow 2LiOH(aq) + H_2(g)$
	Sodium + Water → Sodium hydroxide + Hydrogen
HT	$2Na(s) + 2H_2O(l) \rightarrow 2NaOH(aq) + H_2(g)$
	Potassium + Water → Potassium hydroxide + Hydrogen
HT	$2K(s) + 2H_2O(l) \rightarrow 2KOH(aq) + H_2(g)$

Flame Tests

Lithium, sodium and potassium compounds can be recognised by the colours they produce in a **flame test**.

1. A piece of nichrome (a nickel-chromium alloy) wire is dipped in concentrated hydrochloric acid to clean it.
2. The wire is dipped in the compound.
3. The wire is then put into a Bunsen flame. Each compound will produce a different coloured flame.

Key Word

Oxidation

HT Properties of the Alkali Metals

Although the alkali metals have similar chemical properties, their physical properties alter as you go down the group.

Rubidium is the fourth element in Group 1. Rubidium's reaction with water is...

- very fast
- **exothermic**
- violent (if it's carried out in a glass beaker, the beaker may shatter).

Density increases as you go down the group (with the exception of potassium). Caesium has the greatest density, and lowest melting and boiling points.

Element	Melting Point (°C)	Boiling Point (°C)	Density (g/cm^3)
Lithium, Li	180	1340	0.53
Sodium, Na	98	883	0.97
Potassium, K	64	760	0.86
Rubidium, Rb	39	688	1.53
Caesium, Cs	29	671	1.90

Trends in Group 1

Alkali metals have similar properties because, when they react, an atom **loses** one **electron** to form a **positive ion** with a stable electronic structure.

The alkali metals become **more reactive** because the outer shell gets **further away** from the **influence** of the **nucleus**. This makes it easier for an atom to lose an electron from its outer shell.

The equations for the formation of the Group 1 metal ions are usually written as follows:

$Li \longrightarrow Li^+ + e^-$
$Na \longrightarrow Na^+ + e^-$
$K \longrightarrow K^+ + e^-$

Oxidation involves the loss of electrons by an atom.

Examples of Oxidation

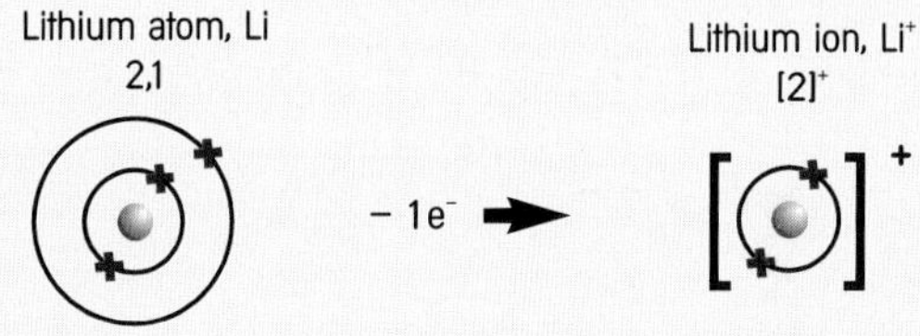

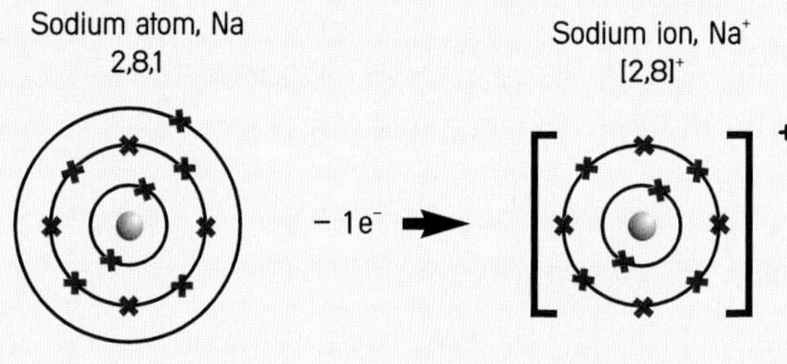

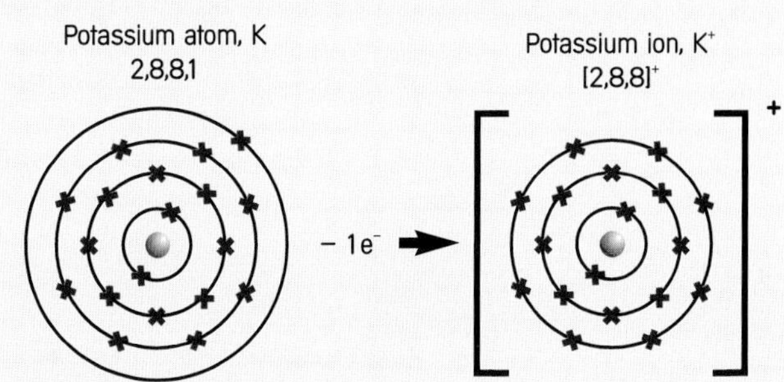

The Group 7 Elements

Group 7 – The Halogens

The five non-metals in Group 7 are known as the **halogens**. They all have seven electrons in their outer shell so they have similar chemical properties.

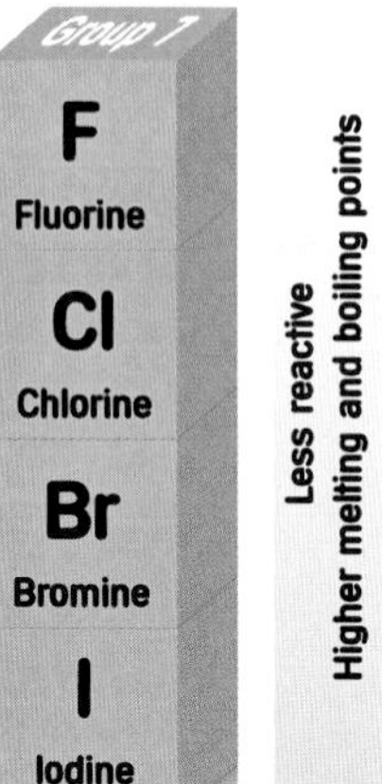

Fluorine, chlorine, bromine and iodine are halogens. At room temperature...

- chlorine is a green gas
- bromine is an orange liquid
- iodine is a grey solid.

Key Words

Halide • Halogens • Oxidation • Reduction

The halogens have many uses:

- **Iodine** is used as an **antiseptic** to sterilise wounds.
- **Chlorine** (extracted from sodium chloride) is used to **sterilise water** and make **pesticides** and **plastics**.
- **Sodium chloride** is used to produce **chlorine**, and as a **flavouring** and **preservative**.

Halogens react vigorously with **alkali metals** to form metal **halides**, for example:

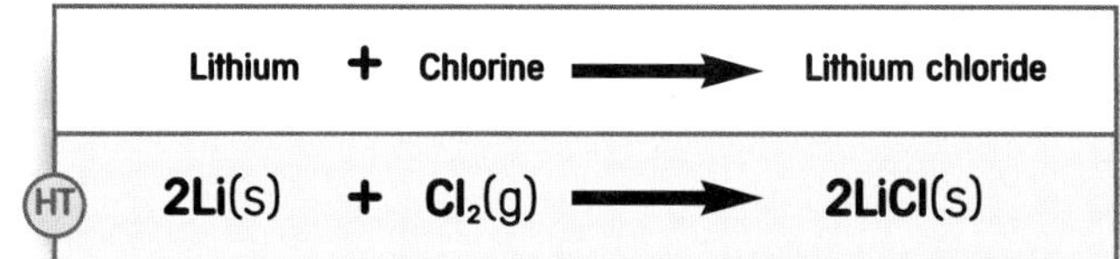

Displacement Reactions

The reactivity of the halogens decreases as you go down the group. So, fluorine is the most reactive halogen and iodine is the least reactive.

A **more reactive** halogen will **displace** a **less reactive** halogen from an aqueous solution of its metal halide. For example...

- chlorine will displace bromides and iodides
- bromine will displace iodides.

If chlorine gas was passed through an aqueous solution of potassium bromide, bromine would be formed due to the displacement reaction.

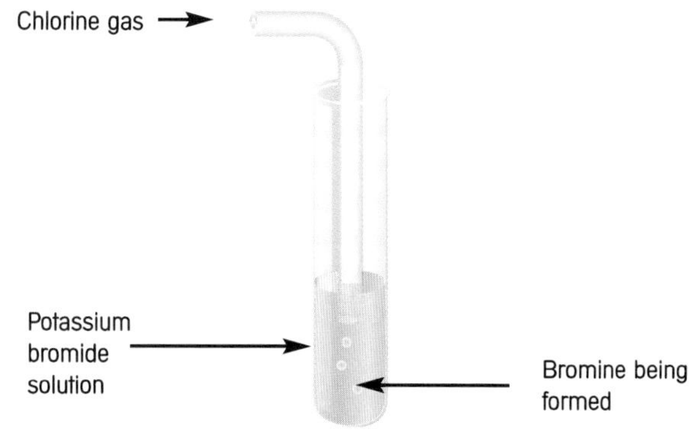

The results of reactions between halogens and aqueous solutions of salts are as follows:

	Potassium Chloride	Potassium Bromide	Potassium Iodide
Chlorine, Cl_2	No change	Potassium chloride	Potassium chloride
Bromine, Br_2	No reaction	No change	Potassium bromide
Iodine, I_2	No reaction	No reaction	No change

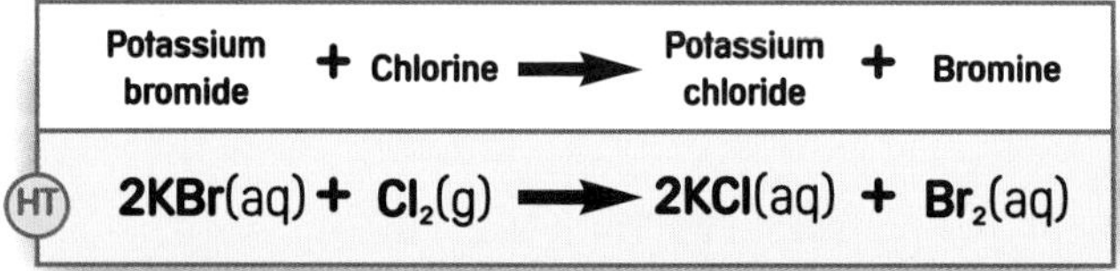

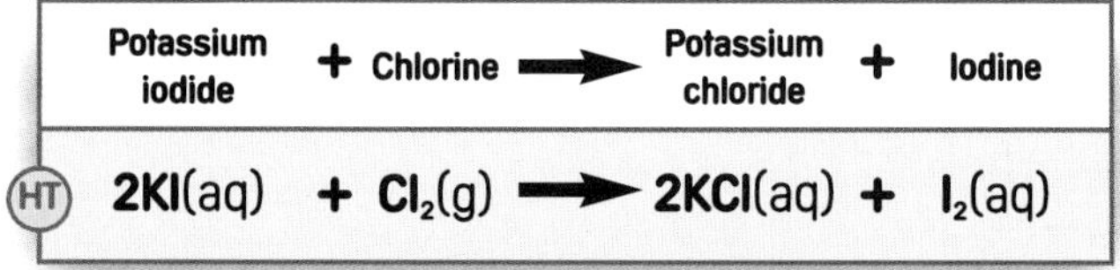

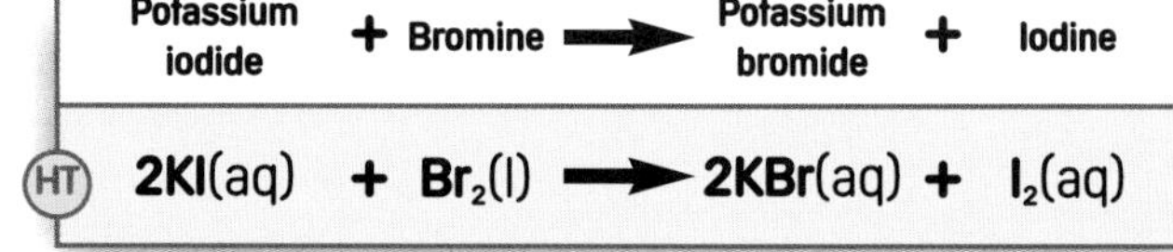

HT Properties of the Halogens

The physical properties of the halogens alter as you go down the group. **Fluorine** is the most reactive element in the group. It will **displace** all of the other halogens from an aqueous solution of their metal halides.

Astatine is a semi-metallic, radioactive element and only very small amounts of it exist naturally. It's the least reactive of the halogens and, theoretically, it would be unable to displace any of the other halogens from an aqueous solution of their metal halides.

Astatine is estimated to have the highest melting and boiling points but its density is not known as it has a very unstable nature.

Element	Melting Point (°C)	Boiling Point (°C)	Density (g/cm³)
Fluorine, F	-220	-188	0.0016
Chlorine, Cl	-101	-34	0.003
Bromine, Br	-7	59	3.12
Iodine, I	114	184	4.95
Astatine, At	302 (estimated)	337 (estimated)	Not known

Trends in Group 7

The halogens have similar properties because, when they react, an atom **gains** one **electron** to form a **negative** ion with a stable electronic structure.

Reduction involves the gain of electrons by an atom, for example:

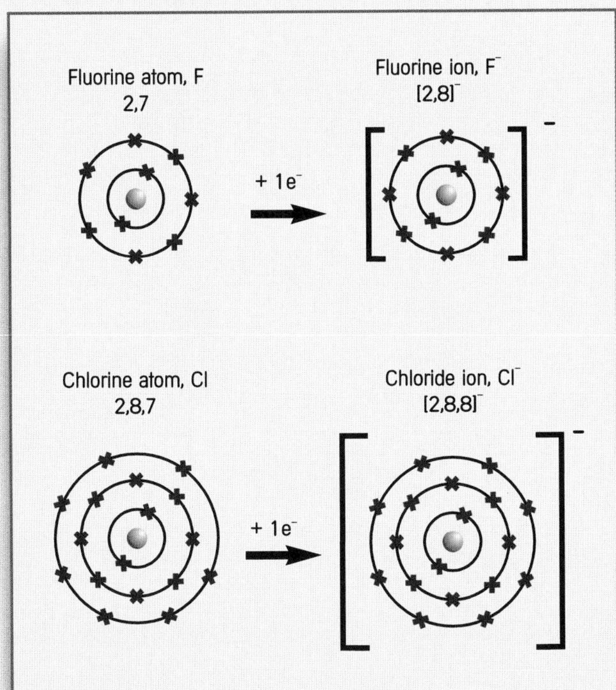

The halogens at the top of the group are **more reactive** than those at the bottom of the group because the outer shell is **closer** to the **influence** of the **nucleus**. This makes it **easier** for an atom to **gain an electron**.

Equations for the formation of the halide **ions** from halogen molecules are usually written as follows:

$$F_2 + 2e^- \longrightarrow 2F^-$$

$$Cl_2 + 2e^- \longrightarrow 2Cl^-$$

By looking at an equation of a reaction, you can decide whether it's oxidation or **reduction**.

- If **electrons** are **added**, it's a **reduction** reaction.
- If **electrons** are **taken away**, it's an **oxidation** reaction.

An easy way to remember the definitions of oxidation and reduction is by remembering **OILRIG**:

- **O**xidation **I**s **L**oss of electrons.
- **R**eduction **I**s **G**ain of electrons.

Electrolysis

Electrolysis

A liquid or solution that **conducts electricity** is called an **electrolyte**. An electrolyte can be separated into its separate parts by **electrolysis**.

When a **direct current** is passed through an electrolyte, the compound will break down.

- Positively charged **ions** (**cations**) move towards the negative **electrode** (**the cathode**).
- Negatively charged ions (**anions**) move towards the positive electrode (**the anode**).

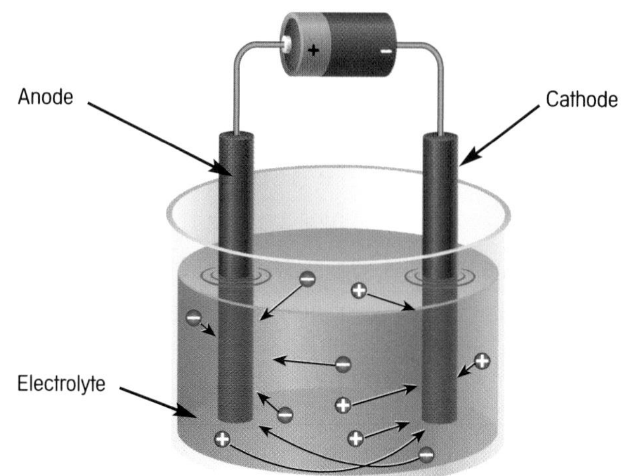

Electrolysis of Sulfuric Acid

Sulfuric acid solution is an electrolyte. It contains **hydrogen ions** (H^+ cations) and **hydroxide ions** (OH^- anions).

When dilute sulfuric acid undergoes electrolysis…

- the **hydrogen cations** are attracted to the **cathode** and form **hydrogen gas**
- the **hydroxide anions** are attracted to the **anode** and form **oxygen gas**.

The products of the electrolysis of sulfuric acid can be **tested** as follows:

- **Hydrogen** burns with a **squeaky pop** when tested with a lighted splint.
- **Oxygen re-lights** a glowing splint.

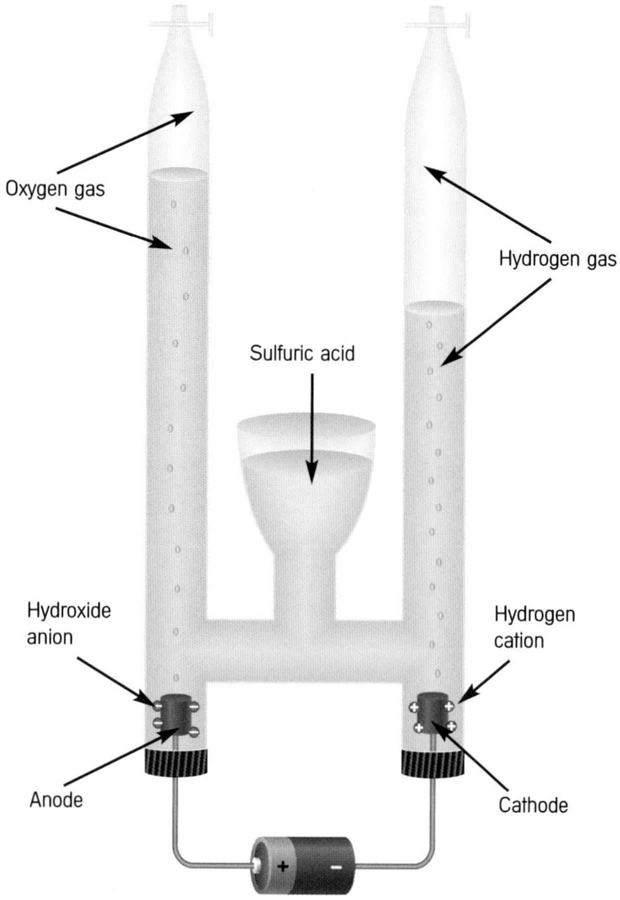

HT The electrolysis of dilute sulfuric acid can be represented by two half-equations:

- At the cathode:

$$2H^+(aq) + 2e^- \xrightarrow{\text{Reduction}} H_2(g)$$

- At the anode:

$$4OH^-(aq) - 4e^- \xrightarrow{\text{Oxidation}} 2H_2O(l) + O_2(g)$$

Key Words

Electrode • Electrolysis • Electrolyte • Ion

Extracting Aluminium

Aluminium is obtained from its mineral ore using electrolysis.

The **electrodes** are made of graphite (a type of carbon). The aluminium ore (bauxite) is purified to leave aluminium oxide, which is then melted.

When a current passes through the molten mixture...

- **positively charged aluminium ions** move towards the negative electrode and form **aluminium**
- **negatively charged oxygen ions** move towards the positive electrodes and form **oxygen**.

The process requires a large amount of **electrical energy**. The anodes gradually wear away and need to be replaced.

The electrolysis of aluminium oxide can be represented by this equation:

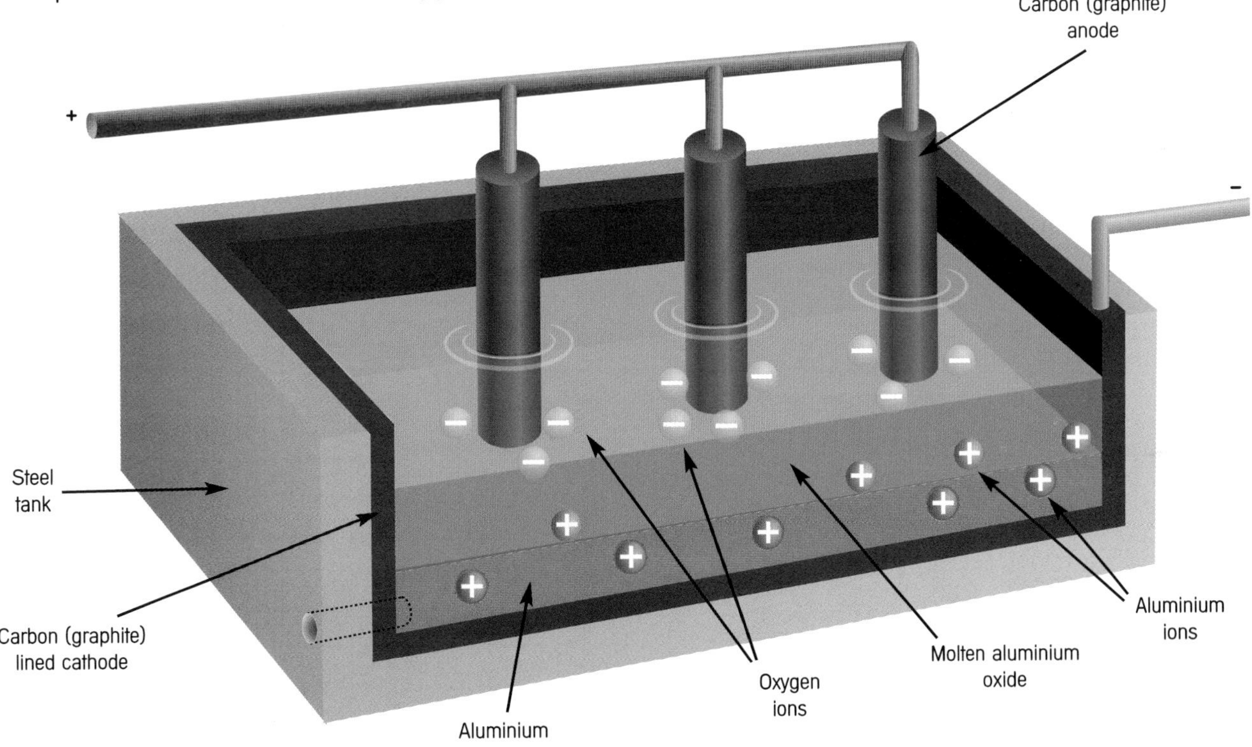

HT During extraction, aluminium oxide is **mixed** with **cryolite** (a compound of aluminium) to **lower** its **melting point**. This **reduces the energy** needed for the process.

However, the extraction still uses **large amounts** of **electricity** which makes aluminium an **expensive** metal.

The electrolysis of molten aluminium oxide can be represented by two half-equations:

- At the cathode:

$$Al^{3+} + 3e^- \xrightarrow{\text{Reduction}} Al$$

- At the anode:

$$2O^{2-} \xrightarrow{\text{Oxidation}} O_2 + 4e^-$$

Transition Elements

The Transition Metals

The **transition metals**, a block of metallic elements, are between Groups 2 and 3 of the periodic table. This block includes iron (Fe), copper (Cu), platinum (Pt), mercury (Hg), chromium (Cr) and zinc (Zn).

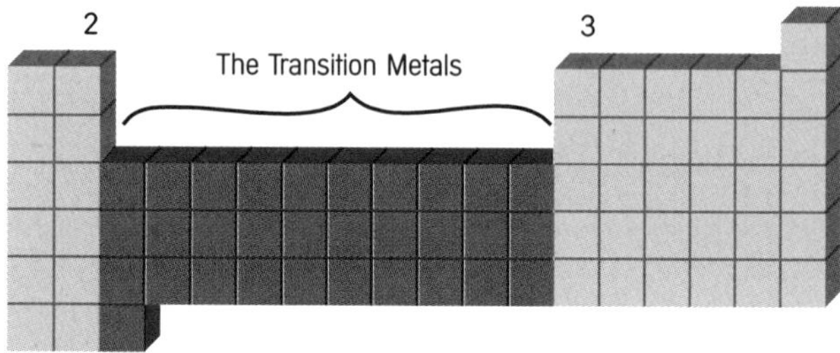

Transition metals have the typical properties of metals. Their compounds are often coloured, for example...

- **copper** compounds are **blue**
- **iron (II)** compounds are **light green**
- **iron (III)** compounds are **orange–brown**.

Many transition metals and their compounds are often catalysts, for example...

- iron is used in the Haber process
- nickel is used in the manufacture of margarine.

Thermal Decomposition

Thermal decomposition is a reaction where a substance is broken down into simpler substances by heating.

When **transition metal carbonates** are heated, a **colour change** occurs and they decompose to form a **metal oxide** and **carbon dioxide**. The test for carbon dioxide is that it **turns limewater milky**.

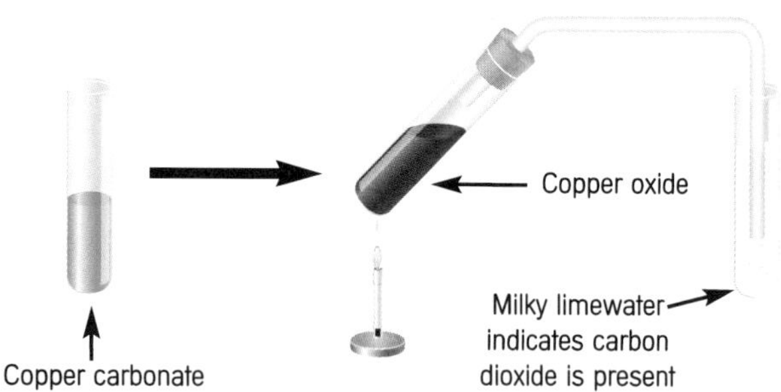

	Copper (II) carbonate	⟶	Copper (II) oxide +	Carbon dioxide
HT	$CuCO_3(s)$	⟶	$CuO(s)$ +	$CO_2(g)$
	Iron (II) carbonate	⟶	Iron (II) oxide +	Carbon dioxide
HT	$FeCO_3(s)$	⟶	$FeO(s)$ +	$CO_2(g)$
	Manganese carbonate	⟶	Manganese oxide +	Carbon dioxide
HT	$MnCO_3(s)$	⟶	$MnO(s)$ +	$CO_2(g)$
	Zinc carbonate	⟶	Zinc oxide +	Carbon dioxide
HT	$ZnCO_3(s)$	⟶	$ZnO(s)$ +	$CO_2(g)$

Identifying Transition Metal Ions

Precipitation is the reaction between **solutions** that makes an **insoluble solid**. Metal compounds in solution contain metal **ions**.

The following ions form coloured **precipitates**:

Metal Ion	Colour of Precipitate	Ionic Symbol Equation
Copper (II), Cu^{2+}	Blue	HT $Cu^{2+} + 2OH^- \rightarrow Cu(OH)_2$
Iron (II) Fe^{2+}	Grey–green	HT $Fe^{2+} + 2OH^- \rightarrow Fe(OH)_2$
Iron (III), Fe^{3+}	Orange–brown	HT $Fe^{3+} + 3OH^- \rightarrow Fe(OH)_3$

Key Words

Ion • Precipitate • Precipitation

Metal Structure and Properties

Metals

Iron and **copper** (transition metals) have many uses, for example...

- **iron** is used to make steel (which is used to make cars and bridges because it's very strong)
- **copper** is used to make electrical wiring because it's a good conductor.

Metals are very useful materials because of their properties. Several of their properties are as follows:

- **Lustrous** (shiny), e.g. gold is used in jewellery.
- **Hard** and with a **high density**, e.g. steel is used to make drill parts.
- **High tensile strength** (able to bear loads), e.g. steel is used to make bridge girders.
- **High melting** and **boiling points**, e.g. tungsten is used to make light bulb filaments.
- **Good conductors** of **heat** and **electricity**, e.g. copper is used to make saucepans and wiring.

Structure of Metals

Metal atoms are packed very close together in a regular arrangement. The atoms are held together by **metallic bonds**.

Metals have **high melting and boiling points** because lots of energy is needed to overcome the strong metallic bonds. As the metal atoms pack together, they build a structure of crystals.

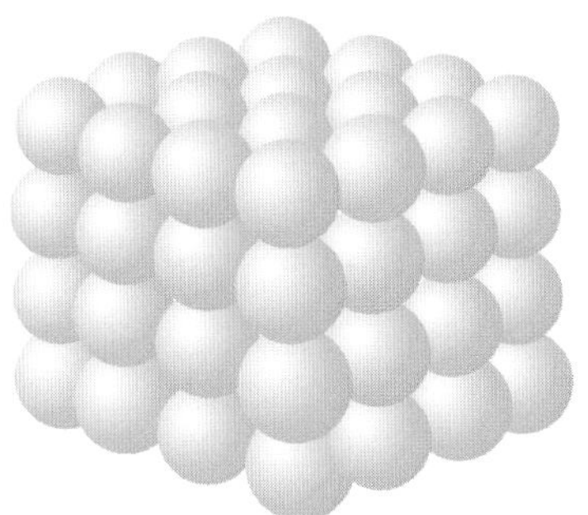

HT The metallic bond structure consists of closely packed positive metal ions in a 'sea' of **delocalised** (free) electrons. The **free movement** of the delocalised electrons allows the metal to **conduct electricity**.

The metal is held together by **strong forces** (the electrostatic attraction between the metal ions and the delocalised electrons). This is why the metal structure has high melting and boiling points.

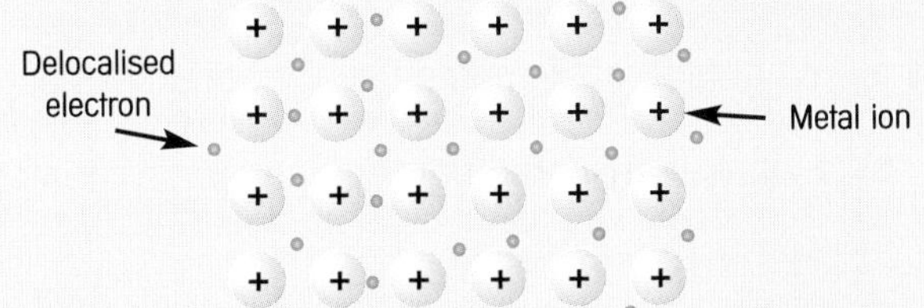

Superconductors

Metals are able to conduct electricity because the atoms are very close together and the electrons can move from atom to atom.

At low temperatures, some metals can become **superconductors**. A superconductor has little, or no, resistance to the flow of electricity. This low resistance is useful for...

- powerful electromagnets, e.g. inside medical scanners
- very fast electronic circuits, e.g. in a supercomputer
- power transmission that doesn't lose energy.

HT The disadvantage of current superconductors is that they only work at temperatures **below -200°C**.

This very low temperature is **costly** to maintain and impractical for large-scale uses. So, there is a need to develop superconductors that will work at room temperature (20°C).

Module C3 Practice Questions

1 a) What type of chemical bonding shares electrons?

b) How many atoms of each element are there in $Mg(NO_3)_2$?

c) Balance the following equation: $Na + H_2O \longrightarrow NaOH + H_2$.

HT d) What is the formula of silver nitrate?

2 a) What charge does a proton have?

b) What are isotopes?

HT c) Briefly explain why an atom has no overall charge.

3 a) What is an ion?

b) How would you make a 2^- ion from a neutral atom?

c) Give two properties of a typical ionic substance such as sodium chloride.

i) ii)

HT d) What is the formula of the ionic compound formed by Fe^{3+} and SO_4^{2-}?

4 a) What type of elements usually bond covalently?

b) Explain why carbon dioxide and water don't conduct electricity.

c) An element has the electronic structure 2,8,4. In which group and period would you find this element?

5 Why are Group 1 metals stored in oil?

b) Write the word equation for the reaction between lithium and water.

c) Alex put a white salt into a Bunsen flame on the end of a wire. The flame changed to a lilac colour. Which metal is in the white salt?

HT d) Write the formula equation for the reaction between potassium and water.

Module C3 Practice Questions

6 **a)** Which gas is used to sterilise water? ....

b) Write the word equation to show the reaction of sodium iodide solution with chlorine gas.

....

HT **c)** Write the formula equation to show the reaction of sodium iodide solution with chlorine gas.

....

d) Write the ionic equation to show the formation of bromide ions from a bromine molecule.

....

7 **a)** What is an electrolyte? ....

b) What is the charge on an anode? ....

c) Write the word equation to show the decomposition of aluminium oxide by electrolysis.

....

HT **d)** Write the ionic equation to show the reaction at the cathode during the electrolysis of molten aluminium oxide. ....

8 **a)** What is thermal decomposition?

....

b) Write the word equation for the thermal decomposition of copper carbonate.

....

c) Which metal ion makes an orange–brown precipitate with sodium hydroxide solution?

....

9 **a)** Why is iron so useful for making cars and bridges? ....

b) How do metals conduct electricity?

....

c) What is a superconductor, and what is the main problem with using them?

....

HT **d)** Briefly explain what metallic bonding is.

....

Speed

Measuring Speed

The **speed** of an object is a measure of how fast it's moving. Speed is measured in...

- metres per second (m/s)
- kilometres per hour (km/h)
- miles per hour (mph).

You can work out the speed of a moving object if you know...

- the **distance** it travels (measured using a measuring tape / trundle wheel)
- the **time it takes** to travel that distance (measured using a stopwatch / stopclock).

The faster the speed of an object, the...

- greater the distance it travels in a particular time
- shorter the time it takes to travel a particular distance.

You can calculate the speed of an object by using this formula:

$$\textbf{Speed (m/s)} = \frac{\textbf{Distance travelled (m)}}{\textbf{Time taken (s)}}$$

$$\frac{d}{s \times t}$$

Example 1

Calculate the speed of a cyclist who travels 2400m in 5 minutes.

$$\text{Speed} = \frac{\text{Distance}}{\text{Time taken}}$$
$$= \frac{2400\text{m}}{300\text{s}} = \mathbf{8m/s}$$

HT You can rearrange the speed formula to calculate either distance or time taken.

Example 2

Calculate the distance a car travels in 90 minutes if it's travelling at a constant speed of 80km/h.

Distance = Speed x Time taken
= 80km/h x 1.5h = **120km**

Example 3

Calculate the time it takes a motorcyclist to travel a distance of 120km at 50km/h.

$$\text{Time taken} = \frac{\text{Distance}}{\text{Speed}}$$
$$= \frac{120\text{km}}{50\text{km/h}} = \mathbf{2h\ 24min}$$

Speed Cameras

Speed cameras generally take **two pictures** of a vehicle a **certain amount of time apart**. The position of the vehicle in relation to the **distance markings** on the road in the two pictures can be used to calculate the vehicle's speed.

$$\textbf{Speed of car} = \frac{\textbf{Distance travelled between pictures}}{\textbf{Time taken between first and second picture}}$$

Distance–Time Graphs

The slope of a **distance–time graph** represents the speed of an object. The **steeper the gradient (slope)**, the **greater the speed**.

This graph shows the movement of three people.

1. A stationary person standing 10m from point (0).
2. A person moving at a constant speed of 2m/s.
3. A person moving at a greater constant speed of 3m/s.

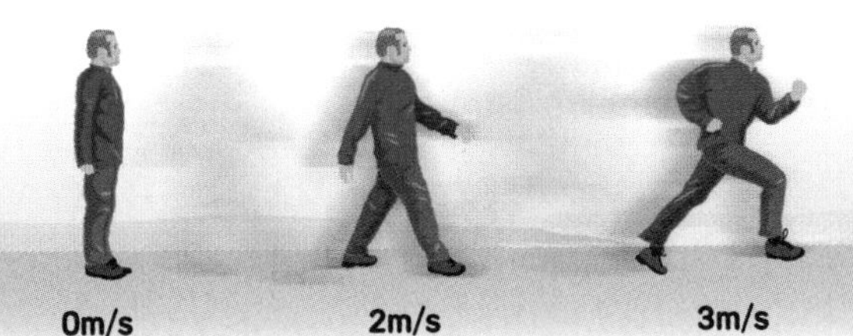

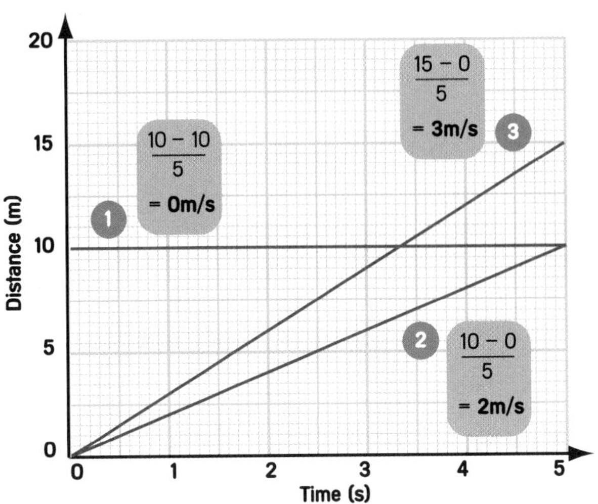

Key Words

Distance–Time graph • Speed

HT Calculating Speed

To work out the speed of an object, take any two points on a distance–time graph and read off the distance travelled for that part of the journey, and the time taken to get there (see Graph 1).

By looking at the graph, you can use the formula to calculate the speed at each part of the journey.

O to A: Speed = $\frac{15 - 0\text{m}}{3\text{s}}$ = **5m/s**

A to B: Speed = $\frac{15 - 15\text{m}}{5\text{s}}$ = **0m/s**

B to C: Speed = $\frac{15 - 0\text{m}}{4\text{s}}$ = **3.75m/s**

So, the object...

- travelled at 5m/s for 3 seconds
- remained stationary for 5 seconds
- travelled at 3.75m/s for 4 seconds back to the starting point.

Graphs can also be drawn for **non-uniform speed** (see Graph 2).

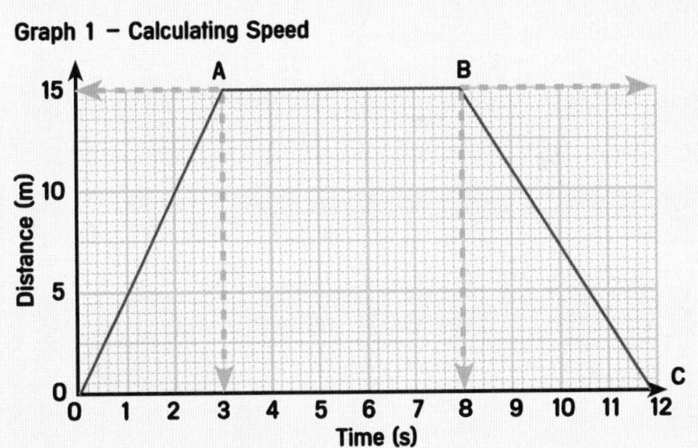

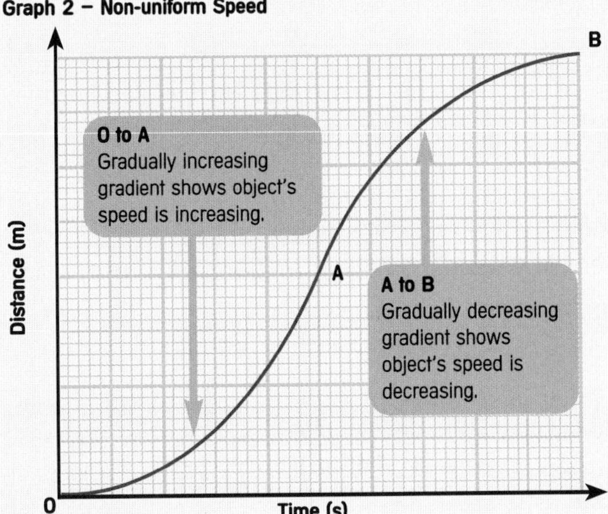

Changing Speed

Measuring Acceleration

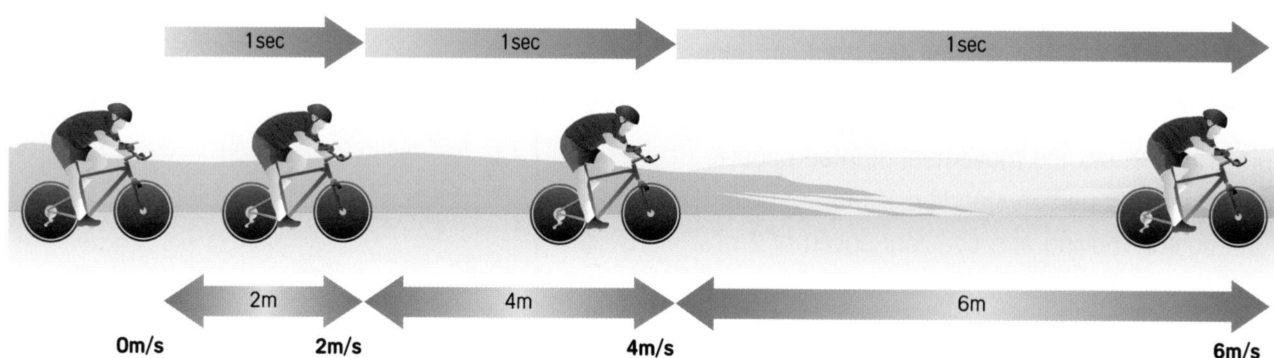

The **acceleration** or **deceleration** of an object is the change in **speed** per second. It's a measure of how quickly an object **speeds up** or **slows down**.

Acceleration is **only** measured in **metres per second squared** (m/s^2).

To work out the acceleration of a moving object you need to know...

- the **change in speed**
- the **time taken** for the change in speed.

You can calculate the acceleration (or deceleration) of an object by using this formula:

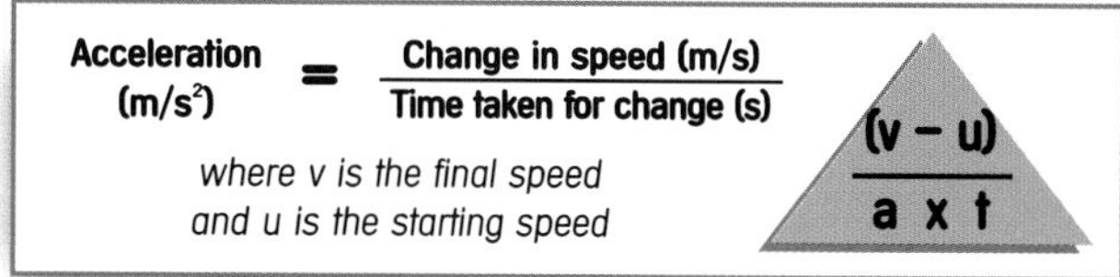

Example 1

A cyclist accelerates uniformly from rest and reaches a speed of 10m/s after 5 seconds. He then decelerates uniformly and comes to rest in a further 10 seconds.

a) Calculate his acceleration.

$$\text{Acceleration} = \frac{\text{Change in Speed}}{\text{Time taken for change}}$$

$$= \frac{10 - 0\text{m/s}}{5\text{s}} = \mathbf{2m/s^2}$$

b) Calculate his deceleration.

$$= \frac{0 - 10\text{m/s}}{10\text{s}} = \mathbf{1m/s^2}$$

HT The acceleration formula can be rearranged to calculate time taken or change in speed.

Example 2

An object falls from the top of a building with an acceleration of $10m/s^2$. It hits the ground with a speed of 25m/s. Calculate how long the object takes to fall.

$$\text{Time taken} = \frac{\text{Change in speed}}{\text{Acceleration}}$$

$$= \frac{25\text{m/s} - 0}{10\text{m/s}^2}$$

$$= \mathbf{2.5s}$$

Example 3

A car accelerates at $1.5m/s^2$ for 12 seconds. Calculate the change in speed of the car.

Change in speed = Acceleration x Time taken

$$= 1.5\text{m/s}^2 \times 12\text{s}$$

$$= \mathbf{18m/s}$$

*N.B. Acceleration can involve a **change of direction** as well as **speed**.*

Key Words

Acceleration • Speed • Speed–Time graph

Speed–Time Graphs

The slope of a **speed–time graph** represents the **acceleration** of the object. A constant acceleration increases the speed.

This graph shows an object moving at a constant speed of 10m/s. It **isn't** accelerating.

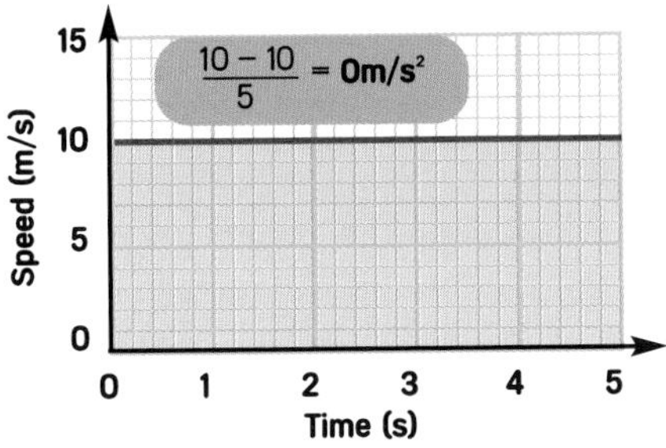

This graph shows an object moving at a constant acceleration of 2m/s^2.

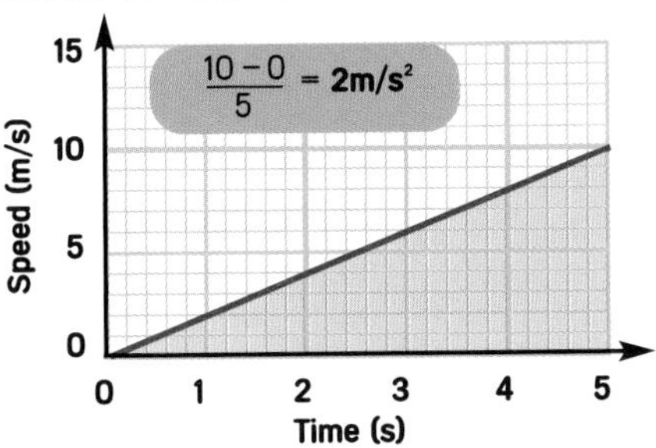

This graph shows an object moving at a greater constant acceleration of 3m/s^2.

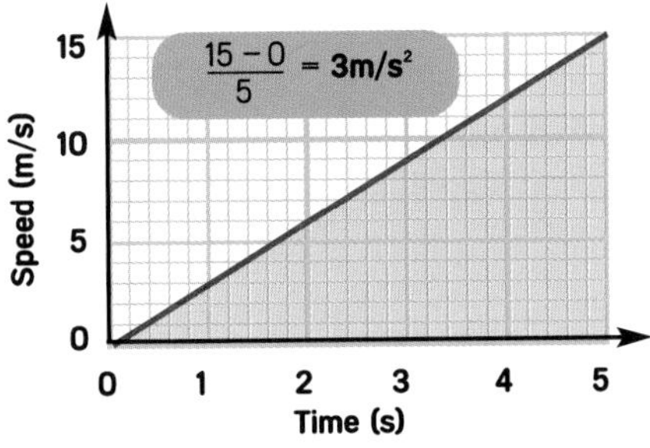

This graph shows an object moving at a constant acceleration of -3m/s^2.

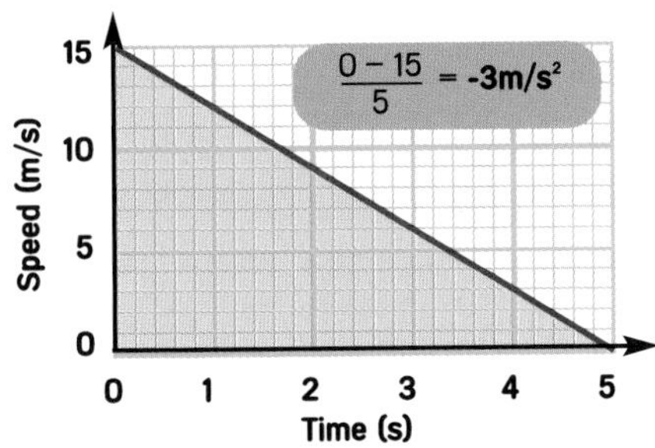

N.B. The ***area underneath the line*** *in a speed–time graph represents the* ***total distance travelled.***

HT To work out the acceleration of an object, take any two points on a speed–time graph and read off the change in speed over the chosen period, and the time taken for this change.

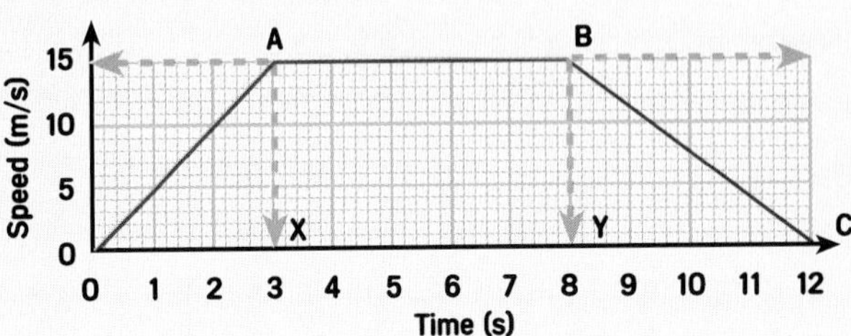

You can use the formula to calculate the acceleration at each part of the journey.

O to A: Acceleration = $\frac{15\text{m/s} - 0\text{m/s}}{3\text{s}}$ = **5m/s^2**

A to B: Acceleration = $\frac{15\text{m/s} - 15\text{m/s}}{5\text{s}}$ = **0m/s^2**

B to C: Acceleration = $\frac{0\text{m/s} - 15\text{m/s}}{4\text{s}}$ = **-3.75m/s^2**

So, the object...

- accelerated at 5m/s^2 for 3 seconds
- travelled at a constant speed of 15m/s for 5 seconds
- decelerated at a rate of 3.75m/s^2 for 4 seconds.

The total distance travelled can be calculated by working out the area under the speed–time graph.

= Area of OAX + Area of ABYX + Area of BCY

= $(\frac{1}{2} \times 3 \times 15) + (5 \times 15) + (\frac{1}{2} \times 4 \times 15)$ = **127.5m**

Graphs can also be drawn to represent **non-uniform** motion.

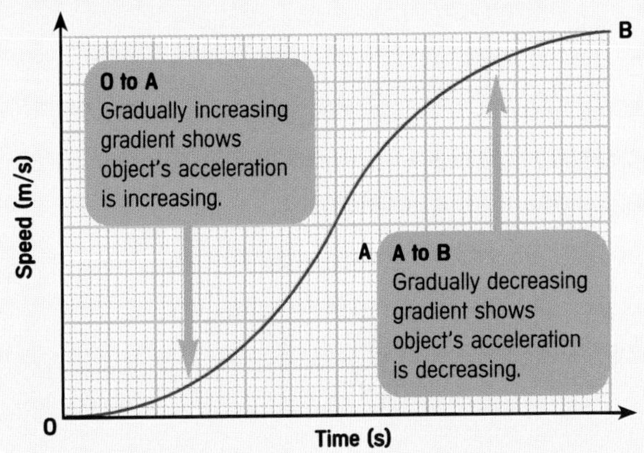

Forces and Motion

Forces in Action

Forces, measured in **newtons** (N), are **pushes** or **pulls**. They may be **different in size** and **act in different directions**.

Forces can cause objects to **accelerate** or decelerate.

For example...

- **weight** causes an apple falling from a tree to speed up as it falls
- **friction** causes a car to slow down
- **air resistance** causes a skydiver to slow down when the parachute opens.

Force, Mass and Acceleration

If an unbalanced force acts, the acceleration of the object will depend on...

- the **size** of the unbalanced force – the **bigger the force** the **greater the acceleration**
- the **mass** of the object – the **bigger the mass** the **smaller the acceleration**.

Example

A boy pushes a trolley. He exerts an unbalanced force which causes the trolley to move and accelerate.

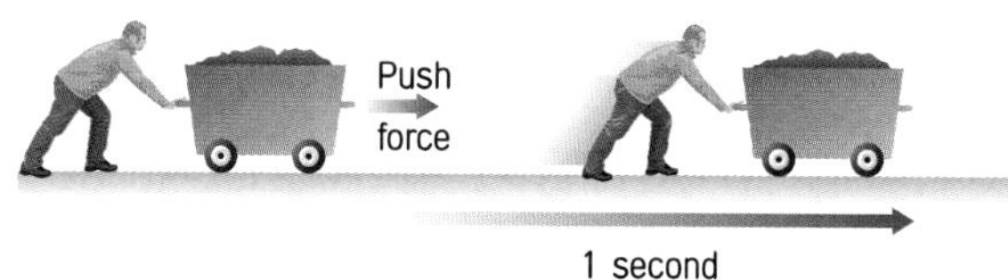

If two boys push the same trolley, it moves with a greater acceleration. (**More force = more acceleration.**)

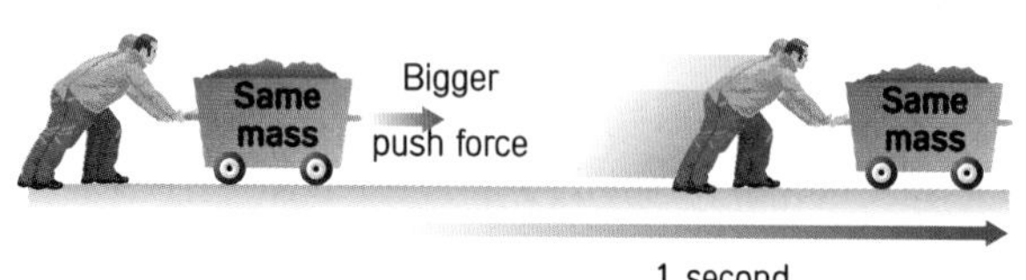

If the first boy now pushes a trolley of bigger mass, it moves with a smaller acceleration than the first trolley. (**More mass = less acceleration.**)

If two trolleys with different masses move with a constant acceleration, the trolley with the larger mass will have more force than the trolley with the smaller mass. (**More mass = more force required.**)

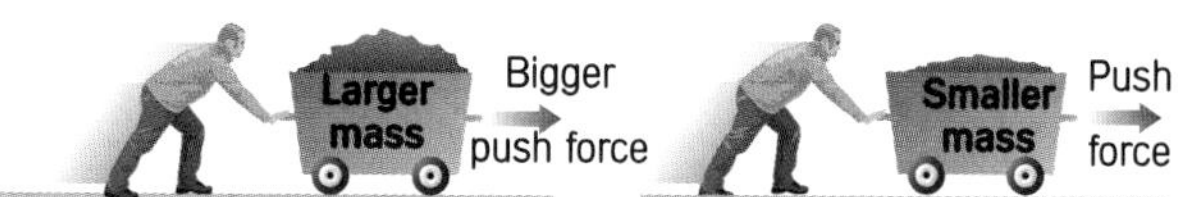

The relationship between force, mass and acceleration is shown in this formula:

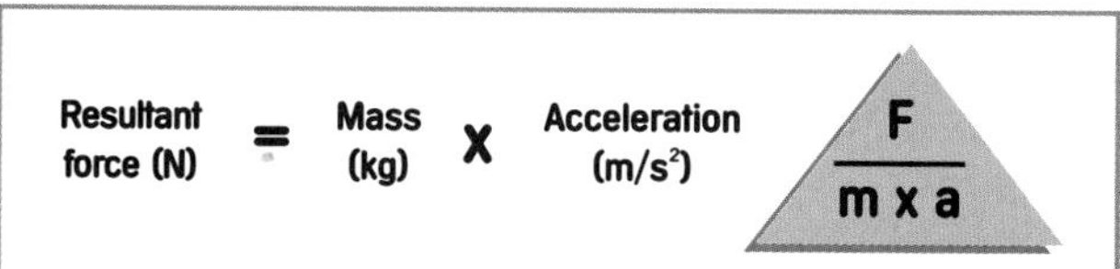

A **newton (N)** can be defined as the force needed to give a **mass of one kilogram** an acceleration of one **metre per second per second** ($1 m/s^2$).

Example

A trolley of mass 400kg is accelerating at $0.5 m/s^2$. What force is needed to achieve this acceleration?

Force = Mass x Acceleration
= $400 kg \times 0.5 m/s^2$
= 200N

HT When object A exerts a force on object B, object B exerts an **equal but opposite** force on object A.

For example, a girl standing still is being **pulled down** to the ground **by gravity**, and the ground is **pushing up** with an **equal force**.

Stopping Distance

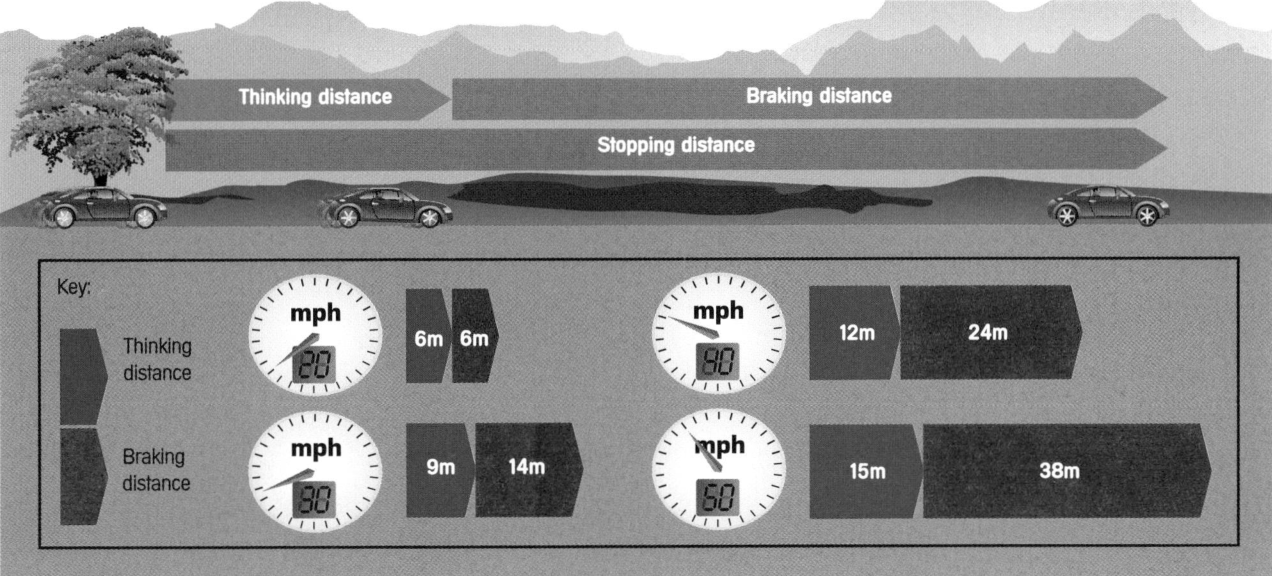

Stopping distance = Thinking distance + Braking distance

The stopping distance of a vehicle depends on...

- the **thinking distance** – the distance travelled by the vehicle from the point the driver realises he needs to brake to when he applies the brakes
- the **braking distance** – the distance it takes the vehicle to stop once the driver applies the brakes.

The **thinking distance** is **increased** if...

- the vehicle is travelling faster
- the driver is ill, tired or under the influence of alcohol or drugs
- the driver is distracted or isn't concentrating
- there is poor visibility.

The **braking distance** is **increased** if...

- the vehicle is travelling faster
- there is poor weather / bad road conditions, e.g. if it's wet, slippery or icy
- the vehicle is in a poor condition, e.g. worn brakes and tyres or under-inflated tyres.

The thinking distance and braking distance of a vehicle under normal driving conditions depend on the vehicle's **speed**.

It takes much longer to stop at faster speeds, so road safety regulations advise you to...

- obey the speed limits
- keep your distance from the car in front
- allow extra room between cars (or drive more slowly) in bad weather or poor road conditions.

HT The braking distance of a vehicle is increased if...

- the **mass** of the vehicle is **increased** – a loaded vehicle has a greater **kinetic energy**
- the **friction** between the tyres and the road is **decreased** – a wet or greasy road surface reduces the amount of friction between the tyres and the road
- the **braking force** applied is **decreased** – a smaller force is exerted by the brake pads on the wheel discs
- the vehicle is **travelling faster** – a faster vehicle has greater kinetic energy.

Key Words

Acceleration • Force • Speed

Work and Power

Work

Work is done whenever a **force** moves an object. You do work and develop power during everyday activities, for example...

- **lifting** weights
- **climbing** stairs
- **pulling** a rubbish bin
- **pushing** a shopping trolley.

Energy is needed to do work. Both energy and work are measured in joules, J.

Work done (J) = Energy transferred (J)

The amount of work done depends on the...

- **size of the force** (in newtons)
- **distance** the object is moved (in metres).

Work done can be calculated using this formula:

Work done (J) = Force applied (N) X Distance moved in direction of force (m)

Power

Power is a measure of how quickly work is done. Power is measured in **watts**, **(W)**.

Some cars have much higher power ratings than others and may also use more fuel. High fuel consumption is...

- expensive for the driver
- damaging to the environment.

Power, work done and time taken are linked by this formula:

$$\text{Power (W)} = \frac{\text{Work done (J)}}{\text{Time (s)}}$$

Example 1

A girl does 2400 joules of work when she runs up a flight of stairs in 8 seconds. Calculate her power.

$$\text{Power} = \frac{\text{Work done}}{\text{Time}} = \frac{2400\text{J}}{8\text{s}} = \textbf{300W}$$

HT The power formula can be rearranged to work out distance moved or time taken.

Example 2

A crane does 200 000J of work when it lifts a load of 25 000N. The power of the crane is 50kW.

a) Calculate the distance moved by the load.

$$\text{Distance} = \frac{\text{Work done}}{\text{Force applied}}$$

$$= \frac{200\ 000\text{J}}{25\ 000\text{N}}$$

$$= \textbf{8m}$$

b) Calculate the time taken to move the load.

$$\text{Time} = \frac{\text{Work done}}{\text{Power}}$$

$$= \frac{200\ 000\text{J}}{50\ 000\text{W}}$$

Power must be in watts

$$= \textbf{4s}$$

Energy on the Move

Kinetic Energy

Kinetic energy is the energy an object has because of its movement. The following all have kinetic energy:

- a ball rolling along the ground
- a car travelling along a road
- a boy running.

The kinetic energy of an object depends on...

- its **mass** (kg)
- its **speed** (m/s).

A moving car has kinetic energy because it has **both mass and speed.**

1. If a car moves with a **greater speed** it has **more kinetic energy.**
2. If a car has **greater mass** it has more **kinetic energy.**

1

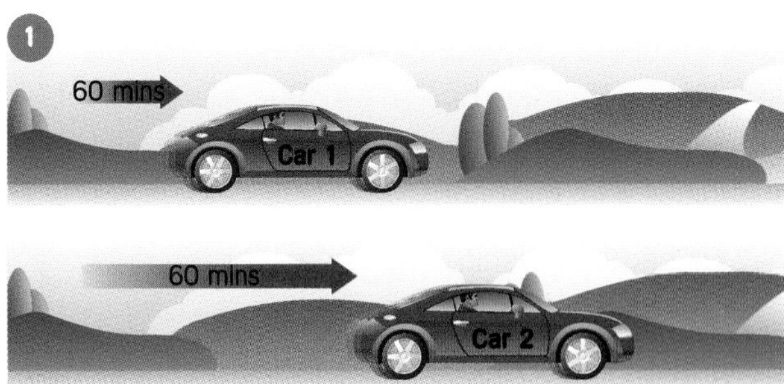

The cars have the same mass, but car 2 has more kinetic energy because it is travelling faster.

2

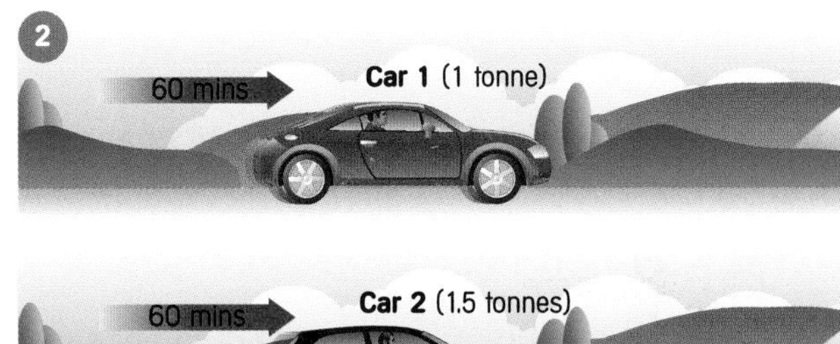

Although they are travelling at the same speed, car 2 has more kinetic energy because it has a greater mass.

HT You can calculate kinetic energy by using this formula:

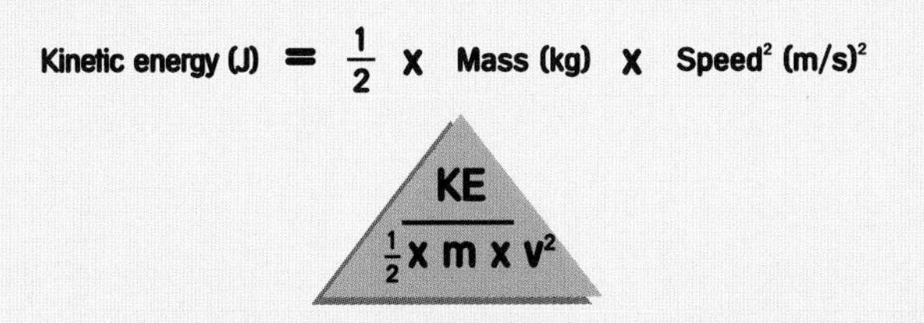

Example

A car of mass 1000kg is moving at a speed of 10m/s. How much kinetic energy does it have?

Kinetic energy $= \frac{1}{2} \times \text{Mass} \times \text{Speed}^2$

$= \frac{1}{2} \times 1000\text{kg} \times (10\text{m/s})^2$

$=$ **50 000J** (or **50kJ**)

Fuel Consumption

Most cars rely on fossil fuels (petrol or diesel) for their energy. But, electricity can also be used, i.e. cars can be driven by...

- battery power
- solar power.

Cars powered by fossil fuels **pollute** the environment at the **point of use**. Battery-powered cars don't do this, but recharging the batteries uses electricity that is generated in power stations. And power stations **do cause pollution**.

HT Car fuel consumption depends on the...

- energy required to increase the kinetic energy
- energy required to work against friction
- driving style and speed
- road conditions.

Key Words

Force • Kinetic energy • Mass • Power • Speed

Crumple Zones

Car Safety Features

Modern cars have **safety features** that absorb energy in a collision, including...

- **seat-belts** to prevent people in the car from being propelled forwards
- **air bags** to cushion the impact for the driver and passengers
- **brakes** to transfer kinetic energy to heat energy, which reduces speed
- **crumple zone**, a part of the car designed to 'crumple' during a collision.

Crumple zones, seatbelts and air bags **all change shape** on impact to **absorb energy**. This **reduces the risk of injury** to the people in the car.

Seatbelts have to be replaced after a crash because they can be damaged by the forces they experience.

Active Safety Features

Active safety features are designed to protect you, and to help you to get out of a crash situation:

- **Anti-lock braking systems** (ABS) prevent the tyres from skidding. This stops the vehicle more quickly and allows the driver to control the steering.
- **Traction control** prevents the car from skidding while accelerating. This helps the driver to quickly get out of a dangerous situation.
- A **safety cage** is a metal cage which strengthens the cabin section of the car. It prevents the vehicle from collapsing when upside down or rolling.

Safety Cage Reinforces Body of Car

Passive Safety Features

Passive safety features help prevent accidents by **reducing distractions**, for example...

- **electric windows** make it easier for drivers to open and close the windows whilst driving
- **cruise control** allows drivers to select a continuous speed which helps to reduce accidental speeding
- **paddle shift controls** allow drivers to keep both hands on the steering wheel when changing gear or adjusting the stereo
- **adjustable seating** allows drivers to sit comfortably and be able to reach the steering wheel and control pedals easily.

Crumple Zones and Falling Safely

HT Reducing Stopping Forces

The stopping forces experienced in a collision can be **reduced** by...

- **increasing** the stopping or **collision time**
- **increasing** the stopping or **collision distance**
- **decelerating**.

All of the standard safety features reduce the stopping forces on the people in the car. This reduces the risk of injury.

Anti-lock braking systems prevent the tyres from skidding. This increases the area of the tyres that is in contact with the road. **Friction** between the two surfaces is increased, so the braking distance is reduced, and the car is able to stop more quickly.

Weight and Gravity

Objects fall because of their **weight**, and they get **faster** as they fall. Weight is a force **pulling us** towards the centre of the planet, in our case, Earth. The strength of weight depends on the **gravity** of the planet.

Gravity is a force of attraction that acts between objects that have mass, i.e. a falling object and the Earth. The weight of an object is the force exerted on it by gravity. It is measured in **newtons (N)**.

Falling objects experience two forces:

- the **downward force** of weight, W (↓), which always stays the same
- the **upward force** of **air resistance**, R, or drag (↑).

When there is no atmosphere, falling objects don't experience drag and their acceleration in free-fall is constant. This is the case on the **Moon** and elsewhere **in space**.

Frictional Forces

Frictional forces, such as **drag**, **friction** and **air resistance**, can act against the movement of the object, slowing it down. These forces can be reduced by...

- changing the shape of the object
- using a lubricant (to make the object slide through the air with less resistance).

The shape of an object can influence its top speed:

- **Badminton shuttlecocks** increase air resistance so they travel slowly.
- **Parachutes** have a larger surface area to increase air resistance.
- **Roof boxes** on cars increase air resistance.
- **Deflectors** on lorries and caravans reduce air resistance.
- **Wedge-shaped** sports cars reduce air resistance.

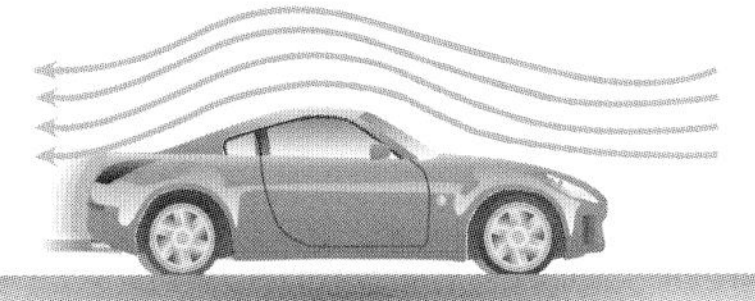

Key Words

Air resistance • Friction • Gravity • Weight

Falling Safely

Terminal Speed

When a skydiver jumps out of an aeroplane, the speed of his descent can be considered in two separate parts:

- **before the parachute opens** (when the skydiver is in free-fall)
- **after the parachute opens** (when air resistance is greatly increased).

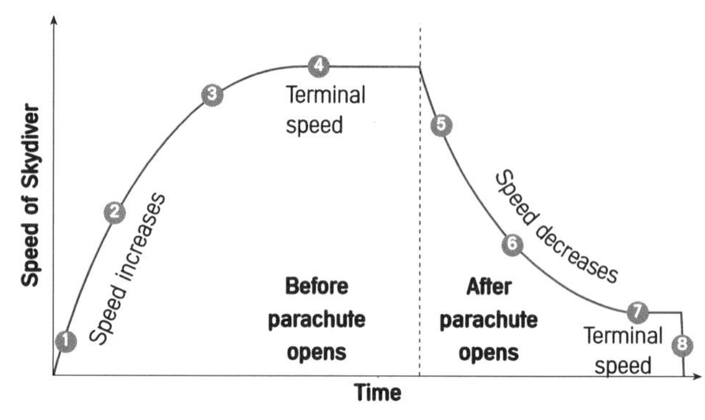

Before the Parachute Opens

1. When the skydiver jumps, he initially accelerates due to the force of **gravity**.
2. As he falls, he experiences the **frictional force of air resistance** (R) in the opposite direction. At this point, **weight** (W) is **greater than R**, so he continues to accelerate.
3. As his speed increases, so does the air resistance acting on him.
4. Air resistance increases until it's equal to W. The force now acting on him is zero and his falling speed becomes **constant**. This speed is called the **terminal speed**.

After the Parachute Opens

5. When the parachute is opened, unbalanced forces act again because the upward force of R is greatly increased and is bigger than W.
6. The increase in R decreases his speed. As his speed decreases, so does R.
7. R decreases until it's equal to W. The forces acting are once again balanced and, for the second time, he falls at a steady speed, although slower than before. This is a **new terminal speed**.

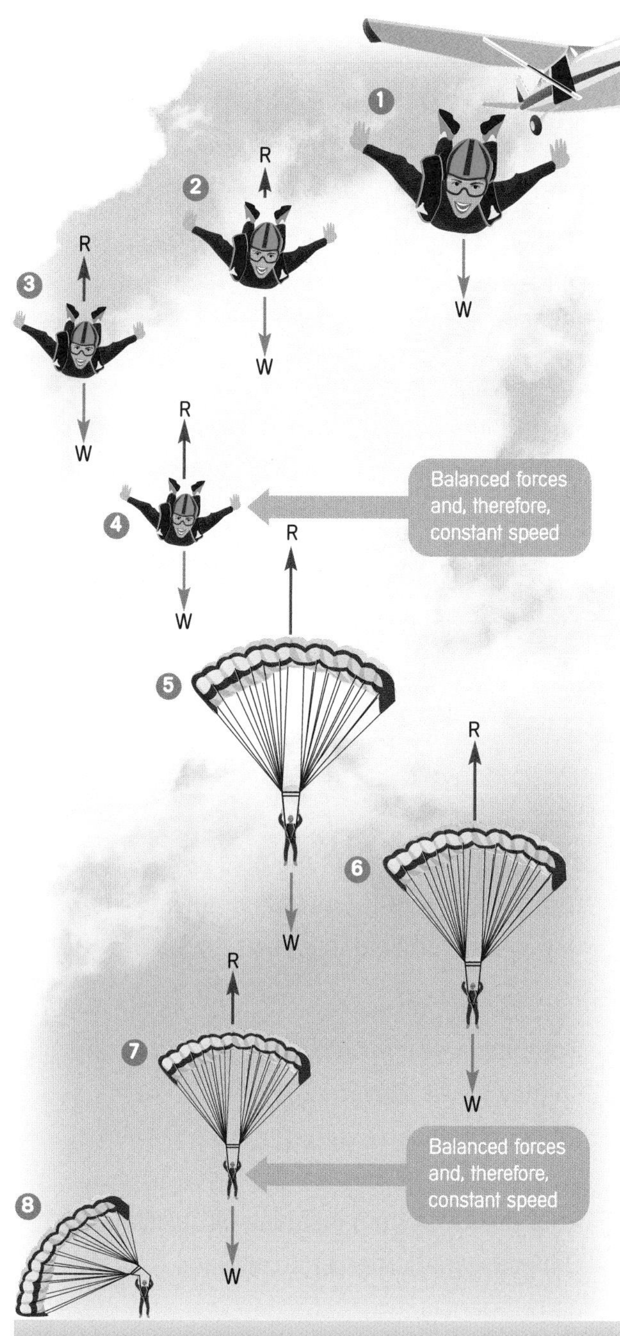

HT At **higher speeds**, falling objects experience **more drag**. If you **increase the area** of the object that's facing downwards, **you increase the drag**. The **terminal speed** occurs when the drag is equal to the weight of the object.

The Energy of Games and Theme Rides

Gravitational Potential Energy

The **gravitational potential energy** (GPE) of an object depends on...

- the energy stored due to its position in the Earth's gravitational field
- its **mass**.

Any object with the **potential** to fall has gravitational potential energy, for example a person standing on a diving board (before they jump off).

1. A man standing on a higher diving board will have **more GPE** than another man standing on a lower diving board (providing they have the same mass). This is because the higher man is further away from the ground.
2. A heavier man standing on the **same diving board** as a lighter man will have **more GPE**. This is because the heavier man has a **bigger mass**.

HT You can calculate GPE using this formula:

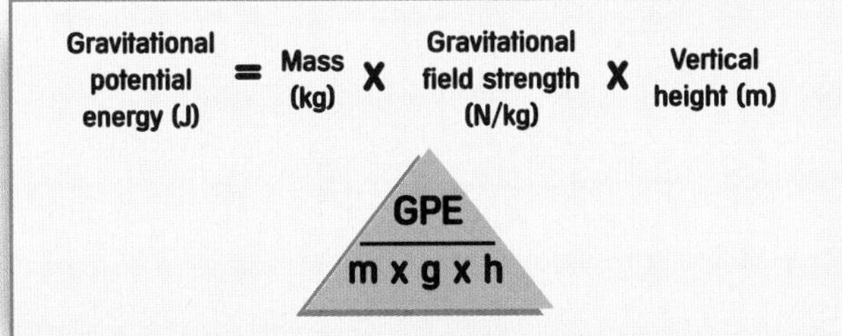

Gravitational potential energy (J) = Mass (kg) X Gravitational field strength (N/kg) X Vertical height (m)

Gravitational field strength, g, is a constant. On Earth it has a value of 10N/kg.

This means that every 1 kg of matter near the surface of the Earth experiences a downwards force of 10N due to gravity.

On planets where the gravitational field strength is higher, the gravitational potential energy is greater.

Key Words

Gravitational potential energy • Mass • Terminal speed

The Energy of Games and Theme Rides

HT Examples of GPE

Example 1

A skier of mass 80kg gets on a ski lift which takes her from a height of 1000m to a height of 3000m. By how much does her gravitational potential energy increase?

$$\text{Gravitational potential energy} = \text{Mass} \times \text{Gravitational field strength} \times \text{Vertical height}$$

$$= 80\text{kg} \times 10\text{N/kg} \times (3000\text{m} - 1000\text{m})$$

$$= 80\text{kg} \times 10\text{N/kg} \times 2000\text{m}$$

$$= \mathbf{1\,600\,000J} \text{ (or } \mathbf{1600kJ}\text{)}$$

N.B. Work done by the ski lift motor has been transferred into gravitational potential energy for the skier.

Example 2

A ball is kicked vertically upwards from the ground. Its mass is 0.2kg and it increases its gravitational potential energy by 30J when it reaches the top point in its flight. What height does the ball reach?

Rearrange the formula...

$$\text{Vertical height} = \frac{\text{GPE}}{\text{Mass} \times \text{Gravitational field strength}}$$

$$= \frac{30\text{J}}{0.2\text{kg} \times 10\text{N/kg}}$$

$$= \mathbf{15m}$$

GPE and Kinetic Energy

When an object falls, it converts **gravitational potential energy** into **kinetic energy** (KE). For example, this happens when...

- a diver jumps off a diving board
- a ball rolls down a hill
- a skydiver jumps out of a plane.

Many theme park rides, for example rollercoasters, also use this transfer of energy.

If the **mass** of the car is **doubled**, the kinetic energy also **doubles**.

If the **speed** of the car is **doubled**, the kinetic energy **quadruples**.

Increasing the **gravitational field strength, g,** will increase the gravitational potential energy. However this couldn't ever happen on Earth as gravitational field strength is **constant**.

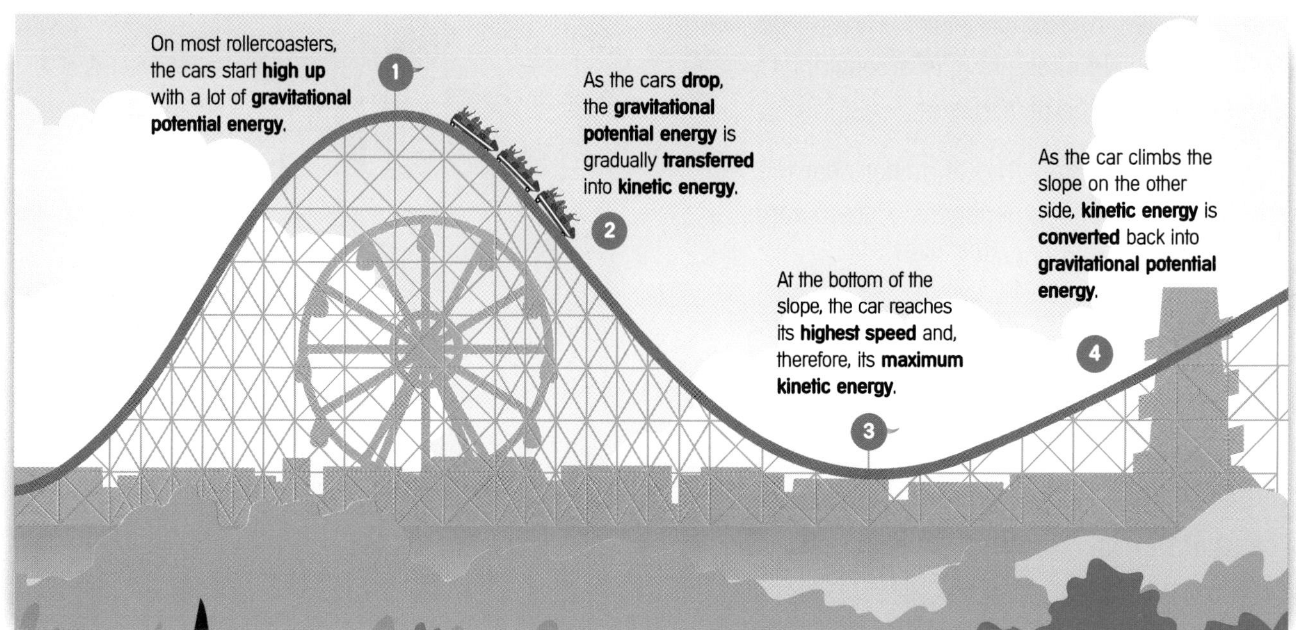

HT Terminal Speed

When an object falls at its **terminal speed**...

- the speed isn't changing so the kinetic energy doesn't increase.
- the GPE decreases as the object does work against friction (GPE is transferred into heat and sound energy).

Weight and Mass

Weight is due to the force of gravity on an object. The **mass** of an object is the amount of matter that it contains. Weight and mass are linked by two related formulae:

Weight (N)	=	Mass (kg)	x	Gravitational field strength (N/kg)	W / m x g

Weight (N)	=	Mass (kg)	x	Acceleration of free-fall (m/s^2)	W / m x g

Without air resistance, a falling object near the Earth's surface would have an acceleration of $10m/s^2$. This is known as the **acceleration of free-fall, g.**

The force which causes this acceleration is the weight of the object. The formula is W = mg.

Example 1

Calculate the weight of a falling stone of mass 0.1kg, if g = $10m/s^2$.

Weight = Mass x Acceleration of free-fall
= 0.1kg x $10m/s^2$
= **1N**

Near the surface of the Earth the gravitational field strength, g, is 10N/kg which means that every 1kg of matter experiences a downwards force, or has a weight, of 10N.

Example 2

Calculate the weight of a stone of mass 0.1kg on Earth, if g is 10N/kg.

Weight = Mass x Gravitational field strength
= 0.1kg x 10N/kg
= **1N**

N.B. Acceleration of free-fall and gravitational field strength are numerically the same, i.e. $10m/s^2$ and 10N/kg. They also both have the same symbol, g.

Key Words

Gravitational potential energy • Kinetic energy • Mass

Module P3 Practice Questions

1 a) Briefly describe what the **speed** of an object is.

b) Calculate the speed of a car which takes 20 seconds to cover a distance of 400 metres.

HT c) If the same car then travels another 400 metres at a speed of 40m/s, how long will it take?

2 Are the following statements **true** or **false**? Explain your answers.

a) A horizontal line on a distance–time graph shows that the object is travelling at a constant speed.

b) An increasingly steep line on a distance–time graph shows that the object's speed is increasing.

3 a) What two things do you need to know in order to calculate the acceleration of an object?

i) ii)

b) Draw lines between the boxes to match each statement with its meaning on a speed–time graph.

Straight line with a positive gradient	Constant speed
Straight line with a negative gradient	Deceleration
Horizontal straight line	Acceleration

4 a) List three forces which can cause objects to speed up or slow down.

i) ii) iii)

b) Calculate the force required for a car of mass 1500kg to accelerate at $5m/s^2$.

5 Draw lines to link each situation with the effect it will have on the stopping distance of a car.

The road is icy.	Only the thinking distance is increased.
The driver is drunk.	Only the braking distance is increased.
The car is travelling too fast.	Both the thinking and braking distance will be increased.

6 **a)** Which two things does the amount of work done depend on?

i) .... **ii)** ....

b) Calculate how much time it will take for a 1000W kettle to do 30kJ of work.

....

7 **a)** Fill in the missing words in the following sentence:

The kinetic energy of an object depends on its .... and the .... it's travelling at.

b) A 2000kg van is travelling at 20m/s. Calculate its kinetic energy.

....

8 List three passive safety features which are fitted to most cars.

a) .... **b)** .... **c)** ....

9 Put the following sentences into the correct order by numbering them **1** to **4**.

a) The skydiver reaches a very high terminal speed where air resistance is equal to his weight. ☐

b) The skydiver slows down to reach a lower terminal speed. ☐

c) As the skydiver falls, his speed increases because his weight is greater than air resistance. ☐

d) When he opens his parachute, the air resistance becomes greater than his weight. ☐

10 **a)** Put a tick next to any object(s) which don't possess gravitational potential energy.

i) A dog sitting by the side of a road. ☐

ii) An apple in a tree. ☐

iii) A rollercoaster at the top of a track. ☐

b) Fill in the missing words in the following sentences:

If the mass of a car is doubled, the kinetic energy is .... But, if the speed is doubled, the kinetic energy is ....

c) Calculate the height of a 100g cricket ball if it has 30J of gravitational potential energy.

....

....

d) An apple falls from a tree with an acceleration of $10m/s^2$. Calculate the weight of the apple if its mass is 80g.

....

Who Planted That There?

Plant Leaves

Cross-Section of Leaf

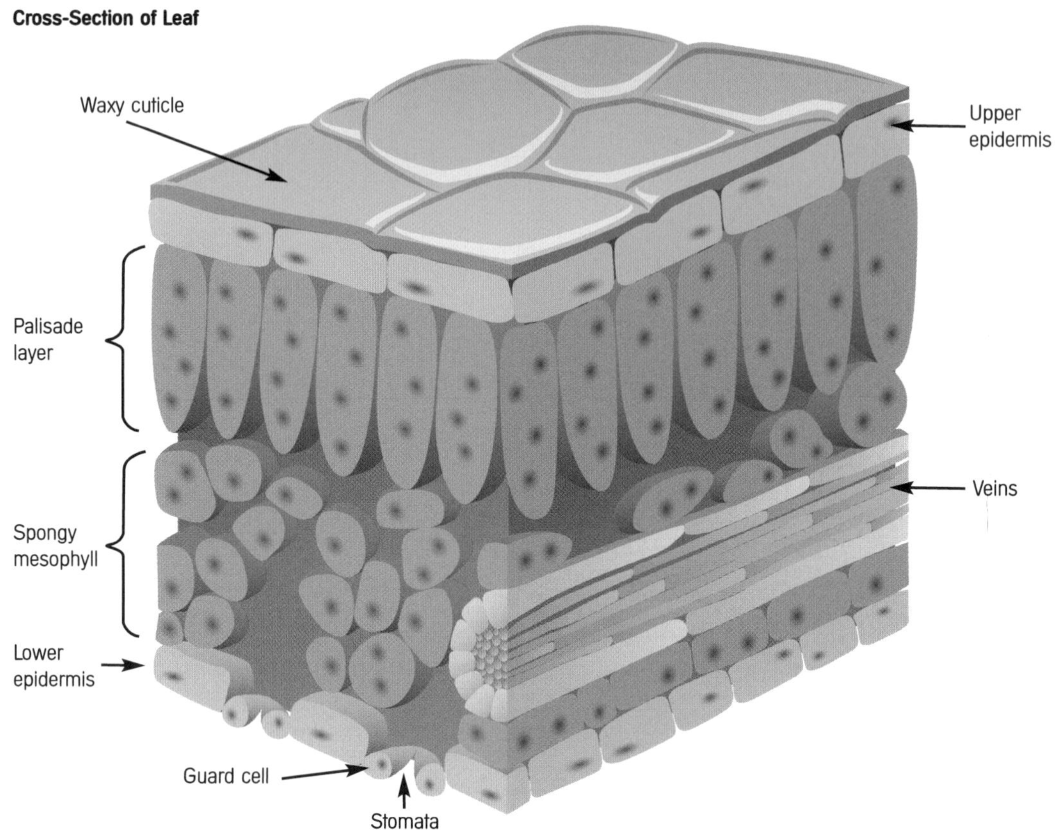

Photosynthesis occurs mainly in the leaves of plants. Leaves are specially adapted for efficiency.

For example, a leaf...

- contains **chlorophyll** (which absorbs light) in millions of chloroplasts
- is **broad** and **flat** to provide a **huge surface area** to absorb sunlight
- has a network of **veins** for **support**, and to **transport** water to the cells and remove the products of photosynthesis, i.e. glucose
- has a **thin structure** so the gases (carbon dioxide and oxygen) only have a short distance to travel to and from the cells
- has **stomata** (tiny pores) on the underside of the leaf to allow the **exchange** of **gases**.

During photosynthesis...

- **carbon dioxide** diffuses in through the **stomata**
- **oxygen** diffuses out through the **stomata**
- water is absorbed through the roots.

A leaf has four distinct layers:

- the **upper epidermis**
- the **palisade layer**
- the **spongy mesophyll**
- the **lower epidermis**.

HT In a typical leaf...

- the **upper epidermis** is **transparent** to allow sunlight through to the layer below
- the **cells** in the **palisade layer** are near the **top** of the leaf and are packed with **chloroplasts** so they can absorb the maximum amount of light
- the **spongy mesophyll** contains lots of **air spaces** connected to the stomata to allow the optimum exchange of gases.

This structure provides a **very large** **surface area: volume ratio** for efficient gaseous exchange.

Water, Water Everywhere

Osmosis

Osmosis is the **diffusion** of water **from high concentration of water** (dilute solution) **to low concentration of water** (concentrated solution) through a **partially-permeable membrane** (a membrane that allows the passage of water molecules but not solute molecules).

Plant cells are surrounded by a **membrane** which allows water to move in and out of the cells. Water and solute molecules move freely through the cellulose cell wall. Its function is to provide support – it doesn't affect the movement of substances in or out of the cell.

HT Net Movement

In osmosis, the water particles move randomly, colliding with each other and passing through the membrane in both directions. But, the **net movement** of molecules is from the area of high water concentration to the area of low water concentration. This gradually **dilutes** the solution.

You can **predict the direction** of water movement if you know what the **concentration** of the water is. Remember, solute molecules can't pass through the membrane, only the water molecules can.

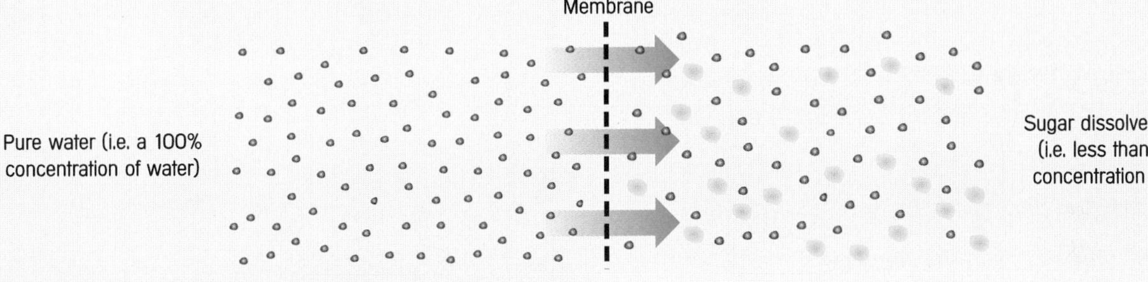

Water in Plants

Plants use water to...

- keep their leaves cool
- transport minerals
- photosynthesise
- keep cells firm and the plant supported.

Plants need to balance the amount of water they take in and lose:

1. Water is **absorbed** by the plant by the root hair cells which have a large surface area to take in water.
2. The water then diffuses through the plant up to the leaves.
3. When it reaches the leaves it can be lost by **transpiration** (evaporation).

Two **adaptations** reduce the rate at which water is lost from leaves:

- A **waxy cuticle** on the surface of the leaf.
- Having the majority of the **stomata** on the **lower surface** of the leaf.

Stomata **open** and **close** to allow the **diffusion** of gases and also to control the **water loss**.

Key Words

Chlorophyll • Diffusion • Osmosis • Photosynthesis • Stomata • Surface area : volume ratio

Water, Water Everywhere

Osmosis in Plant Cells

Plant cells have **inelastic cell walls** which, together with the **water inside the cells**, are essential for the **support** of young non-woody plants. The cell wall...

- prevents cells from bursting due to excess water
- contributes to rigidity.

A lack of water can cause plants to **droop** (**wilt**). As the amount of water inside the cells reduces, the cells become less rigid due to reduced pressure.

HT As water moves into plant cells **by osmosis**, the **pressure inside the cell increases**. The inelastic cell walls can withstand the pressure and the cell becomes very **turgid** (rigid).

When all the cells are fully turgid, the plant is firm and upright. But, if water is in short supply, cells will start to lose water **by osmosis**. They lose turgor pressure and become **flaccid** (not rigid), and the plant begins to wilt.

When cells lose a lot of water, the inside of the cell contracts. This is called **plasmolysis**.

Osmosis in Animal Cells

Water also diffuses in and out of animal cells by osmosis. But, animal cells don't have a cell wall, so too much water entering a cell could cause the cell to burst.

Example – Red blood cells

1. When red blood cells are in solutions with the same concentration as their cytoplasm, they retain their shape.
2. When in weaker solution, they absorb water and swell up, and may burst.
3. When in more concentrated solution, they lose water and shrivel up.

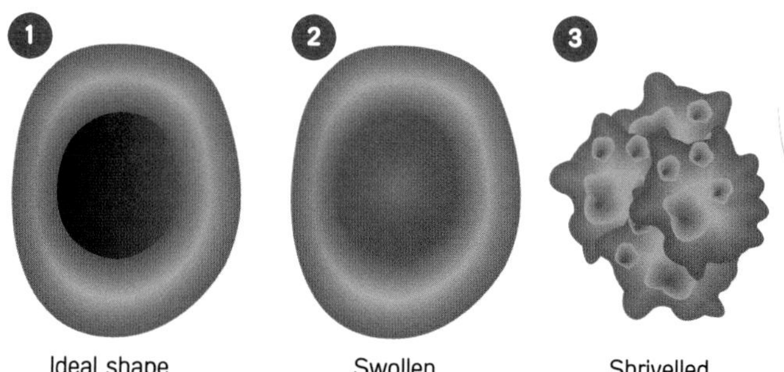

Key Words

Crenated • Flaccid • Lysis • Plasmolysis • Turgid

Water, Water Everywhere

HT More on Osmosis in Animal Cells

Animal cells, unlike plant cells, **don't have an inelastic cell wall.**

Blood cells in a pure water solution will gain water by osmosis. Without a cell wall to prevent water entering the cell, they absorb more and more water until eventually they burst. This is called **lysis**.

Blood cells in a concentrated solution (very little water) will lose water by osmosis. Without a cell wall to prevent water loss, they can shrivel up and become **crenated** (have rough edges).

Water Loss from Leaves

Transpiration and **water loss** are an unavoidable consequence of photosynthesis. Although **stomata** are **needed** for the **exchange of gases** during photosynthesis, they also allow water molecules to pass out of the leaf.

But, the **leaf** is **adapted** to be able to **reduce** water loss:

- The **number**, **position**, **size** and **distribution** of stomata vary between plants, depending on their environment (which affects the amount of water they need).
- The **turgidity** of guard cells changes in relation to the **light intensity** and **availability** of water, in order to alter the size of the stomatal openings.

During photosynthesis, the guard cells become **turgid** and the stomata are fully open. But, if there is a lack of water, the guard cells become **flaccid** and the stomata close to prevent unnecessary water loss and photosynthesis.

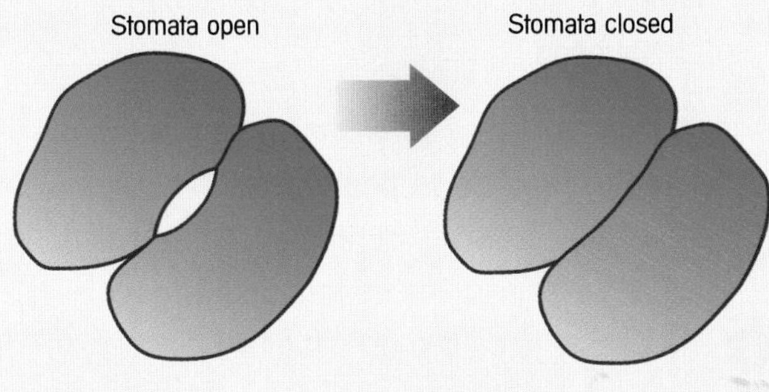

High light intensity causes the stomata to open – this increases rate of water evaporation.

High temperatures increase the movement of the water molecules – this speeds up transpiration.

Increased air movement blows the water molecules away from stomata – this increases transpiration.

High humidity decreases the concentration gradient – this slows down transpiration.

Transport in Plants

The Structure of a Plant

Flower – this contains the **reproductive** organs of the plant (needed to make seeds).
Leaves – are broad, thin and flat to provide a large surface area to absorb sunlight for **photosynthesis**.
Stem – in most plants, the stem **supports** the plant and **transports substances** from the roots to the leaves by the **transport tissues**: **xylem** and **phloem**.
Roots – they **anchor** the plant firmly in the ground and absorb water and minerals. The root hair cells have an enormous surface area for absorbing water.

Stems

The **xylem** and **phloem** form a continuous system of tubes from roots to leaves.

- **Xylem** transports water and soluble mineral salts from the roots to the leaves (**transpiration**).
- **Phloem** allows the movement of food substances (sugars) around the plant (**translocation**).

HT **Xylem vessels** are tubes made from dead plant cells. They have a hollow lumen. The cellulose cell walls are thickened and strengthened with a waterproof substance. **Phloem** cells are long columns of living cells.

Cross-section of a Stem

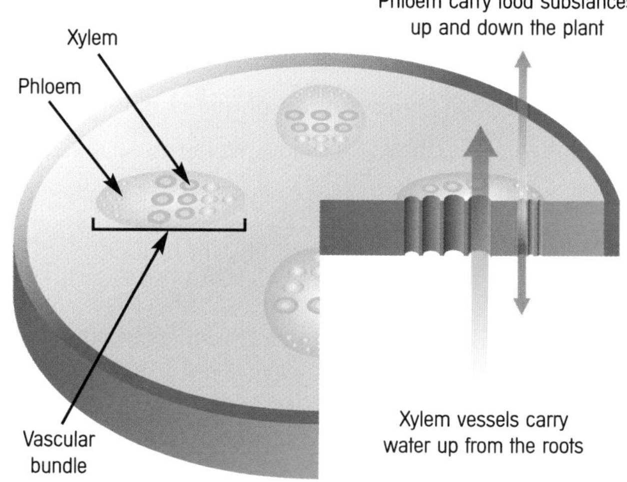

Transpiration

Transpiration is the **diffusion** and **evaporation** of water from inside a leaf. The transpiration stream is powered by the evaporation of water from the leaf:

1. Water evaporates from the internal leaf cells through the stomata.
2. Water passes by osmosis from the xylem vessels to leaf cells, which pull the thread of water in that vessel upwards by a very small amount.
3. Water enters the xylem from root tissues, to replace water which has moved upwards.
4. Water enters root hair cells by osmosis to replace water which has entered the xylem.

The rate of **transpiration** can be affected by...

- **light** – more light increases the rate of photosynthesis and transpiration
- **air movement** (**wind**) – as the movement of the air increases, transpiration increases
- **heat** – heat increases the rate of photosynthesis and transpiration
- **humidity** – high humidity decreases the rate of transpiration.

A leafy shoot's rate of transpiration can be measured using a **mass photometer**.

1. The plant's roots are submerged in a sealed bag of water and placed in a beaker.
2. The beaker is placed on a digital balance.
3. Readings are then taken to see how much water is lost by the plant during transpiration.

Plants Need Minerals Too

Essential Minerals

Essential minerals are needed to keep plants healthy and growing properly. Plants absorb essential minerals (as **ions** dissolved in water) through their root hairs.

The minerals are **naturally present** in the soil, although usually in quite **low concentrations**. So, farmers use **fertilisers** containing essential minerals to make sure that plants get all the minerals they need.

Each mineral is needed for a different purpose:

- **nitrates** – to make proteins for cell growth
- **potassium** – for respiration and photosynthesis
- **phosphates** – for respiration and cell growth
- **magnesium** – for photosynthesis.

If one or more of the essential minerals is missing from the soil, the growth of the plant will be affected.

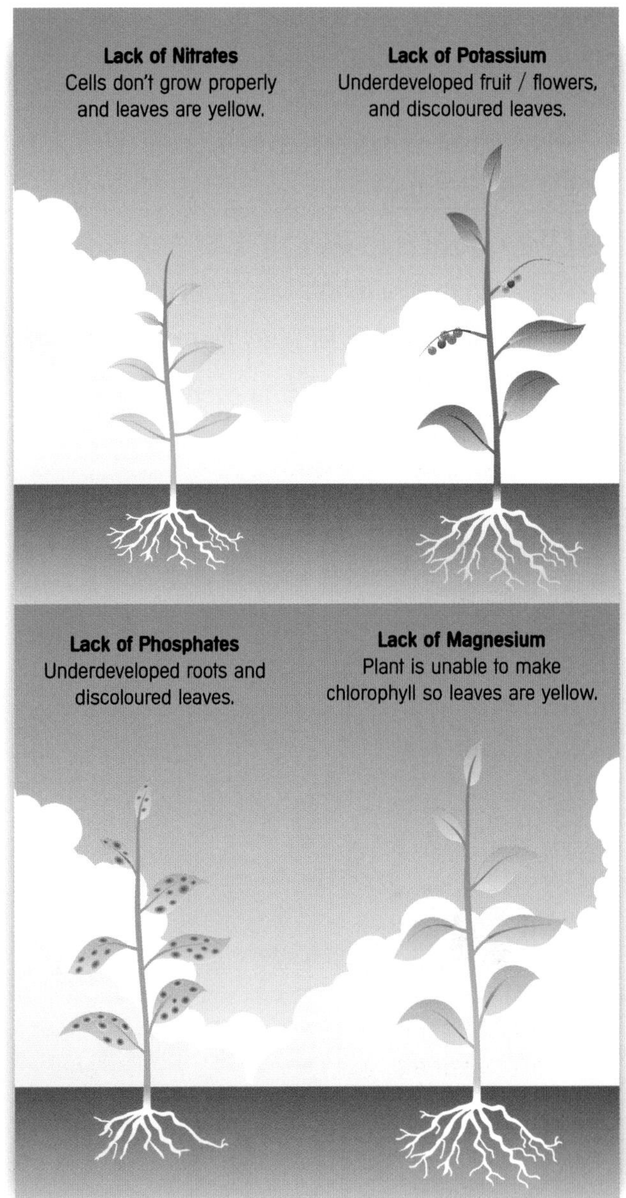

HT **Nitrates** are used to make amino acids, that form proteins. **Potassium** is used to help the enzymes in respiration and photosynthesis. **Phosphates** are used to make DNA and cell membranes. **Magnesium** is used to make the chlorophyll for photosynthesis.

Key Words

Active transport • **Diffusion** • **Ion** • **Phloem** • **Photosynthesis** • **Translocation** • **Transpiration** • **Xylem**

HT Active Transport

Substances sometimes need to be absorbed from a **low** to a **high concentration** area, i.e. against a concentration gradient.

This is called active transport and it requires **energy** from **respiration**.

Plants absorb mineral ions through their root hairs by active transport.

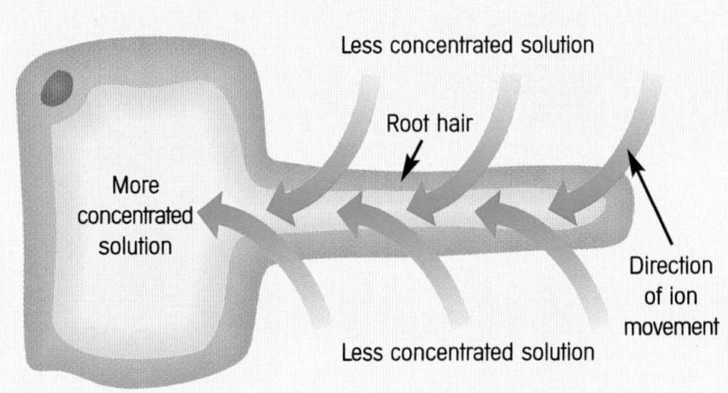

Energy Flow

Food Chains

Food chains show the **transfer of energy** and materials from organism to organism. Energy from the Sun flows through a food chain...

- when green plants absorb sunlight
- through feeding.

Green plants are **producers** because they produce **biomass** during **photosynthesis**. **Consumers** are organisms which eat other organisms.

Biomass and energy are lost at every stage (trophic level) of a food chain because...

- materials and energy are lost in an organism's faeces during **egestion**
- energy is lost through **movement** and **respiration**, especially in birds and mammals.

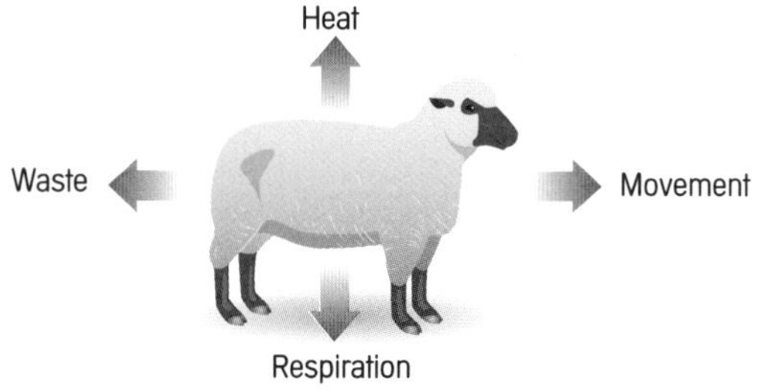

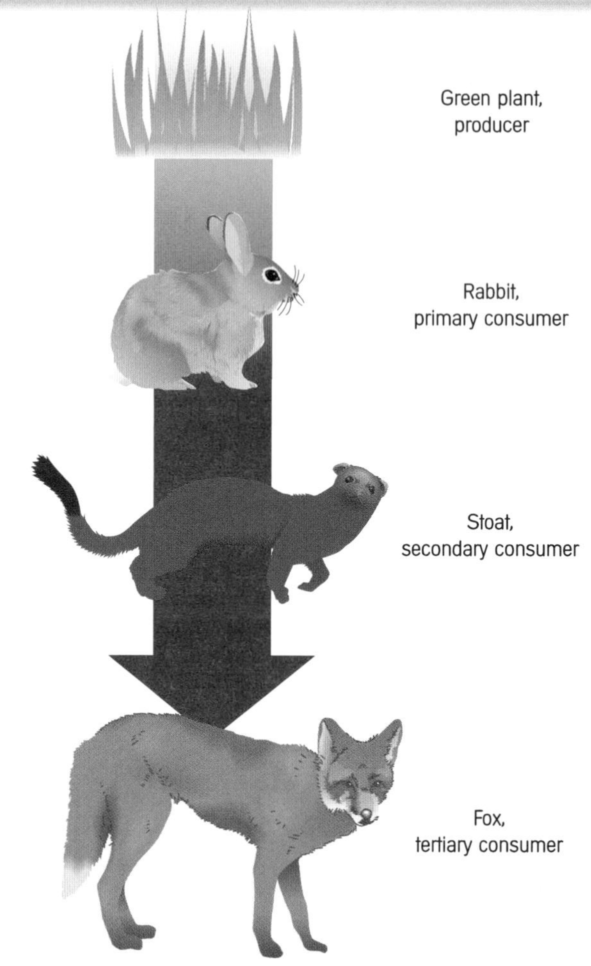

HT Efficiency of Energy Transfer

The length of a food chain depends on the **efficiency of energy transfer**:

- A fraction of the Sun's energy is captured by the producers.
- The rabbits respire and produce waste products. They pass on a tenth of the energy they get from the grass.
- The stoats respire and produce waste products. They pass on a tenth of the energy they get from the rabbits.
- The fox gets the last tiny bit of energy left after all the others have had a share.

So, food chains rarely have fourth degree or fifth degree consumers because there isn't enough energy to pass on.

If you know how much energy is stored in the living organisms at each level of a food chain, you can calculate the efficiency of energy transfer using this formula:

$$\text{Energy efficiency} = \frac{\text{Energy converted to biomass}}{\text{Total energy taken in}} \times 100$$

Example

A sheep eats 100kJ of energy in the form of grass, but only 9kJ becomes new sheep tissue. The rest is lost as faeces, urine or heat. Calculate the efficiency of energy transfer in the sheep.

$$\text{Energy efficiency} = \frac{9}{100} \times 100 = \mathbf{9\%}$$

Pyramid of Numbers

The number of organisms at each stage in the food chain be shown as a **pyramid of numbers**.

The number of organisms decreases as you go up the pyramid – i.e. a lot of grass feeds a few rabbits, which feed even fewer stoats, which feed just one fox.

For simplicity, pyramids of numbers usually look like this:

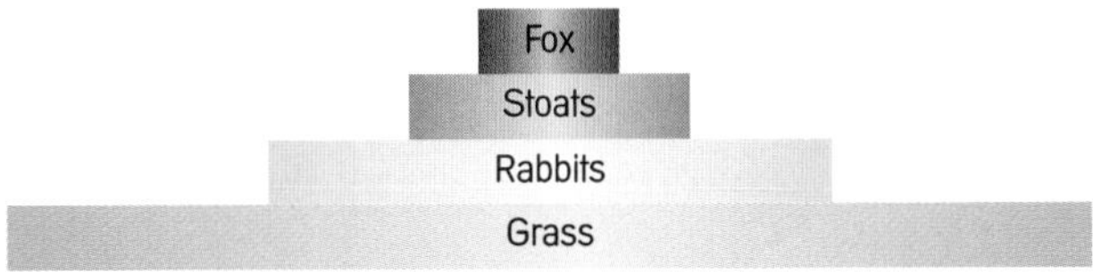

Pyramids of numbers don't take into account the **mass** of the organisms, so it's possible to end up with some odd-looking pyramids.

For example, if lots of slugs feed on one lettuce, the base of the pyramid is smaller than the next stage. This happens because the lettuce is a large organism compared to the slug. This situation also happens when trees are at the bottom of a food chain

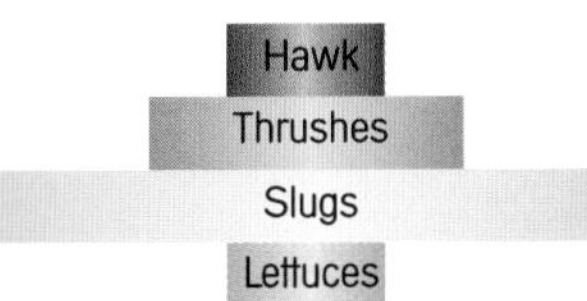

The Pyramid of Numbers

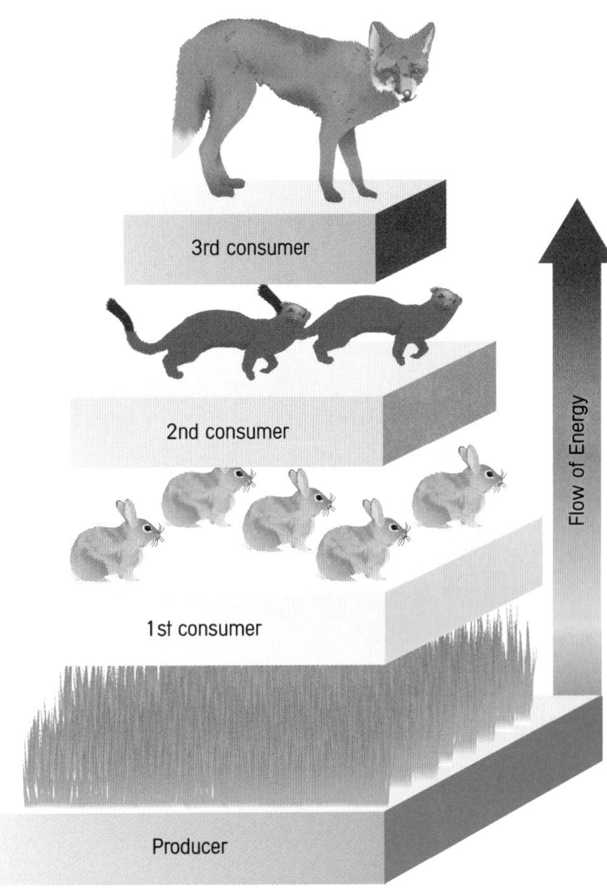

Pyramid of Biomass

Pyramids of biomass show the mass of living material at each stage in the chain. They're always pyramid shaped because they take the **mass** of the **organisms into account**.

If enough information is given, the pyramid of biomass can be drawn to scale.

HT The efficiency of energy transfer **explains the shape of biomass pyramids**. Biomass is lost through the stages.

- A lot of biomass remains in the ground as the root system.
- The rabbits lose biomass in faeces and urine.
- The stoats lose biomass in faeces and urine.
- The fox gets the remaining biomass.

Key Words

Biomass • Consumers • Egestion • Photosynthesis • Producers

Energy Flow

Biofuels

Plants grow new plant tissues by using some of the glucose from **photosynthesis** to produce starch and cellulose. This new plant material is **biomass**.

Biomass can be **burned** to release energy to be used as a **fuel**. Some examples of biomass fuels are...

- **fast-growing trees**, e.g. pine burned to release energy
- **manure** or **other waste** – broken down by **bacteria** or **yeast** in a **fermenter** to release methane (**biogas**) which can be used to power electricity generators
- **corn** or **sugar cane** – broken down by yeast in a fermenter to produce alcohol
- **bio-ethanol** – used to fuel some cars.

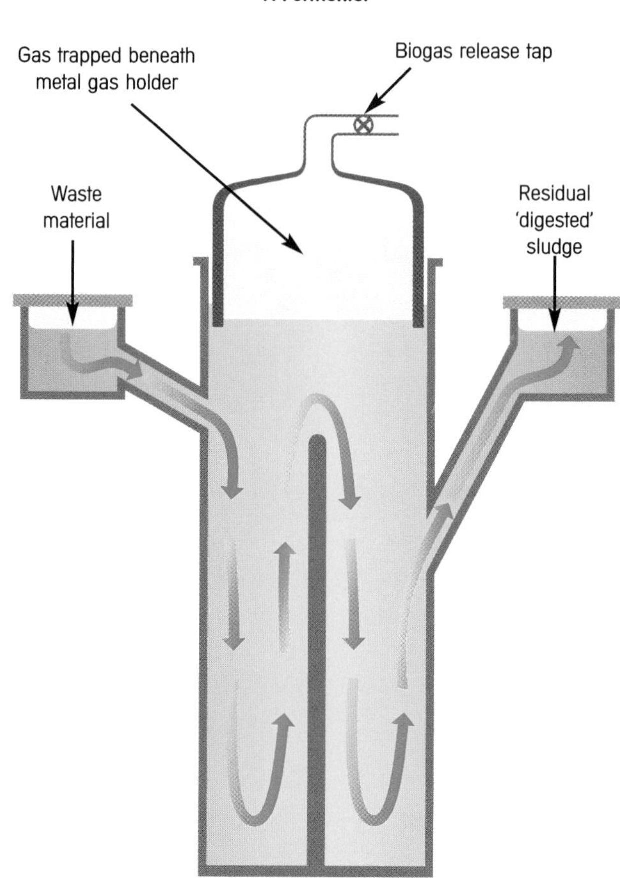

HT A crop like maize (corn) produces a lot of biomass which can be used for...

- feed for livestock
- food for humans
- biofuel (after being fermented)
- seeds to grow more biomass.

HT Advantages of Biofuels

There are many advantages to using biofuels:

- Biofuels are **renewable** – new plants can be grown quickly and easily.
- Biofuels are relatively clean fuels – they produce less air pollution than fossil fuels when burned, and new plants use up the CO_2 made when the biofuels are burned.
- Countries can produce their own biofuel and aren't dependent on oil-producing countries for their energy supplies.

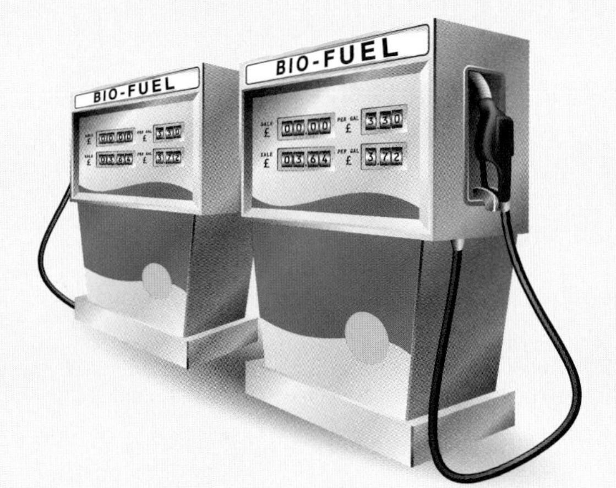

Key Words

Biomass • Photosynthesis

Intensive Farming

Intensive farming methods aim to produce as much food as possible from the available land, plants and animals. These methods use...

- **pesticides** – used to kill pests that can damage crops or farm animals
- **insecticides** (types of pesticide) – used to kill insect pests
- **fungicides** (types of pesticide) – used to kill fungi
- **herbicides** – used to kill weeds which compete with crops for water and nutrients.

But, care needs to be taken with pesticides because...

- they can harm other organisms (non-pests)
- they can build up (accumulate) in food chains, harming animals at the top.

Intensive farming can **increase productivity** by keeping animals in carefully controlled environments where their temperature and movement are limited. For example...

- fish farms breed huge numbers of fish in enclosed nets in the sea or lakes
- battery farms raise chickens in cages.

But, this can raise **ethical dilemmas**. Some people find this **morally unacceptable** because the animals have a poor quality of life.

Use of Pesticides

Intensive Farming

HT Accumulation of Pesticides

Herbicides and pesticides kill weeds and pests, which reduces the energy taken by competing plants and pests. But, they can cause problems.

Pesticides can flow into rivers where they are absorbed by algae (tiny plants). The algae are eaten by small aquatic organisms, which in turn are eaten by larger organisms.

The pesticide increases in concentration along the food chain and the accumulation could kill the larger organisms.

Example of Accumulation

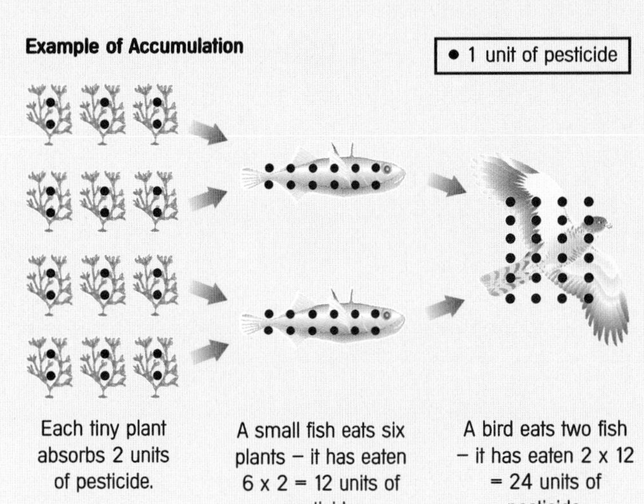

Farming

Organic Farming

Organic farming methods aim to produce high quality food whilst maintaining the welfare of the animals and minimising the impact on the environment.

These methods include...

- using natural fertilisers like animal manure or compost
- growing nitrogen-fixing crops (e.g. peas or clover)
- rotating crops to maintain soil fertility
- avoiding chemical pesticides by weeding and using **biological controls**
- varying seed planting times to discourage pests.

HT **Advantages** of organic farming:

- Food crops and the environment aren't contaminated with artificial fertilisers or pesticides.
- Soil erosion is limited, and fertility is maintained through the use of organic fertilisers.
- Biodiversity is promoted because hedgerows and other habitats are conserved.
- Livestock have space to roam.

Disadvantages of organic farming:

- It's less efficient because some crops are lost to pests and diseases.
- Organic fertilisers take time to rot and they don't supply a specific balance of minerals.

Hydroponics

Hydroponics is a way of growing plants without using soil. The plants are grown with their roots in a **solution** containing the minerals needed for growth. This growing method is useful for **greenhouses** or areas which have very **thin or barren soil**.

Certain plants, e.g. tomatoes, can be grown hydroponically in greenhouses. Conditions such as temperature, light intensity and carbon dioxide concentration can be controlled.

HT **Advantages** of hydroponics:

- The mineral levels added to the solution can be carefully controlled and adjusted to the type of plant.
- There is a reduced risk of the plants becoming diseased.

Disadvantages of hydroponics:

- The plants have to be supported as they have no anchorage for their roots.
- Expensive fertilisers are needed to supply the plant with minerals.

Biological Control

Food Web

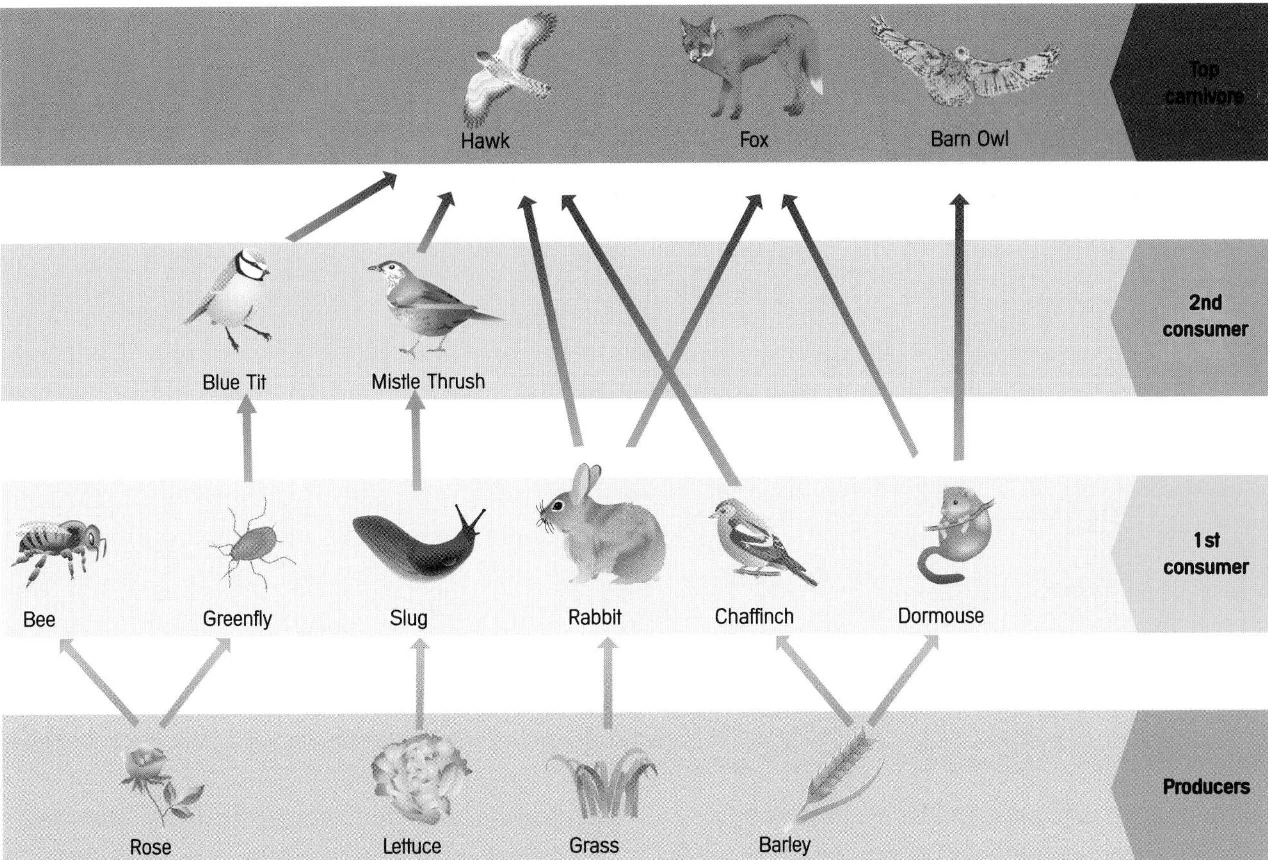

Some farmers prefer to **introduce a predator,** instead of using a pesticide, to reduce the number of pests. This is called **biological control**.

For example, the cottony cushion scale (an insect) was a pest that attacked citrus fruit crops in America. Farmers introduced the ladybird beetle and the pest's numbers were significantly reduced.

But, it's important to remember that when biological controls or pesticides are used to get rid of pests, the **effect** on the **rest** of the **organisms** in the **food chain** or web **must be considered**.

For example, if a pest control was to target rabbits, this would have an effect not only on the rabbits, but also on hawks and foxes (who eat rabbits).

Advantages of biological control:

- The predator selected only usually attacks the pest (i.e. it's species-specific).
- Once introduced, the predator can have an impact over many years.
- The pest can't become resistant to the predator (unlike pesticides).

Disadvantages of biological control:

- A lot of time, research and cost is involved in developing control agents.
- Only about one fifth of the biological controls are totally successful.
- The pest is reduced but it isn't completely removed.

Key Words

Biological control • Hydroponics

Decay

Decay

Decay is a process involving the breakdown of complex substances into simpler ones by microorganisms. The rate of decay is affected by several factors:

- Changing **temperature** – microorganisms responsible for decay work best at 40°C.
- **Amount of oxygen** – microorganisms' rate of activity increases as the amount of oxygen in the air increases.
- **Amount of water** – microorganisms prefer moist conditions.

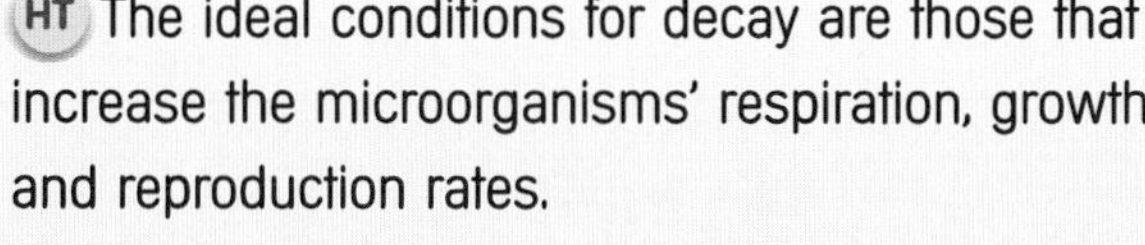

HT The ideal conditions for decay are those that increase the microorganisms' respiration, growth and reproduction rates.

Temperature – microorganisms work slowly at low temperatures, but at high temperatures (above 40°C) they are denatured and decay stops.

Amount of oxygen – increasing the amount of oxygen increases the microorganisms' rate of respiration, which means they produce more energy, enabling them to grow and reproduce more quickly. The more oxygen there is, the faster they grow.

Amount of water – microorganisms grow quickest in moist conditions. Too much or too little water will slow down their growth and, therefore, the rate of decay.

Decomposers

Dead organisms or waste materials decay and release minerals which can be re-used by other living organisms.

Earthworms, woodlice and maggots, known as **detritivores**, feed on...

- dead organisms
- waste (**detritus**) produced by living organisms.

Detritivores speed up the process of decay by breaking detritus down into small particles which have a large surface area. This makes it easier for decomposers to feed on. The faeces of detritivores provide food for **decomposers** like bacteria and fungi.

Microorganisms are used to break down...

- human waste in sewage treatment works
- plant waste in compost heaps.

HT Bacteria and fungi are **saprophytes** – they feed on dead organic material by secreting **enzymes** onto the material and then absorbing the digested products. Saprophytes are essential for decay.

A Garden Composter

Food Preservation

When food is exposed to air, moisture and warmth, microorganisms will quickly grow on it. Storing food in dry, cold conditions prevents microorganisms and fungi from growing.

Food can be preserved by removing the **oxygen, heat** or **moisture** that the microorganisms need in order to grow or survive. Food can be...

- **sealed** inside sterile cans or bottles – this removes the oxygen
- kept at **low temperatures** in a fridge or freezer – this slows down microorganisms' growth
- **pickled** in vinegar – the low pH **denatures** the microorganisms' enzymes
- **preserved** in sugar (or salt) – this makes the conditions too concentrated for the microorganisms to survive
- **dried** – this reduces the moisture.

Food Preservation Experiment

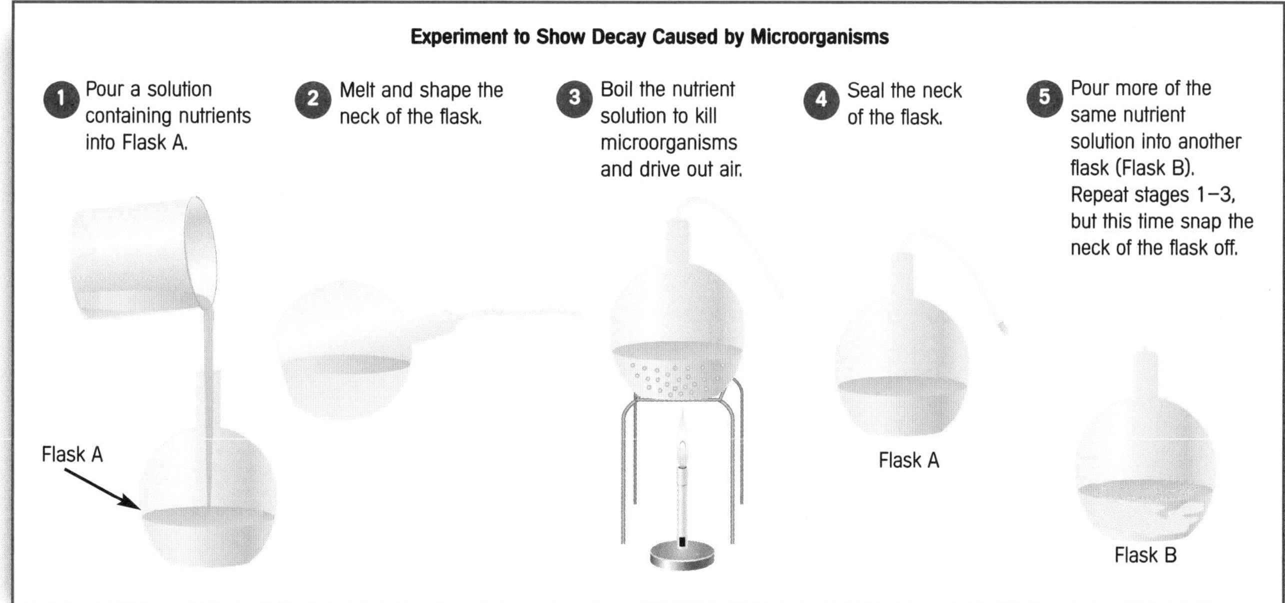

The solution in the flask that had the neck snapped off (Flask B) will start to decay within days because microorganisms will be able to enter the flask. But, the solution in the other flask (Flask A) will show no signs of decay as long as it remains sealed.

Key Words

Denature • Detritus • Detritivores • Saprophytes

Recycling

Recycling

In a stable community, the removal of materials is balanced by the return of materials. So materials are constantly being recycled:

- When animals and plants **grow**, they **take in** elements from the soil which are incorporated into their bodies.
- When animals **die** and **decay**, these mineral elements are **released** and can be taken up by other living organisms to allow them to grow.

Carbon and **nitrogen** are two recycled elements.

The Carbon Cycle

The constant recycling of carbon is called the **carbon cycle**.

1. Carbon dioxide is removed from the atmosphere by green plants for photosynthesis.
2. Plants and animals respire, releasing carbon dioxide into the atmosphere.
3. Microorganisms feed on dead plants and animals, causing them to break down, decay and release carbon dioxide into the air. (The microorganisms respire as they feed.)

The burning of fossil fuels also releases carbon dioxide into the air.

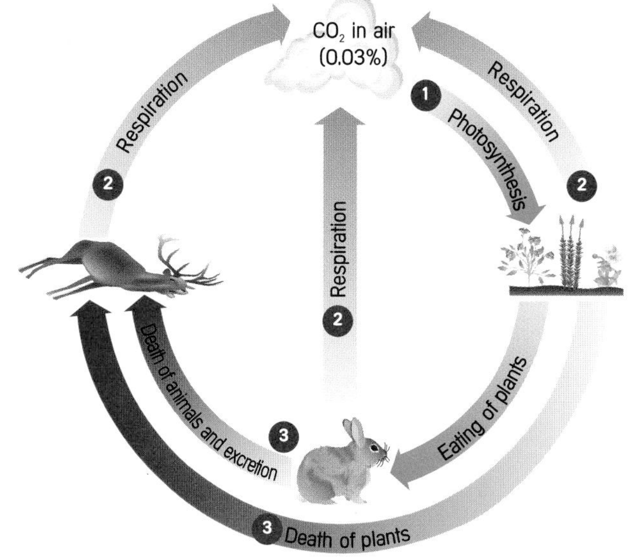

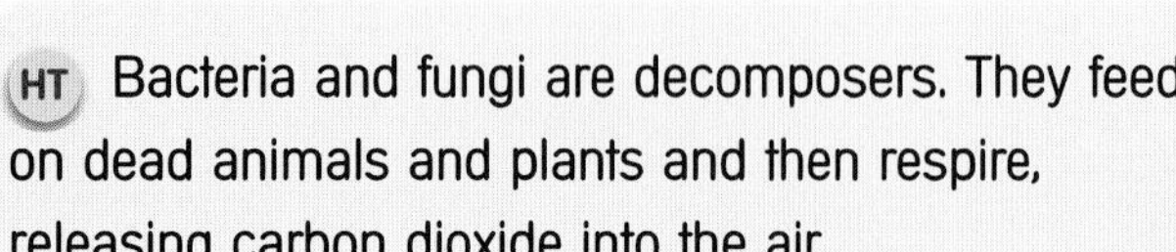

HT Bacteria and fungi are decomposers. They feed on dead animals and plants and then respire, releasing carbon dioxide into the air.

Carbon is also recycled in the sea.

1. Marine organism shells are made of carbonates. The shells drop to the sea bed as the organisms die.
2. The shells fossilise to become limestone rock.
3. Volcanic eruptions heat the limestone and release carbon dioxide into the atmosphere.
4. Acid rain weathers buildings and rocks, releasing carbon dioxide.

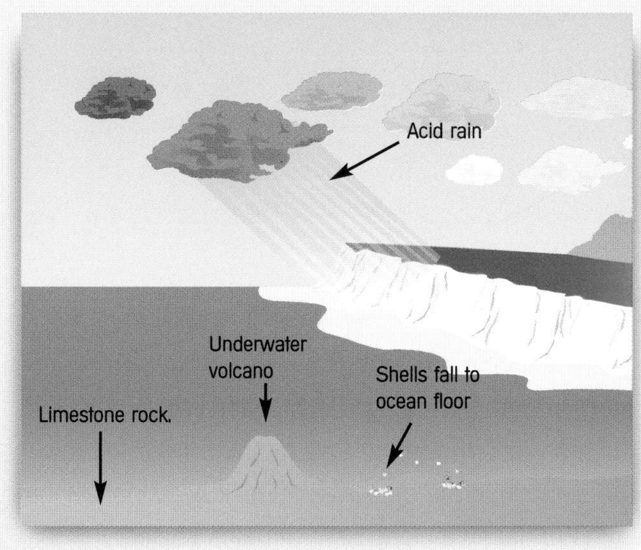

The Nitrogen Cycle

The air contains approximately 78% **nitrogen**. Nitrogen is a vital element used in the production of proteins, which are needed for growth in plants and animals. A lot of nitrogen is stored in the air, but animals and plants can't use it because it's so **unreactive**.

The **nitrogen cycle** shows how nitrogen and its compounds are recycled in nature:

1. Plants absorb nitrates from the soil to make protein for growth.
2. Animals eat plants and use the nitrogen to make animal protein.
3. Dead animals and plants are broken down by decomposers, releasing nitrates back into the soil.

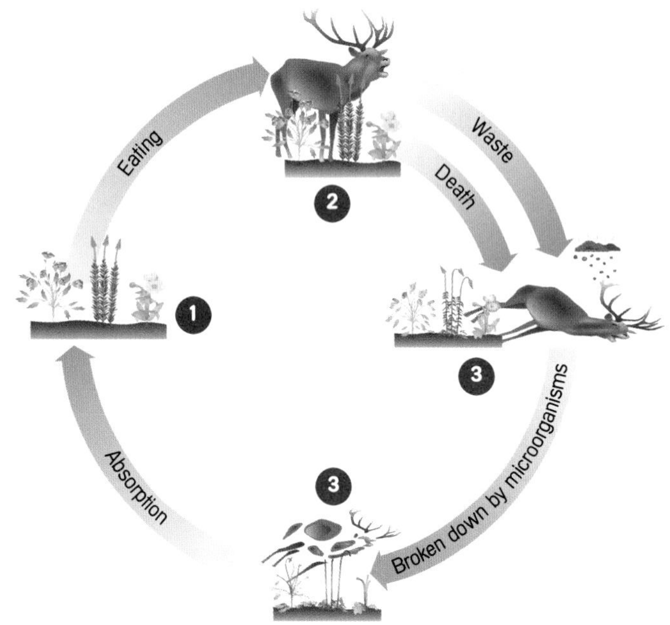

HT The Role of Bacteria

Nitrogen-fixing bacteria convert atmospheric nitrogen into nitrates in the soil. Some of these bacteria live in the soil while others are associated with the root systems of certain plants.

Nitrifying bacteria convert ammonium compounds into nitrates in the soil.

Denitrifying bacteria convert nitrates and ammonium compounds into atmospheric nitrogen.

N.B. The energy released by lightning causes oxygen and nitrogen in the air to combine to form nitrogen oxides which dissolve in water.

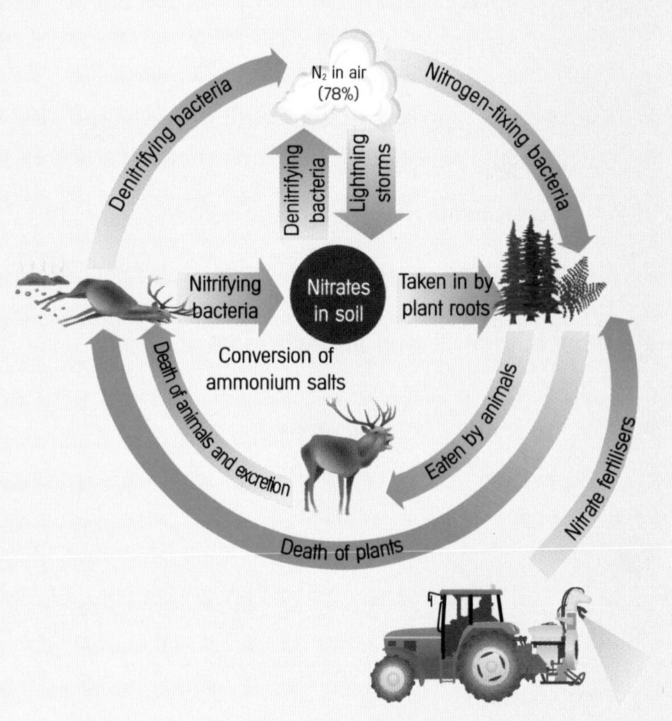

Key Words

Carbon cycle • Nitrogen cycle

Module B4 Practice Questions

1 **a)** Through which part of the plant does water enter a plant during photosynthesis? Tick the correct option.

- **i)** Through the leaves. ☐
- **ii)** Through the roots. ☐
- **iii)** Through the stomata. ☐
- **iv)** Through the guard cells. ☐

HT **b)** What is the name of the process by which carbon dioxide and oxygen enter or exit a plant?

....

c) Describe how the structure of the palisade cells allows them to absorb sunlight to fuel photosynthesis.

....

2 What is osmosis?

....

HT **3** Fill in the gaps in the following sentences, using the words below.

flaccid **osmosis** **plasmolysis** **turgor** **inelastic** **turgid**

Plants rely on the .... cell wall surrounding each of their cells for support to stay upright. They also use the .... pressure created by filling their cells with water.

Water is drawn into the cell by .... The cells become full of water which creates pressure on the cell wall, and the cell becomes ....

If water is in short supply, the plant cells start to lose water and the pressure drops. The cell is then .... Eventually the inside of the cell contracts which is called ....

4 What is transpiration and why does it occur?

....

....

5 A plant left at room temperature for 4 days took in 5cm^3 of water. If the plant had been left in a more humid atmosphere, would you have expected it to take in more or less water? Explain your answer.

....

6 A plant has poor root growth and discoloured, purple leaves. Which mineral is the plant short of?

....

HT **7** What is active transport?

8 **a)** Where do producers in a food chain get their energy from?

b) Give two ways in which biomass and energy are lost at every stage of a food chain.

i) **ii)**

9 What does a pyramid of biomass show?

10 What happens to the amount of available energy and biomass as you move up the food chain? Tick the correct option.

a) It stays the same. ☐

b) It increases. ☐

c) It decreases. ☐

d) It depends on the animals in the chain. ☐

11 Give two examples of biomass fuels.

a) **b)**

12 *Intensive farming methods consider the welfare of animals to be the main priority.*

Is this statement **true** or **false**?

13 **a)** List three key factors that decomposers need to thrive and cause decay.

i) **ii)** **iii)**

b) Explain how detritivores increase the rate of decay.

14 Describe two methods of preserving food and explain how they work to prevent the growth of decomposer microorganisms.

a)

b)

Fundamental Chemical Concepts

HT Fundamental Chemical Concepts

In addition to the concepts covered in Chemistry Module 3, you also need to know the formulae for the following compounds:

Acids	
Hydrochloric acid	HCl
Nitric acid	HNO_3
Sulfuric acid	H_2SO_4
Carbonates	
Calcium carbonate	$CaCO_3$
Sodium carbonate	Na_2CO_3
Chlorides	
Ammonium chloride	NH_4Cl
Barium chloride	$BaCl_2$
Potassium chloride	KCl
Silver chloride	$AgCl$
Sodium chloride	$NaCl$

Hydroxides	
Potassium hydroxide	KOH
Sodium hydroxide	$NaOH$
Sulfates	
Ammonium sulfate	$(NH_4)_2SO_4$
Barium sulfate	$BaSO_4$
Potassium sulfate	K_2SO_4
Sodium sulfate	Na_2SO_4
Others	
Ammonia	NH_3
Copper (II) oxide	CuO
Silver nitrate	$AgNO_3$

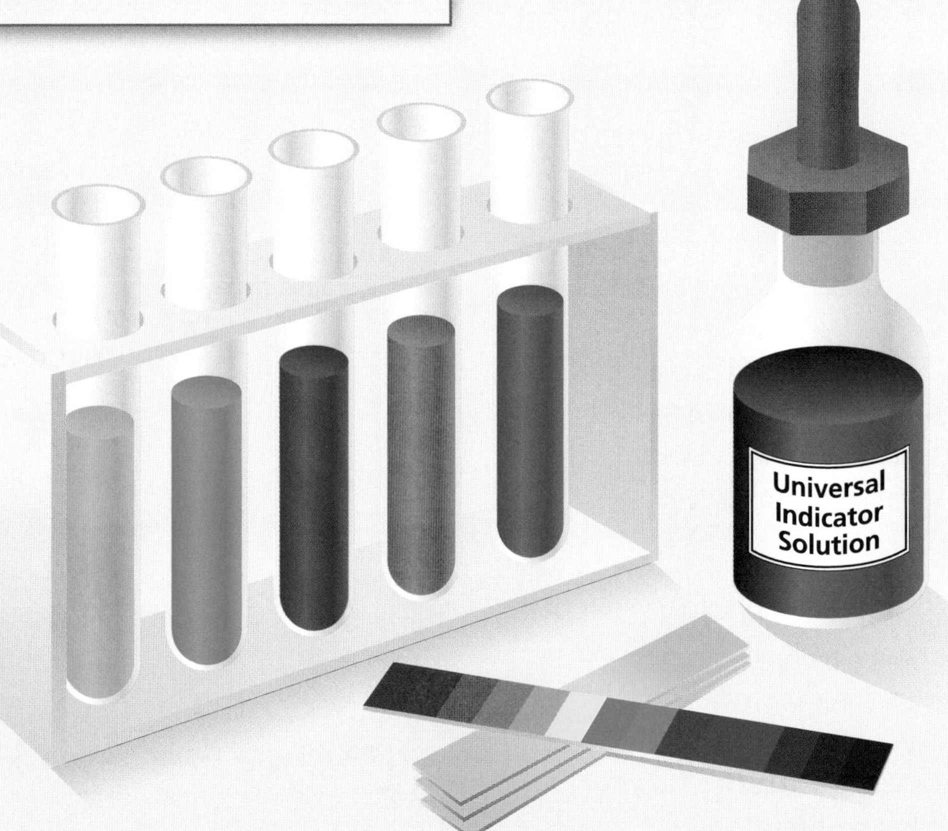

Acids and Bases

Acids are substances with a pH of **less than 7**. **Bases** are the oxides and hydroxides of metals.

Soluble bases are called **alkalis**, and they have a pH **greater than 7**.

You can find the pH of a solution by using **universal indicator**. You can add a few drops of universal indicator to the solution and compare the resulting colour against a **pH colour chart**.

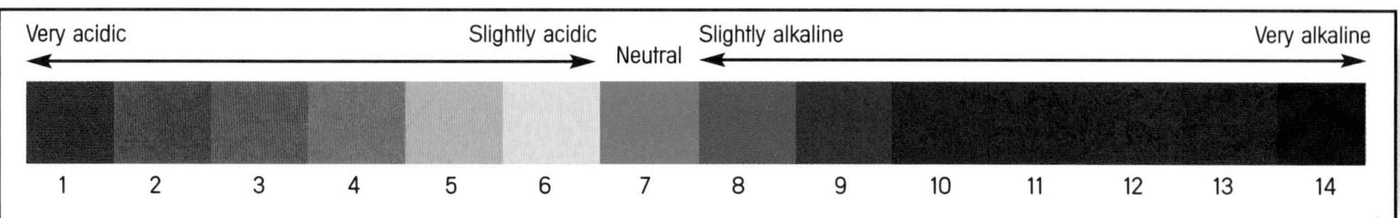

Neutralisation

Acids and bases / alkalis are chemical opposites. When added together in the correct amounts, they can cancel each other out. This is called **neutralisation** because the solution that remains has a **neutral** pH of 7.

As an **acid** is added to an **alkali**, the **pH** of the solution **decreases** because the acid neutralises the alkali to reach pH 7.

As an **alkali** is added to an **acid**, the **pH** of the solution **increases** because the alkali neutralises the acid to reach pH 7.

Salts

Carbonates neutralise **acids** to produce a **salt**, water and carbon dioxide gas.

The **first name** of a salt comes from the name of the **base or carbonate** used, for example...

- **sodium** hydroxide will make a **sodium** salt
- **copper** oxide will make a **copper** salt
- **calcium** carbonate will make a **calcium** salt
- **ammonia** will make an **ammonium** salt.

The **second name** of the salt comes from the **acid** used, for example...

- hydro**chlor**ic acid will produce a **chlor**ide salt
- **sulf**uric acid will produce a **sulf**ate salt
- **nitr**ic acid will produce a **nitr**ate salt.

For example, neutralising **potassium** hydroxide with **nitric** acid will produce **potassium nitrate**.

Sulfuric Acid

Sulfuric acid has many uses, for example...

- to clean / prepare metals before they are painted or coated
- in the manufacture of fertilisers
- in car and motorbike batteries.

Key Words

Acid • Alkali • Base • Neutralisation • Salt • Universal indicator

Acids and Bases

HT More on Neutralisation

Alkalis in solution contain **hydroxide ions, OH^-**(aq).

Acids in solution contain **hydrogen** ions, H^+(aq).

So, neutralisation can be described using the ionic equation:

$$H^+(aq) + OH^-(aq) \longrightarrow H_2O(l)$$

Producing Salts

You should be able to construct any of the following word equations and balanced formula equations for producing salts.

Acid + Base

	Hydrochloric Acid (HCl)	Sulfuric Acid (H_2SO_4)	Nitric Acid (HNO_3)
Sodium Hydroxide (NaOH)	Sodium chloride + Water	Sodium sulfate + Water	Sodium nitrate + Water
	$NaOH + HCl \rightarrow NaCl + H_2O$	$2NaOH + H_2SO_4 \rightarrow Na_2SO_4 + 2H_2O$	$NaOH + HNO_3 \rightarrow NaNO_3 + H_2O$
Potassium Hydroxide (KOH)	Potassium chloride + Water	Potassium sulfate + Water	Potassium nitrate + Water
	$KOH + HCl \rightarrow KCl + H_2O$	$2KOH + H_2SO_4 \rightarrow K_2SO_4 + 2H_2O$	$KOH + HNO_3 \rightarrow KNO_3 + H_2O$
Copper (II) Oxide (CuO)	Copper (II) chloride + Water	Copper (II) sulfate + Water	Copper (II) nitrate + Water
	$CuO + 2HCl \rightarrow CuCl_2 + H_2O$	$CuO + H_2SO_4 \rightarrow CuSO_4 + H_2O$	$CuO + 2HNO_3 \rightarrow Cu(NO_3)_2 + H_2O$
Ammonia (NH_3)	Ammonium chloride	Ammonium sulfate	Ammonium nitrate
	$NH_3 + HCl \rightarrow NH_4Cl$	$2NH_3 + H_2SO_4 \rightarrow (NH_4)_2SO_4$	$NH_3 + HNO_3 \rightarrow NH_4NO_3$

Acid + Carbonate

	Hydrochloric Acid (HCl)	Sulfuric Acid (H_2SO_4)	Nitric Acid (HNO_3)
Sodium Carbonate (Na_2CO_3)	Sodium chloride + Water + Carbon dioxide	Sodium sulfate + Water + Carbon dioxide	Sodium nitrate + Water + Carbon dioxide
	$Na_2CO_3 + 2HCl \rightarrow 2NaCl + H_2O + CO_2$	$Na_2CO_3 + H_2SO_4 \rightarrow Na_2SO_4 + H_2O + CO_2$	$Na_2CO_3 + 2HNO_3 \rightarrow 2NaNO_3 + H_2O + CO_2$
Calcium Carbonate ($CaCO_3$)	Calcium chloride + Water + Carbon dioxide	Calcium sulfate + Water + Carbon dioxide	Calcium nitrate + Water + Carbon dioxide
	$CaCO_3 + 2HCl \rightarrow CaCl_2 + H_2O + CO_2$	$CaCO_3 + H_2SO_4 \rightarrow CaSO_4 + H_2O + CO_2$	$CaCO_3 + 2HNO_3 \rightarrow Ca(NO_3)_2 + H_2O + CO_2$

Reacting Masses

Relative Atomic Mass, A_r

The **relative atomic mass**, A_r, of a particular atom is its mass compared with one twelfth of the mass of a carbon atom.

Each element in the periodic table has two numbers. The **larger** of the two numbers is the A_r.

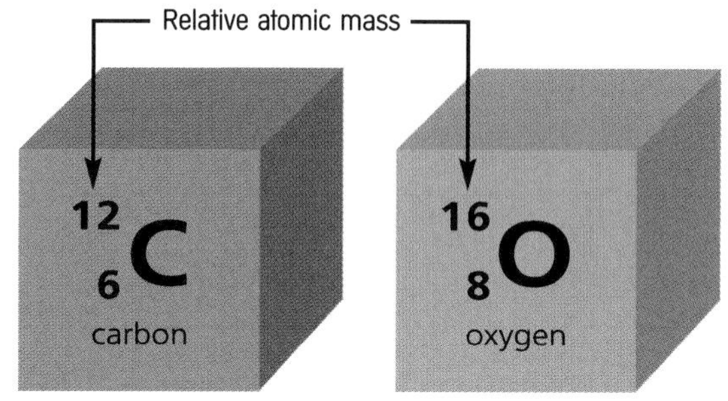

Relative Formula Mass, M_r

The **relative formula mass**, M_r, of a compound is the relative atomic masses of all its elements added together.

To calculate the M_r you need to know...

- the formula of the compound
- the A_r of all the atoms involved.

Example

Calculate the relative formula mass of H_2SO_4.

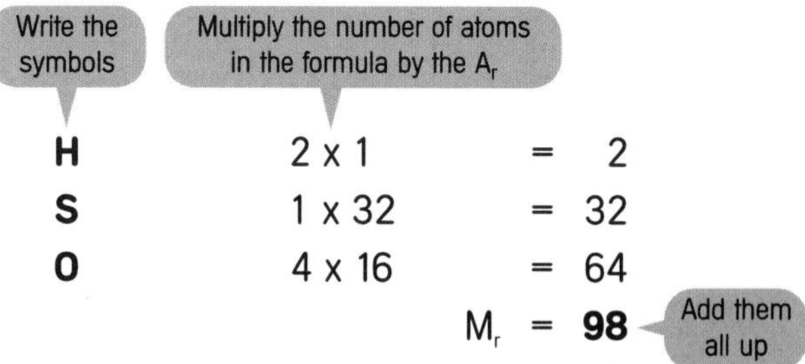

Calculating Reactants and Products

To calculate how much substance a reaction will produce (**product**), or the amount of starting materials (**reactant**) you need, you must remember that...

- the total mass of the reactants always equals the total mass of the products
- the more reactants you start with, the greater the amount of product formed.

Substances react in simple **ratios**. You can use the ratio to calculate how much of each reactant is needed to produce a certain amount of product.

Example

Nitric acid and ammonia react with each other, in the mass ratio 63 : 17, to make ammonium nitrate:

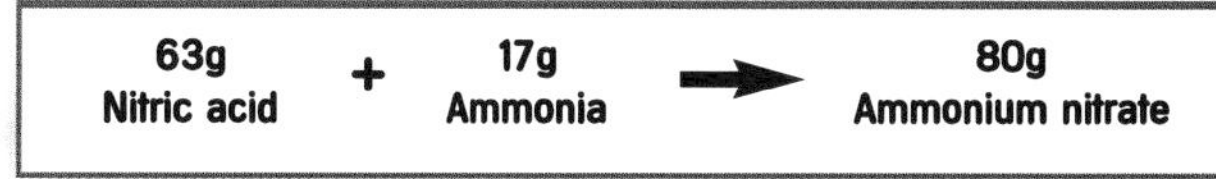

a) Calculate how much of each reactant you would need to make 80kg of product.

1kg = 1000g, so multiply all the quantities by 1000 to get the amounts in kg.

63kg Nitric acid + **17kg** Ammonia → **80kg** Ammonium nitrate

b) Calculate how much of each reactant you would need to make 16g of product.

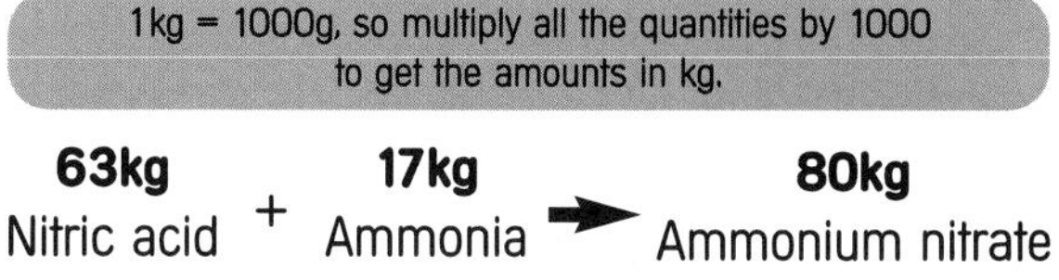

12.6g Nitric acid + **3.4g** Ammonia → **16g** Ammonium nitrate

Key Words

Ion • Product • Reactant • Relative atomic mass • Relative formula mass

Reacting Masses

HT Products and Reactants

The **total mass** of **reactants equals** the **total mass** of **products** because **no atoms** are **gained** or **lost** in a chemical reaction.

There is exactly the same number of atoms; they are just rearranged into different substances.

To work out how much of a substance is used up or produced, you need to know...

- the **relative formula mass**, M_r, of the reactants and products (or the **relative atomic mass**, A_r, of all the elements)
- the balanced symbol equation for the reaction.

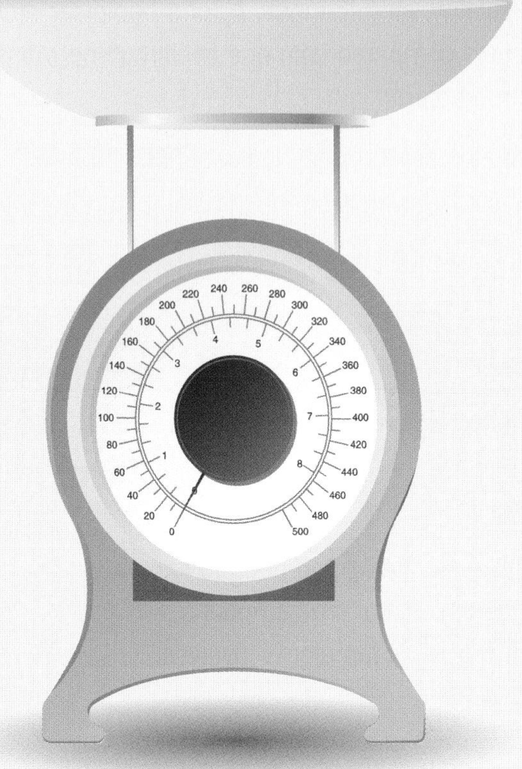

Calculating the Mass of a Product

Example

Calculate how much calcium oxide can be produced from 50kg of calcium carbonate.

(Relative atomic masses: Ca = 40, C = 12, O = 16).

1. Write down the equation.
2. Work out the M_r of each substance.
3. Check that the total mass of reactants equals the total mass of the products. If they aren't the same, check your work.
4. The question only mentions calcium oxide and calcium carbonate, so you can now ignore the carbon dioxide. You just need the ratio of mass of reactant to mass of product.
5. Use the ratio to calculate how much calcium oxide can be produced.

1

$$CaCO_3 \xrightarrow{\text{Heat}} CaO + CO_2$$

2

$$40 + 12 + (3 \times 16) \rightarrow (40 + 16) + [12 + (2 \times 16)]$$

3

$$100 \rightarrow 56 + 44 \checkmark$$

4

100 : 56

5

If 100kg of $CaCO_3$ produces 56kg of CaO, then 1kg of $CaCO_3$ produces $\frac{56}{100}$kg of CaO, and 50kg of $CaCO_3$ produces $\frac{56}{100} \times 50$ **= 28kg of CaO.**

HT Calculating the Mass of a Reactant

Example

Calculate how much aluminium oxide is needed to produce 540 tonnes of aluminium.

(Relative atomic masses: Al = 27, O = 16).

1. Write down the equation.
2. Work out the M_r of each substance.
3. Check that the total mass of reactants equals the total mass of the products. If they aren't the same, check your work.
4. The question only mentions aluminium oxide and aluminium, so you can now ignore the oxygen. You just need the ratio of mass of reactant to mass of product.
5. Use the ratio to calculate how much aluminium oxide is needed.

1. $2Al_2O_3 \rightarrow 4Al + 3O_2$
2. $2[(2 \times 27) + (3 \times 16)] \rightarrow (4 \times 27) + [3 \times (2 \times 16)]$
3. $204 \rightarrow 108 + 96$ ✔
4. 204 : 108
5. If 204 tonnes of Al_2O_3 produces 108 tonnes of Al, then $\frac{204}{108}$ tonnes is needed to produce 1 tonne of Al, and $\frac{204}{108} \times 540$ tonnes is needed to produce 540 tonnes of Al
   = **1020 tonnes of Al_2O_3.**

Percentage Yield

Percentage yield is a way of comparing the amount of product made (**actual yield**) to the amount of product expected to be made (**predicted yield**).

You can calculate percentage yield by using this formula:

$$\textbf{Percentage yield} = \frac{\textbf{Actual mass}}{\textbf{Predicted mass}} \times 100$$

- A 100% yield means that no product has been lost (actual yield is the same as predicted yield).
- A 0% yield means that no product has been made (actual yield is zero).

Example

A reaction was expected to produce a mass of 10g. But, the actual mass produced was 8g. Calculate the percentage yield.

$$\text{Percentage yield} = \frac{\text{Actual mass}}{\text{Predicted mass}} \times 100$$

$$= \frac{8g}{10g} \times 100 = \mathbf{80\%}$$

There are several reasons why the percentage yield is less than the expected yield. The products could be lost in...

- evaporation
- filtration
- the transfer of liquids
- heating.

Evaporation

Filtration

Transferring liquids

Heating

Key Word

Yield

Fertilisers and Crop Yield

Fertilisers

Fertilisers are chemicals that provide plants with **essential chemical elements** needed for growth. Fertilisers...

- make crops grow faster and bigger
- increase the crop **yield**.

The three main essential elements found in fertilisers are **nitrogen (N)**, **phosphorus (P)** and **potassium (K)**. **Urea** can also be used as a fertiliser.

Fertilisers must be **soluble in water** in order for them to be taken in by the roots of plants in solution.

HT Fertilisers **increase crop yield** by...

- **replacing essential elements** in the soil that have been used up by a previous crop
- **increasing the amount** of essential elements available
- **providing nitrogen** in the form of soluble nitrates which are used by the plant to make protein for growth.

Making Fertilisers

Some fertilisers can be manufactured by **neutralising** an **acid** with an **alkali**:

- **ammonium sulfate** – neutralise sulfuric acid with ammonia
- **ammonium nitrate** – neutralise nitric acid with ammonia
- **ammonium phosphate** – neutralise phosphoric acid with ammonia
- **potassium nitrate** – neutralise nitric acid with potassium hydroxide.

You should be able to recognise and label the apparatus needed to prepare a fertiliser by neutralisation:

- burette
- measuring cylinder
- filter funnel.

HT A fertiliser, e.g. potassium nitrate, can be made by producing a salt from neutralisation:

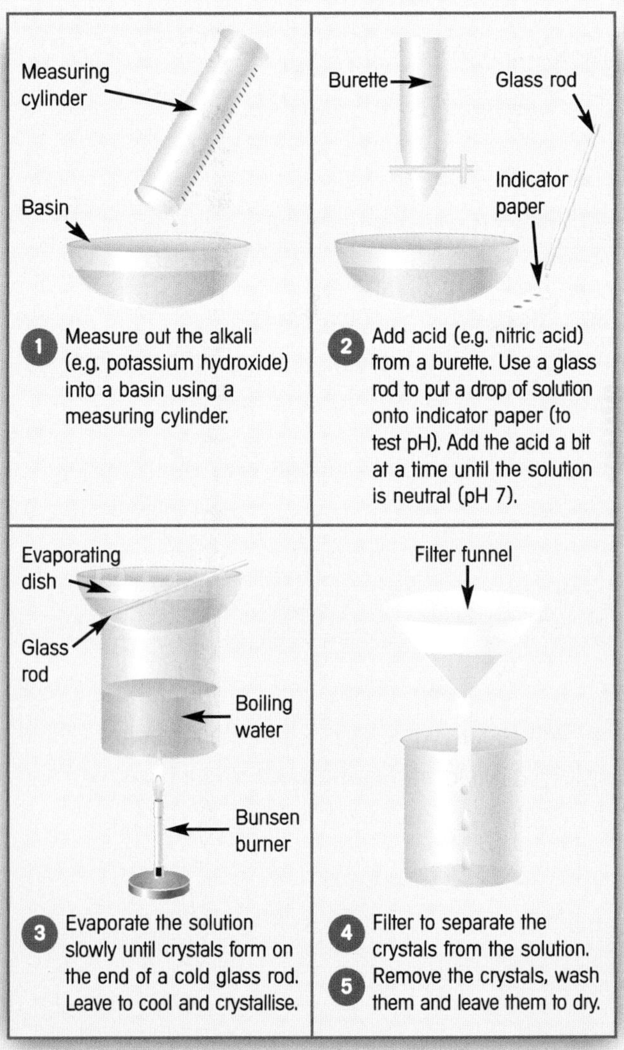

1. Measure out the alkali (e.g. potassium hydroxide) into a basin using a measuring cylinder.
2. Add acid (e.g. nitric acid) from a burette. Use a glass rod to put a drop of solution onto indicator paper (to test pH). Add the acid a bit at a time until the solution is neutral (pH 7).
3. Evaporate the solution slowly until crystals form on the end of a cold glass rod. Leave to cool and crystallise.
4. Filter to separate the crystals from the solution.
5. Remove the crystals, wash them and leave them to dry.

Key Words

Acid • Alkali • Eutrophication • Neutralisation • Relative formula mass • Yield

Calculating Mass

You need to be able to calculate the **relative formula mass** of a fertiliser if you are given its chemical formula.

Example

Calculate the M_r of the fertiliser that is represented by the chemical formula NH_4NO_3.

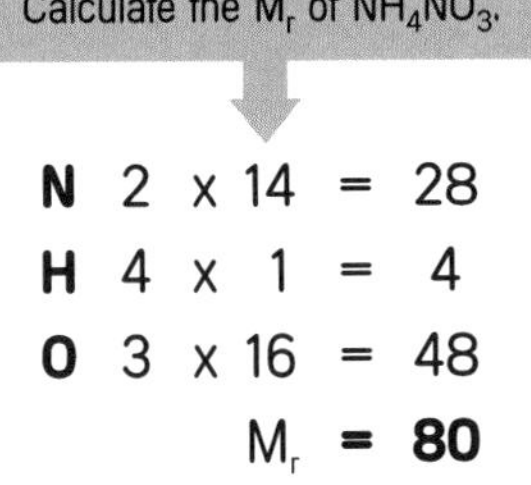

HT You can calculate the **percentage mass** of an element in a fertiliser by using this formula:

$$\text{Percentage mass} = \frac{\text{Mass of element}}{\text{Relative formula mass}} \times 100$$

Example

Calculate the percentage mass of nitrogen in ammonium nitrate (NH_4NO_3) fertiliser.

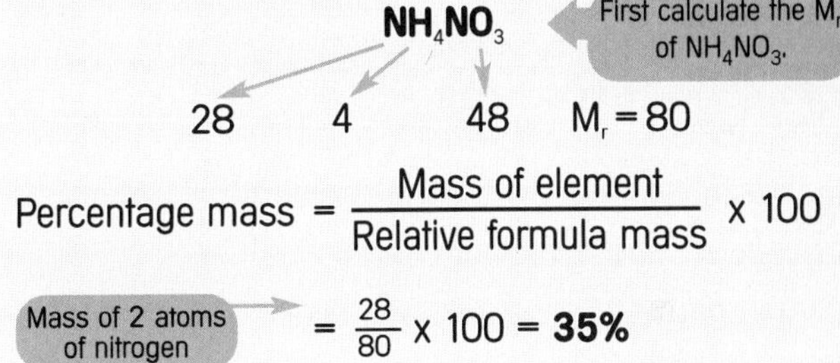

$$\text{Percentage mass} = \frac{\text{Mass of element}}{\text{Relative formula mass}} \times 100$$

Mass of 2 atoms of nitrogen → $= \frac{28}{80} \times 100 =$ **35%**

HT Eutrophication

Eutrophication is the process by which the careless overuse of fertilisers causes stretches of water to become stagnant.

1. Fertilisers used by farmers may be washed into lakes and rivers. This increases the levels of nitrates and phosphates in the water and increases the growth of simple algae.
2. The algal bloom blocks off sunlight to other plants, causing them to die and rot.
3. Aerobic bacteria feed on the dead organisms and increase in number. They quickly use up the oxygen until nearly all the oxygen is removed. There isn't enough oxygen left to support the larger organisms, such as fish and other aquatic animals, so they suffocate.

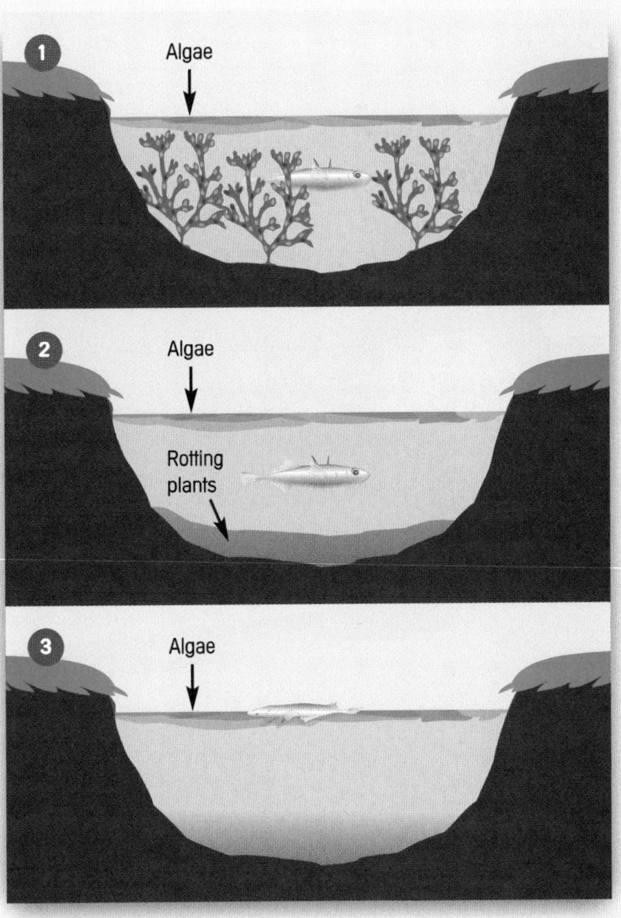

Making Ammonia – Haber Process and Costs

Ammonia

Ammonia (NH_3) is an alkaline gas made from nitrogen and hydrogen. It can be used to make...

- cleaning fluids
- nitric acid
- fertilisers (cheap fertilisers are very important in helping to produce enough food for the growing world population).

The reaction which produces ammonia is a **reversible reaction**. So, nitrogen and hydrogen can combine to form ammonia, and ammonia can decompose to form hydrogen and nitrogen.

Reversible reactions have the symbol $\rightleftharpoons$ in their equation to show that the reaction can take place in either direction.

The Haber Process

Ammonia is made on a large scale in the **Haber process**. The raw materials are...

- nitrogen (obtained from the air)
- hydrogen (from natural gas or the cracking of crude oil).

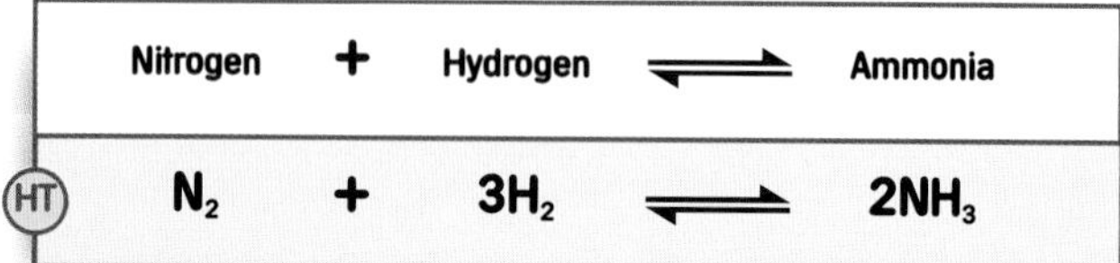

	Nitrogen	+	Hydrogen	$\rightleftharpoons$	Ammonia
HT	N_2	+	$3H_2$	$\rightleftharpoons$	$2NH_3$

Optimum conditions aren't used as they would be very expensive to maintain, so a compromise is reached:

- The nitrogen and hydrogen mixture is under a **high pressure** of 200 atmospheres.
- The gases are passed over an iron **catalyst** at **450°C**.

About 28% of the gases are converted into ammonia, which is separated from the unreacted gases by cooling, and then collected as a liquid. The unreacted gases are recycled.

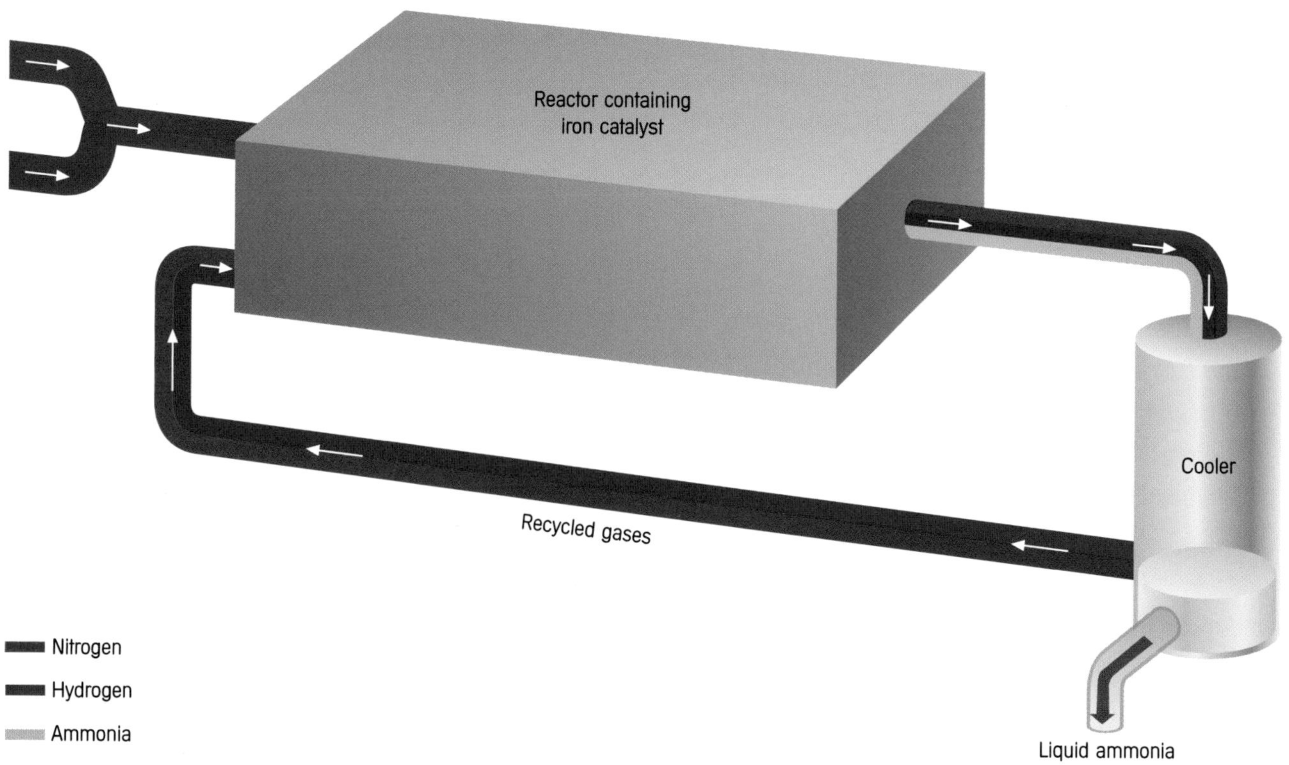

Making Ammonia – Haber Process and Costs

Interpreting Data

You need to be able to interpret data relating to percentage yield in reversible reactions, and changes in conditions.

Example
The graph and table explain how temperature and pressure affect the rate of reaction in the Haber process.

For example, from the information given you should be able to pick out that the yield falls when temperature is increased, and that the yield increases as pressure increases.

HT You may also be asked to interpret data on other industrial processes in terms of rate, percentage yield and cost.

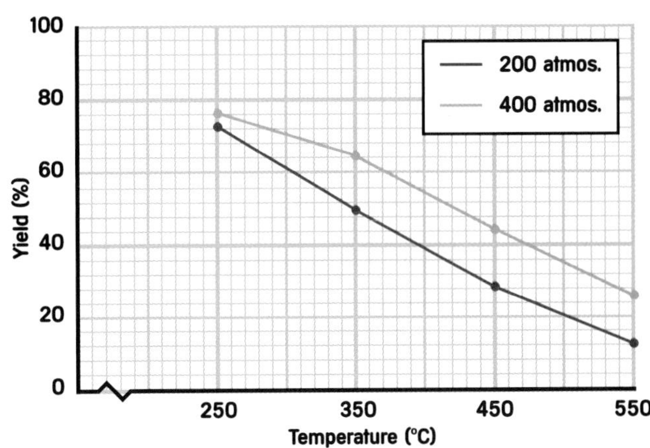

% Yield Pressure	Temperature			
	250°C	350°C	450°C	550°C
200 atmos.	73%	50%	28%	13%
400 atmos.	77%	65%	45%	26%

Cost and Factors Affecting Cost

The cost of making a new substance depends on...

- the price of energy (gas and electricity)
- labour costs (wages for employees)
- how quickly the new substance can be made
- the cost of starting materials (reactants)
- the cost of equipment needed (plant and machinery).

There are various factors that affect the cost of making a new substance, including...

- the **pressure** required – the higher the pressure, the higher the plant cost
- the **temperature** required – the higher the temperature, the higher the energy cost
- the **catalysts** required – catalysts can be expensive to buy, but production costs are reduced because they increase the rate of reaction
- the **number of people** required to operate machinery – automation reduces the wages bill
- the **amount of unreacted material** that can be recycled – recycling reduces costs.

Key Words

Catalyst • Reversible reaction

Making Ammonia – Haber Process and Costs

HT Economic Considerations

Economic considerations determine the conditions used in the manufacture of chemicals:

- The **rate of reaction** must be high enough to produce a sufficient daily yield of product.
- The **percentage yield** achieved must be high enough to produce a sufficient daily yield of product (a low percentage yield is acceptable providing the reaction can be repeated many times with **recycled starting materials**).
- The **optimum conditions** should be used to give the most economical reaction (this could mean a slower reaction or a lower percentage yield at a lower cost).

HT Economics of the Haber Process

It's important that the **maximum amount** of ammonia is produced in the **shortest possible time** at a **reasonable cost**. This requires a **compromise**.

Temperature – a low temperature favours the production of ammonia and produces a greater yield. Increasing the temperature increases the rate of reaction in both directions, but reduces the yield.

$$N_2 + 3H_2 \rightleftharpoons 2NH_3$$

Pressure – a high pressure produces a faster reaction rate and increases the percentage yield. Although this high pressure favours the production of ammonia, as the pressure becomes higher it becomes more expensive to maintain.

Catalyst – using a catalyst increases the rate of the reaction, but it doesn't affect the percentage yield. Using a catalyst can reduce costs, although there is still the initial purchase cost.

So, in summary...

- a low temperature increases yield but the reaction is too slow
- a high pressure increases yield but becomes more expensive as yield increases
- a catalyst increases the rate of reaction but doesn't change the percentage yield.

So, a compromise is reached of...

- temperature – 450°C
- pressure – 200 atmospheres
- catalyst – iron.

Key Words

Soluble • Solution • Solvent

Washing Powder

The main components of a washing powder have specific jobs:

- **Active detergent** does the cleaning.
- **Bleach** removes coloured stains.
- **Water softener** softens hard water.
- **Optical brightener** makes whites appear brighter.
- **Enzymes** break up food and protein stains in low-temperature washes.

When clothes are washed, the...

- water is the **solvent** (the liquid that does the dissolving)
- washing powder is the **solute** (the solid that dissolves) because it's **soluble** (it dissolves) in water
- resulting mixture of solvent and solute is a **solution**.

Low-temperature washes are used because they...

- can be used to wash delicate fabrics (that would shrink in a hotter wash or have a dye that could run)
- don't denature enzymes in biological powders
- save energy.

All your clothes will have washing symbols on the labels which tell you the washing conditions required.

Wash at 40°C

Hand-wash only

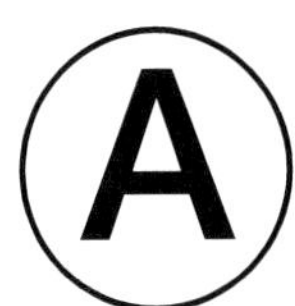

Dry clean – any solvent

Stain Removal

Different solvents dissolve different stains. The table shows which solvents can remove stains.

Although you don't need to learn this information, you might be asked to use similar information to choose which solvent to use to remove a stain. Some stains are **insoluble** (they will not dissolve) in water.

Dry cleaning solvents are used for these kinds of stain. The solvent is a liquid, but it doesn't contain water.

Stain	Solvent
Ball-point pen	Methylated spirits (ethanol) then biological washing powder in water
Blood	Biological washing powder in water
Shoe polish	White spirit then biological washing powder in water
Coffee	Biological washing powder in water
Correcting fluid	White spirit

HT Dry-Cleaning Solvents

The molecules making up a stain are held together by **weak intermolecular forces** (forces between the molecules).

The stain will dissolve in a **dry-cleaning solvent** if the intermolecular forces holding it together are overcome. The new intermolecular forces between the stain molecules and the solvent molecules are stronger than the ones between the stain.

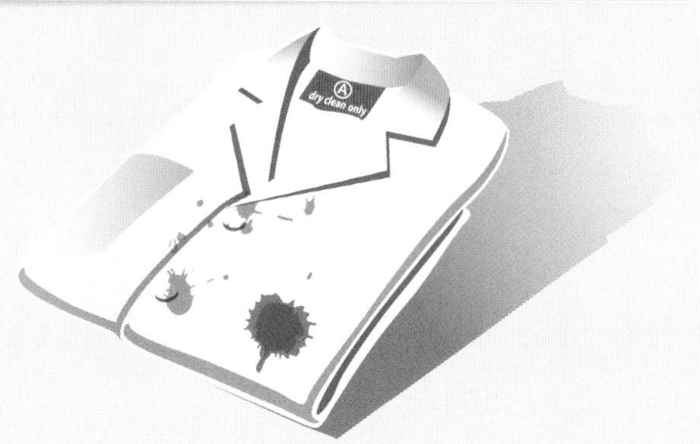

Detergents

Washing-Up Liquid

Washing-up liquid contains...

- **active detergent** – to do the cleaning
- **water** – to dissolve and dilute the detergent so that it's easy to pour
- **water softener** – to soften hard water
- **rinse agent** – to help the water drain off the crockery so it dries quickly
- **colour and fragrance** – to make the product more attractive to buy and use.

The detergent is often a **salt** made by **neutralising** an acid with an alkali.

HT Detergent Molecules

A detergent molecule is **non-polar** (i.e. it has a balanced overall charge). This is what happens when the molecule is dissolved in water:

1. The positively charged **sodium ion** comes away from the 'head' of the detergent molecule.
2. This leaves the molecule head negatively charged, so it's attracted to water molecules. It's known as **hydrophilic** (**water-loving**).
3. The hydrocarbon tail is non-polar and so it isn't attracted to water molecules. It's known as **hydrophobic** (**water-hating**).

Detergent Molecule

Charged hydrophilic head

Detached sodium ion

Carbon

Sulfur

Hydrogen

Oxygen

Non-polar hydrophobic tail

This is how washing-up liquid detergents work:

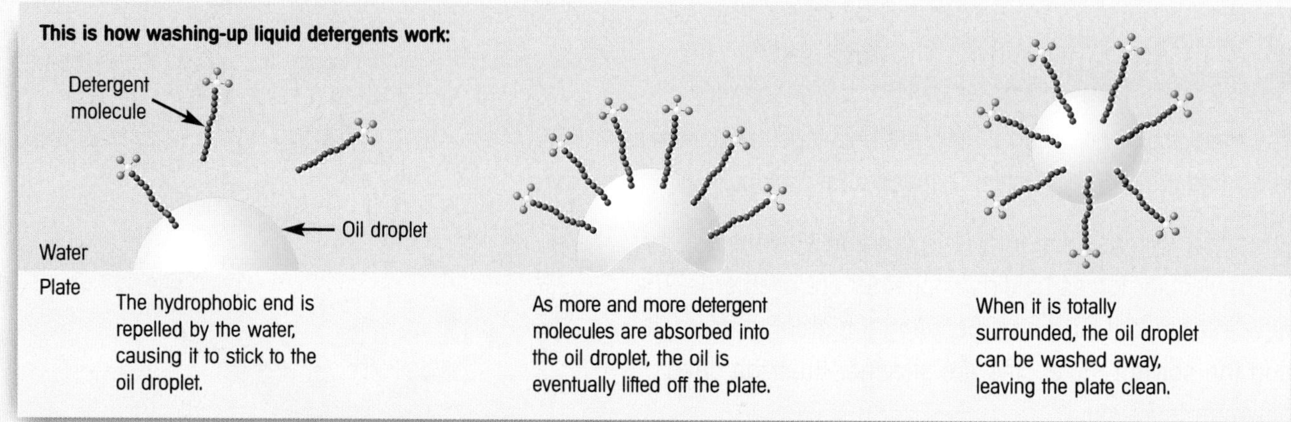

The hydrophobic end is repelled by the water, causing it to stick to the oil droplet.

As more and more detergent molecules are absorbed into the oil droplet, the oil is eventually lifted off the plate.

When it is totally surrounded, the oil droplet can be washed away, leaving the plate clean.

Batch or Continuous

Batch and Continuous Processes

In a **batch process**, reactants are put into a reactor and the product is removed at the end of the reaction. Medicines and pharmaceutical drugs can be made in this way. Batch processes...

- make a product on demand and on a small scale
- can be used to make a variety of products
- are labour intensive – the reactor needs to be filled, emptied and cleaned.

In a **continuous process**, reactants are continually fed into the reactor as the products are removed. The production of ammonia in the Haber process is made in this way. Continuous processes...

- make a product on a large scale
- are dedicated to making just one product
- operate all the time
- can run automatically.

Making and Developing Medicines

The materials used to make a medicine can be...

- **manufactured** (synthetic)
- extracted from **natural** sources such as plants.

Chemicals can be extracted from plant materials by...

- **crushing** – using a pestle and mortar
- **dissolving** – using a suitable solvent
- **chromatography** – using chromatography paper to separate a concentrated solution.

Developing a new pharmaceutical drug is very expensive, and takes a long time. The drug must also be approved for use, and satisfy all the legal requirements set out by the government.

The costs include...

- **materials** needed – they could be rare or may require expensive extraction from plants
- **research** and **testing**
- **labour** – highly qualified staff are needed. It can't be automated (carried out by machines) as only small quantities are made.
- **energy**
- **marketing**.

Key Words

Batch process • Continuous process • Hydrophilic • Hydrophobic • Neutralisation • Salt

HT Research and development can take a few years, but it can take even longer to carry out **safety tests**, including testing on human volunteers. There are very strict legal rules which a new medicine must satisfy before it can be put on the market.

A pharmaceutical company may invest hundreds of millions of pounds to develop one drug and only have a limited time to recoup their investment before they lose exclusive rights to produce the medicine. If the number of people using the medicine is small, then the cost of buying the drug would be very high.

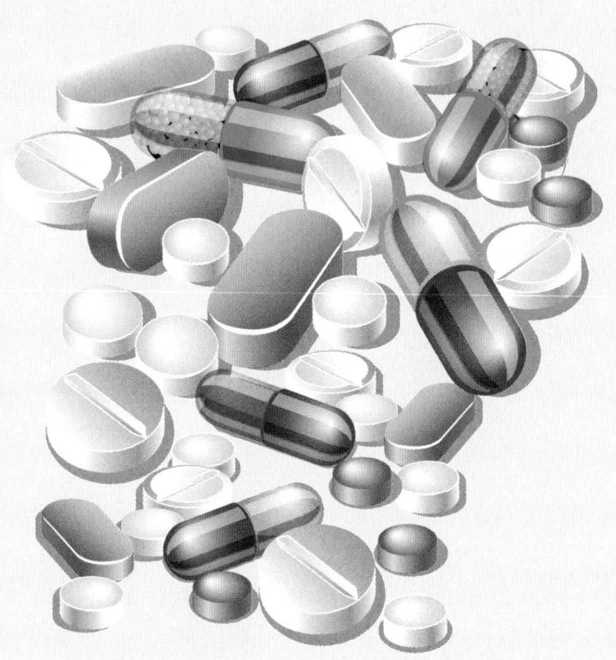

Nanochemistry

Carbon

There are three forms of carbon:

- diamond
- graphite
- buckminster fullerene (buckyballs).

HT Diamond, graphite and the fullerenes are allotropes of **carbon**. **Allotropes** are different forms of the same element with atoms arranged in different molecular structures.

Diamond

Diamond has a rigid structure:

- It's insoluble in water and doesn't conduct electricity.
- It's used in jewellery because it's colourless, clear (transparent) and lustrous (shiny).
- It can be used in cutting tools because it's very hard and has a very high melting point.

HT **Diamond** is made of carbon atoms bonded to four other carbon atoms by strong **covalent bonds**.

- It's hard and has a high melting point because of the large number of covalent bonds.
- It doesn't have any free electrons so it doesn't conduct electricity.

The Structure of Diamond

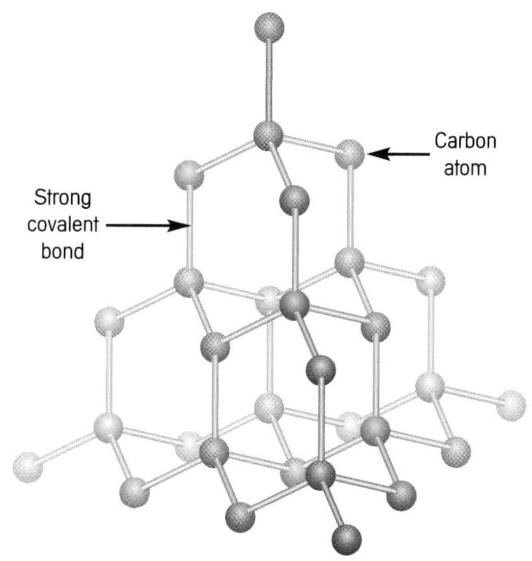

Graphite

Graphite has a layered structure:

- It's insoluble in water.
- It's black, which is why it's used in pencils.
- It is lustrous and opaque (light can't travel through it).
- It conducts electricity and has a very high melting point, so is used to make electrodes for electrolysis.
- It's slippery, so it's used in lubricants.

HT **Graphite** is made of layers of carbon atoms that are bonded to three other carbon atoms by strong **covalent bonds**.

- The layers are held together by weak intermolecular forces, allowing each layer to slide easily.
- It conducts electricity because it has **free** (delocalised) **electrons**.
- It has a high melting point because it has many strong covalent bonds to break.

The Structure of Graphite

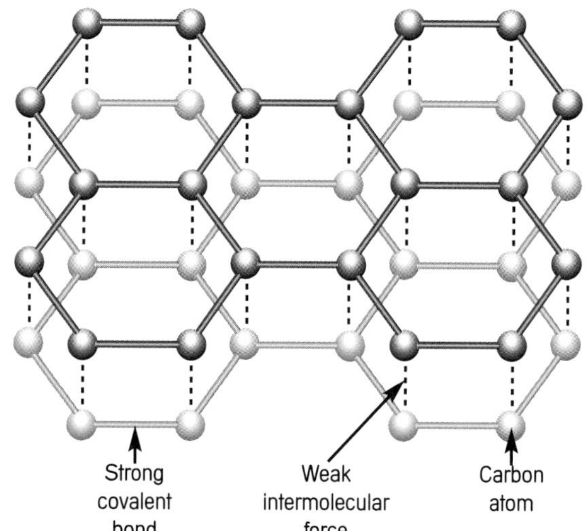

Key Words

Allotropes • **Nanochemistry**

Nanochemistry

Chemistry deals with materials on a **large scale**, but **nanochemistry** deals with materials on an **atomic scale** (i.e. individual atoms). The properties of particles on this very small scale are very different to the properties of the bulk material.

Two forms of carbon are of special interest to nanochemists, because of their properties at the atomic scale. The forms are **buckminster fullerenes** and **nanotubes**.

Buckminster Fullerene

A buckminster fullerene (C_{60}) consists of 60 carbon atoms arranged in a sphere:

- It's a black solid.
- It makes a red solution when dissolved in petrol.

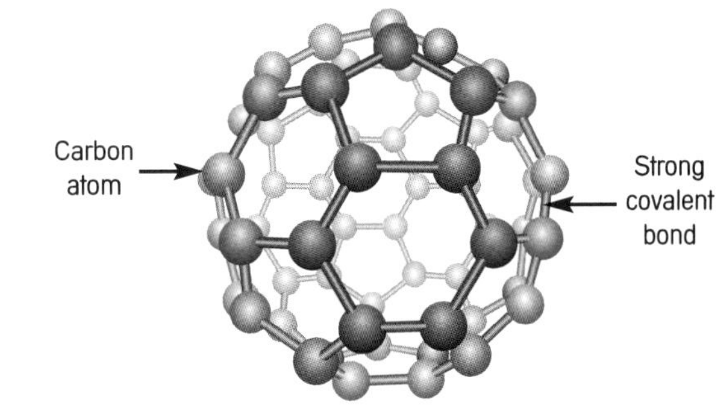

Nanotubes

Chemists discovered that **nanotubes** could be made by joining fullerenes together. Nanotubes conduct electricity and are very strong. They are used to...

- reinforce graphite tennis rackets because of their strength
- make connectors and semiconductors in the most modern molecular computers because of their electrical properties
- develop more efficient industrial catalysts.

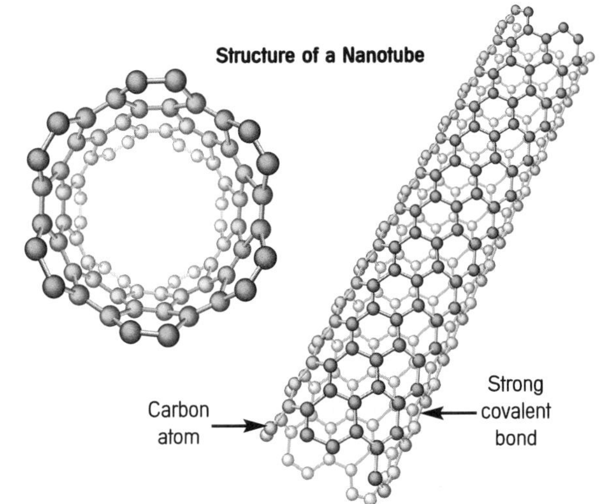

HT More on Nanochemistry

Fullerenes and nanotubes can be used to 'cage' other molecules because their shape allows them to trap other substances, for example...

- **drugs**, e.g. a major new HIV treatment uses buckyballs to deliver a material which disrupts the working of the HIV virus
- **catalysts** – by attaching catalyst material to a nanotube, a massive surface area can be achieved, making the catalyst very efficient.

Fullerenes and nanotube molecules are manufactured by a variety of processes:

- Lasers can be used to vaporise carbon which then deposits onto a molecule and builds up the structure piece by piece.
- Matter can be removed from a big structure to produce nanoscale features.

How Pure is Our Water?

Water

The four main sources of water are...

- rivers
- lakes
- reservoirs
- aquifiers (wells and bore holes).

Water is an important resource for industry as well as being essential for drinking, washing, etc. The chemical industry uses water...

- as a coolant
- as a solvent
- as a raw material.

In some parts of Britain, the **demand** for water is **higher than the supply**, so it's important to **conserve** and not waste water.

Many parts of the developing world don't have access to clean water (water without disease-carrying microorganisms). The World Health Organisation estimates that...

- over 2 million people worldwide die every year from water-borne diseases
- nearly 20% of the world's population doesn't have access to clean drinking water.

Water Treatment

Water Treatment Process

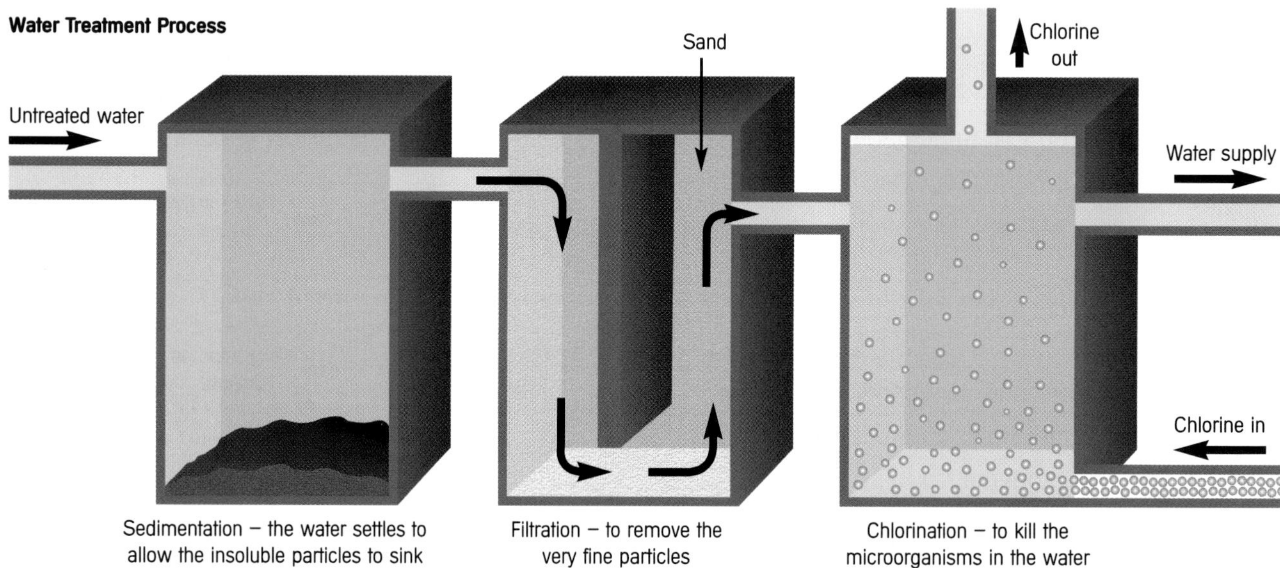

Water has to be treated to purify it and make sure it's safe to drink. Untreated (raw) water can contain...

- **insoluble** particles
- pollutants
- microorganisms
- dissolved **salts** and minerals.

Key Words

Distillation • Insoluble • Ion • Pollutant • Precipitation • Salt

HT Tap water isn't pure – it contains soluble materials that aren't removed by the normal water treatment process. Some of these materials could be poisonous, so extra steps must be taken to remove them.

To obtain pure water, it must be **distilled**, but this process uses a lot of energy and is expensive.

The equipment and energy use needed to **distil sea water** would be very expensive. The cost of making drinking water out of sea water is too high to make it a realistic option.

How Pure is Our Water?

Pollutants in Water

Pollutants that can be found in water supplies are often difficult to remove. They include...

- **nitrates** from the run-off of fertilisers
- **lead compounds** from old pipes in the plumbing
- **pesticides** from spraying crops near to the water supply.

Dissolved Ions

The dissolved **ions** of some salts are easy to identify as they will undergo **precipitation** reactions. A precipitation reaction occurs when a solid is made from mixing two solutions together.

Sulfates can be detected using barium chloride solution – a white precipitate of barium sulfate forms. For example...

Sodium sulfate + Barium chloride → Barium sulfate (white) + Sodium chloride

HT $Na_2SO_4(aq) + BaCl_2(aq) \rightarrow BaSO_4(s) + 2NaCl(aq)$

Silver nitrate solution is used to detect **halide ions**. Halides are the ions made by the halogens (Group 7).

With silver nitrate...

- chlorides form a white precipitate
- bromides form a cream precipitate
- iodides form a pale yellow precipitate.

Sodium chloride + Silver nitrate → Silver chloride (white) + Sodium nitrate

HT $NaCl(aq) + AgNO_3(aq) \rightarrow AgCl(s) + NaNO_3(aq)$

Sodium bromide + Silver nitrate → Silver bromide (cream) + Sodium nitrate

HT $NaBr(aq) + AgNO_3(aq) \rightarrow AgBr(s) + NaNO_3(aq)$

Sodium iodide + Silver nitrate → Silver iodide (pale yellow) + Sodium nitrate

HT $NaI(aq) + AgNO_3(aq) \rightarrow AgI(s) + NaNO_3(aq)$

Interpreting Data

In your exam, you may be asked to interpret data about water resources in the UK. For example, this table shows some pollutants and the maximum amounts allowed in drinking water.

You don't have to remember the data, but you might, for example, be asked to pick out which pollutant has the smallest allowed concentration, or transfer this data onto a graph.

Pollutant	Maximum Amount Allowed
Nitrates	50 parts in 1 000 000 000 parts water
Lead	50 parts in 1 000 000 000 parts water
Pesticides	0.5 parts in 1 000 000 000 parts water

Module C4 Practice Questions

HT **1 a)** Ammonia has the formula NH_3. How many atoms of each element does it contain?

b) Draw a line to match each acid to its correct formula.

Hydrochloric acid	H_2SO_4
Nitric acid	HNO_3
Sulfuric acid	HCl

c) What is the name of $(NH_4)_2SO_4$?

2 a) Briefly describe what happens to the pH of an alkaline solution when an acid is slowly added to it until there is an excess of acid.

b) Name the salt made by reacting nitric acid with…

i) sodium carbonate **ii)** ammonium hydroxide

iii) copper oxide.

HT **c)** Which ion is always found in an acid?

3 a) Using the periodic table at the back of the book to help you, calculate the relative formula mass of each compound.

i) Na_2CO_3

ii) $(NH_4)_2SO_4$

b) A neutralisation reaction was expected to produce a salt with a mass of 15g. The actual mass was 9g. Calculate the percentage yield.

4 a) Which element is present in all of the following fertilisers: ammonium sulfate, ammonium chloride, ammonium phosphate and potassium nitrate?

HT **b)** What role do aerobic bacteria play in eutrophication?

c) Calculate the percentage mass of nitrogen in $(NH_4)_2SO_4$.

Module C4 Practice Questions

5 **a)** Name the two raw materials used for making ammonia.

b) What type of reaction has the symbol $\rightleftharpoons$ in the equation?

c) The Haber process reaction would give a bigger yield if the temperature is lower than 450°C. Why isn't a lower temperature used?

6 **a)** What is the purpose of a rinse agent in a washing-up liquid?

HT **b)** Briefly describe how washing-up liquid cleans a plate.

7 **a)** Briefly explain why the materials needed to make a new medicine are expensive.

b) Give two of the advantages of using a batch process to make a chemical.

i)

ii)

8 **a)** Which element are diamond, buckminster fullerene and graphite all forms of?

HT **b)** Why can graphite conduct electricity?

c) Use ideas about bonding and structure to explain why diamond has a high melting point and doesn't conduct electricity.

9 **a)** List three ways in which water is used as a resource in the chemical industry.

i)

ii)

iii)

b) Describe how you would test a sample of water to show it contained chloride ions.

HT **c)** Write the balanced symbol equation for the reaction of barium chloride solution with potassium sulfate solution.

Sparks

Generating Static Electricity

An insulating material can become electrically **charged** if it's rubbed with another insulating material. Electrons transfer from one material to the other, leaving...

- one material with a **positive** charge
- one material with a **negative** charge.

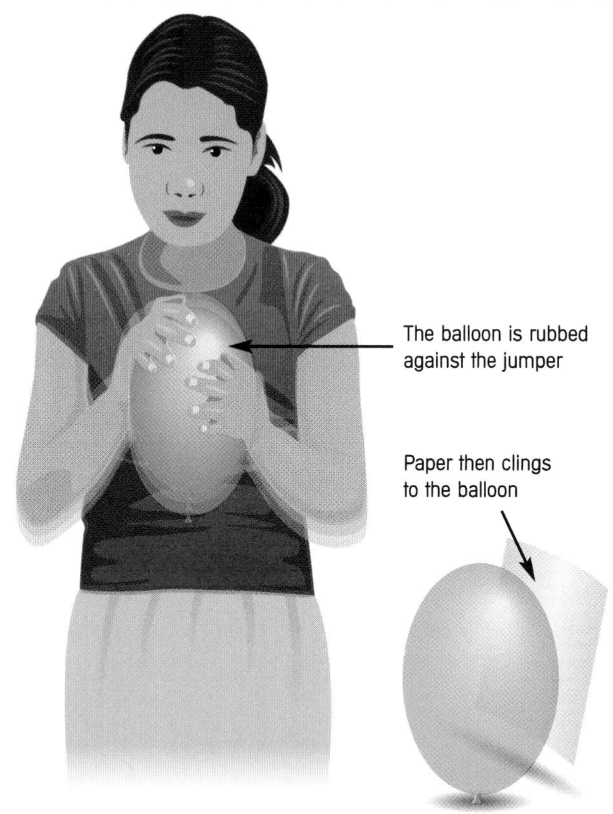

You can generate static electricity by rubbing a balloon, comb or strip of plastic against a jumper. The electrically charged object will attract very small objects, e.g. pieces of paper or cork.

Dusting brushes can be charged so that they attract dust when they pass over it.

Synthetic clothing can become charged due to friction between the clothing and the person's body when the clothes are put on. When the clothing is removed from the body, static sparks are sometimes produced.

Discharging Static Electricity

A **charged object** can be **discharged** (i.e. have the excess charge removed) by earthing it. When an object discharges, electrons are transferred from the charged object to earth.

If you become charged and then earthed, you could get an **electrostatic shock**.

For example, **touching water pipes** – you can become charged by friction between the soles of your feet and the floor if you're walking on an insulator such as carpet or vinyl. If you then touch a water pipe, e.g. a radiator, the charge is earthed and discharge occurs.

Problems of Static Electricity

In some situations, static electricity can be a **nuisance**. For example, static can cause...

- dirt and dust to be attracted to insulating materials, e.g. television screens and computer monitors
- some materials to cling to your skin.

Key Words

Attraction • Earthed • Electron • Repulsion • Static electricity

In other situations, static electricity can be very **dangerous**:

- Flour mills and petrochemical factories have atmospheres that can contain extremely flammable gases (or vapours), or high concentrations of oxygen. A discharge of static electricity (i.e. a spark) can lead to an explosion.
- Static is dangerous in any situation where large amounts could flow through your body to earth, for example, lightning.

Repulsion and Attraction

Two insulating materials with the **same charge** will repel each other. For example, a **positively charged** Perspex rod is held near to a suspended **positively charged** Perspex rod, the suspended rod will be **repelled**. The same thing would happen if both rods had a negative charge.

Two insulating materials with **different charges** will attract each other. For example, if a **negatively charged** ebonite rod is held near to a suspended **positively charged** Perspex rod, the suspended rod will be **attracted** to the ebonite rod. This would also happen if the charges were the other way round.

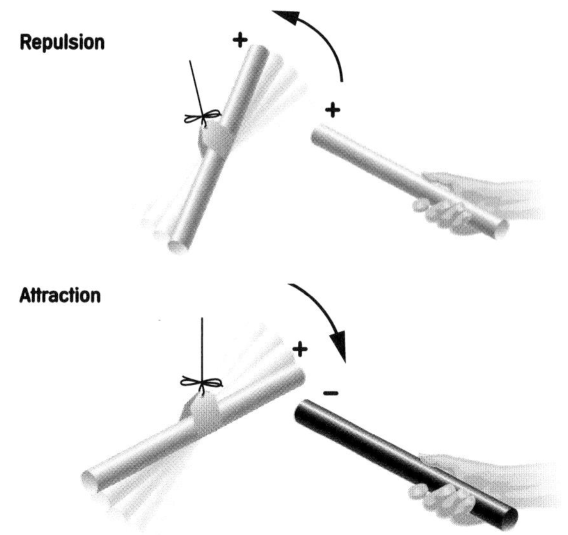

HT Why Objects Become Charged Up

Electric or static charge builds up when **electrons** (negatively charged) are rubbed off one material onto another.

- The material that **receives** the electrons becomes **negatively charged** due to an **excess of electrons**.
- The material **giving up the** electrons becomes **positively charged** due to a **loss of electrons.**

A Perspex rod rubbed with a cloth gives up electrons and becomes positively charged. The cloth receives the electrons and becomes negatively charged.

An ebonite rod rubbed with fur receives electrons and becomes negatively charged. The fur gives up electrons and becomes positively charged.

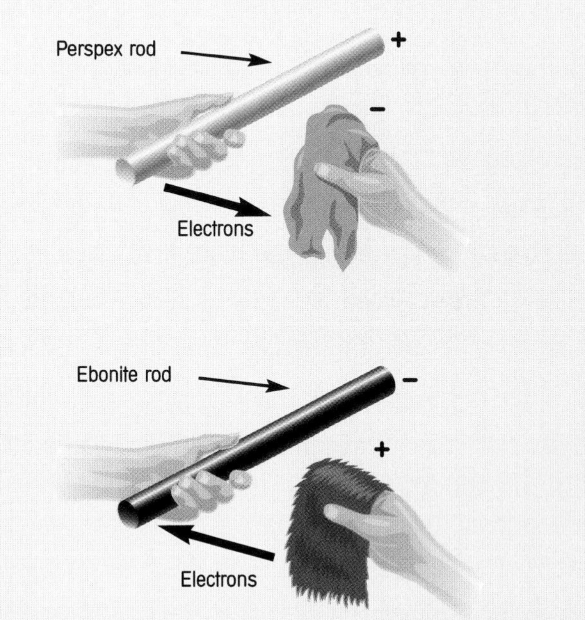

Reducing the Danger

The chance of receiving an electric shock can be **reduced** by...

- making sure appliances are correctly earthed
- using insulation mats effectively
- wearing shoes with insulating soles.

Lorries that contain inflammable gases, liquids or powders need to be earthed before unloading, as friction can cause a build-up of charge. This charge could lead to a spark, which could then ignite the flammable substance.

Anti-static sprays, liquids and cloths help to reduce the problems of static electricity by preventing the transfer of charge from one insulator to another. If there is no build-up of charge, there can't be any discharge.

Uses of Electrostatics

Using Static in Everyday Life

Static electricity is used in many ways in everyday life:

Photocopiers – an image of the page to be copied is projected onto a positively charged plate. Light causes charge to leak away, leaving an electrostatic impression of the page. The charged impression on the plate attracts tiny specks of black powder, which are transferred from the plate to paper. Heat fixes the final image on the paper.

Laser printers – a printer cartridge contains a charged rotating drum. As the drum rotates, a laser beam discharges parts of the drum to leave behind an image of text and graphics. The drum then rotates past charged toner which is attracted to the discharged parts of the drum. The toner is transferred from the drum onto paper, which is heated to fix the final image.

Defibrillators – electricity can be used to start the heart when it has stopped. Two paddles are charged and are put in good electrical contact with the patient's chest. Taking care not to shock the operator, charge is then passed through the patient to make the heart contract.

Spray painting – the paint particles are given a negative charge so that they repel each other, forming a fine spray. This ensures that the paint is applied evenly. The panel to be sprayed is positively charged so it attracts the negatively charged paint. This means that less paint is wasted and even the back and sides of the object, in the shadow of the spray, receive a coat of paint.

Smoke precipitators – electrostatic dust precipitators can remove smoke particles from chimneys. Metal plates / grids are installed in the chimney and are connected to a high potential difference (voltage). The dust particles are attracted to the plates / grids, where they form large particles that fall back down the chimney when they are heavy enough.

Defibrillation

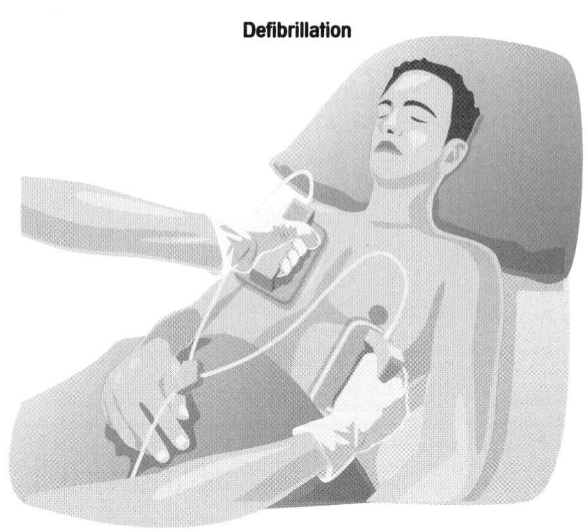

Spray Painting

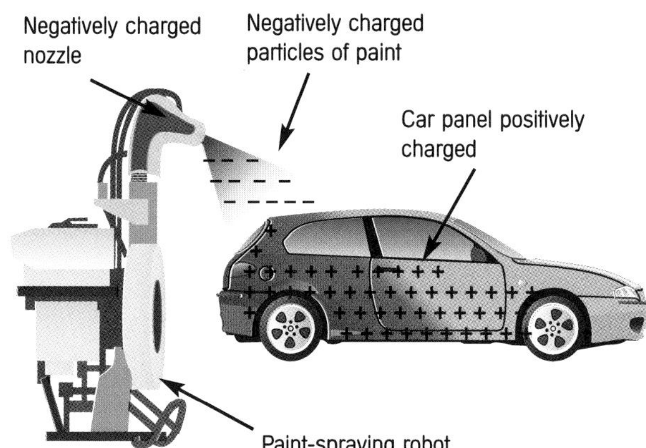

Smoke Precipitator

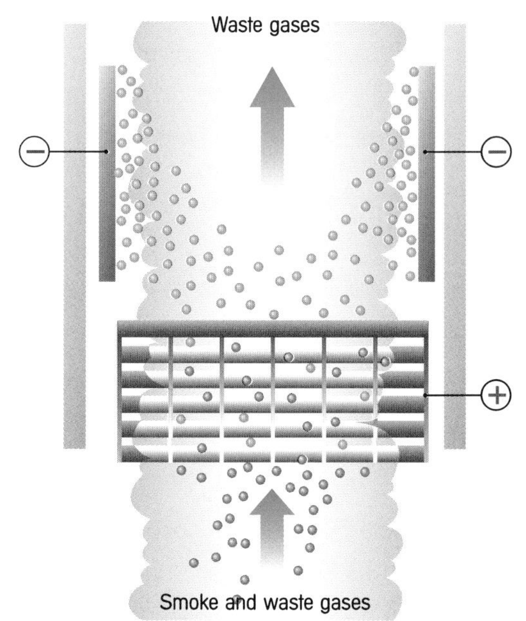

Circuits

A **circuit** is a complete loop that allows an **electrical current** to flow. Electrons flow around the circuit from the **negative electrode** of the power source to the **positive electrode**. But, this was only discovered recently so circuit diagrams show the current flowing from the positive to the negative electrode.

Fixed and Variable Resistors

Resistance is a measure of how hard it is to get a current through a **component** in a circuit at a particular voltage (potential difference). Resistance is measured in **ohms** (Ω).

The current through a circuit can be controlled by varying the resistance. There are two types of resistor:

- **Fixed resistor** – a component with **constant** resistance. The bigger the resistance, the smaller the current that flows for a particular voltage.
- **Variable resistor** (or rheostat) – a component with **changeable** resistance. The flowing current can be changed by moving the sliding contact of the variable resistor.

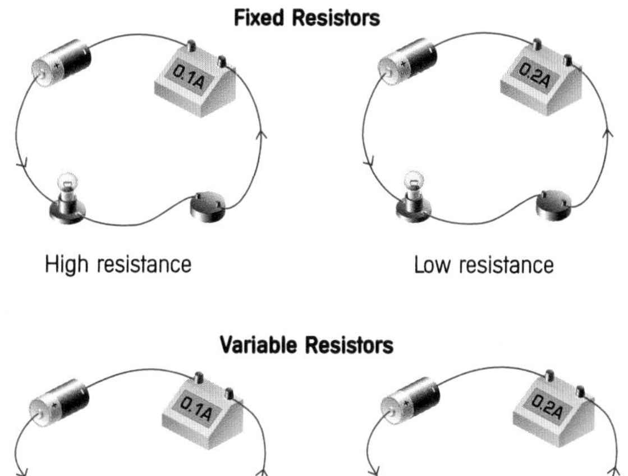

High resistance Low resistance

Current, Voltage and Resistance

For a **given resistor, current increases** as **voltage increases** (and vice versa). For a **fixed voltage, current decreases** as **resistance increases** (and vice versa).

Current, voltage and resistance are related by this formula:

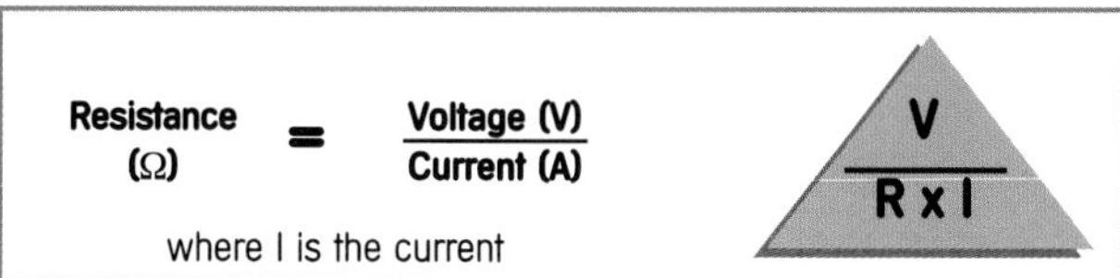

N.B. You need to remember this formula as it will not be given to you in the exam.

Key Words

Current • Electron • Resistance • Static electricity • Voltage

Example 1

Calculate the resistance of the lamp in the following circuit:

$$\text{Resistance} = \frac{\text{Voltage}}{\text{Current}} = \frac{3\text{V}}{0.2\text{A}} = \mathbf{15\Omega}$$

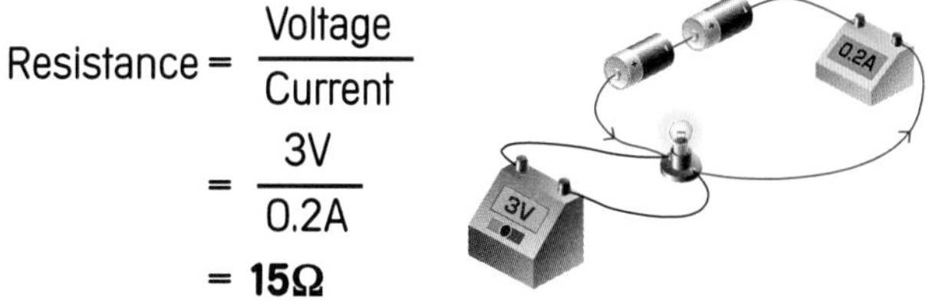

HT **Example 2**

Calculate the reading on the ammeter in the circuit below if the bulb has a resistance of 20 ohms.

$$\text{Current} = \frac{\text{Voltage}}{\text{Resistance}} = \frac{6\text{V}}{20\Omega} = \mathbf{0.3A}$$

Safe Electricals

Live, Neutral and Earth Wires

Electrical appliances are connected to mains electricity by a cable and 3-pin plug. Most cables and plugs contain three wires:

- **live wire** (brown) – carries current to the appliance at a high voltage (230V)
- **neutral wire** (blue) – completes the circuit and carries current away from the appliance
- **earth wire** (green and yellow) – safety wire that stops the appliance becoming live.

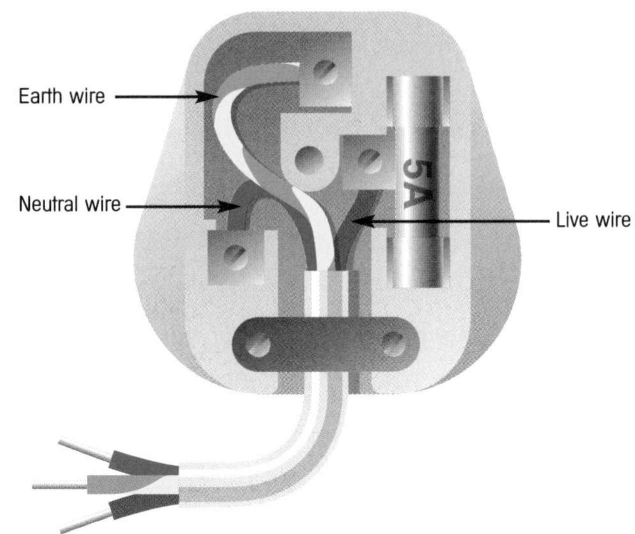

Double Insulation

All appliances with outer metal cases (conductors) have an **earth wire**, so they are earthed. An earthed conductor can't become live.

Some appliances have **cases made of insulators** so they don't have an earth wire (although they still have a fuse). These appliances are **double insulated** and they don't need to be earthed because they can't become live.

HT Earthing

Electrical appliances with outer metal cases are earthed in order to protect the appliance and the user. The earth wire and fuse work together.

1. A fault in the appliance causes the casing to become live.
2. The circuit **short-circuits** (i.e. the path of the flow of charge changes) because the earth wire offers less resistance.
3. The fuse wire melts.
4. The circuit is broken.
5. The appliance and the user are protected.

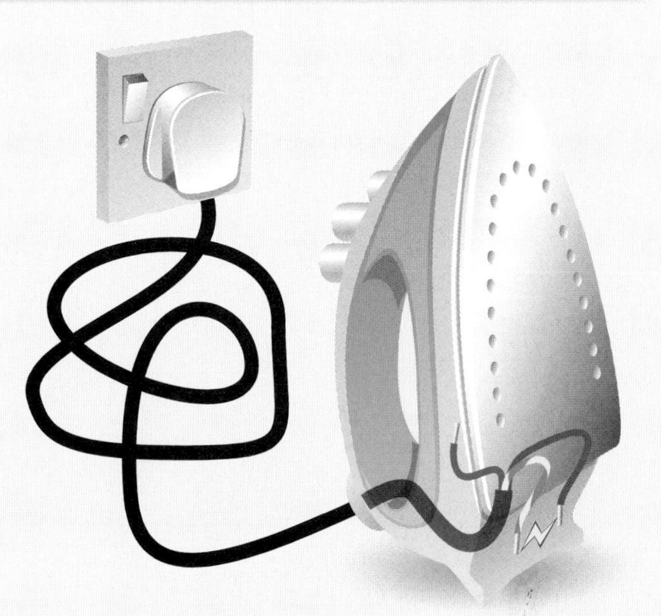

Key Words

Earthed • Fuse

Fuses and Circuit Breakers

Fuses and circuit breakers are **safety devices** designed to break a circuit if a fault occurs. This can prevent fires, injuries and deaths.

A **fuse** is a short, thin piece of wire with a low melting point. It's used to prevent cables or appliances from overheating. To work properly, the current rating of the fuse must be **just above** the normal current that flows through the appliance.

1. A fault causes the current in the appliance to exceed the current rating of the fuse.
2. The fuse wire gets hot and melts or breaks.
3. The circuit is broken so the current is unable to flow.
4. The appliance and user are protected.

A **circuit breaker** acts in a similar way to a fuse, but it can be easily **reset**.

HT Example of a Fuse in Action

1. If the current flowing through an appliance is **below** the **current rating** of the fuse, the appliance will work properly.
2. But, if a fault occurs inside the appliance, the live wire will make contact with the neutral wire. The current flowing would then be **higher** than the **current rating** of the fuse due to lower resistance.
3. This causes the fuse wire to get hotter and hotter until it melts and breaks the circuit. The current is unable to flow so there is no danger of the flex overheating (resulting in a fire). Further damage to the appliance, or injury to the user, is prevented.

Fuses and circuit breakers prevent...
- fires as they stop cables and flexes from overheating
- injury and death as they stop appliances from becoming 'live'
- damage to the components of an appliance because they break the circuit if a higher than normal current flows through the appliance.

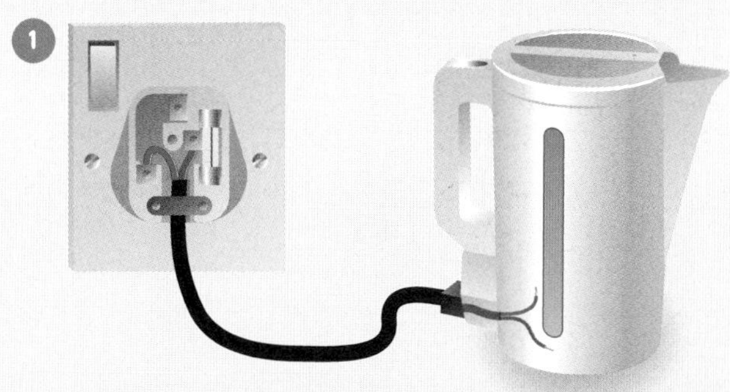

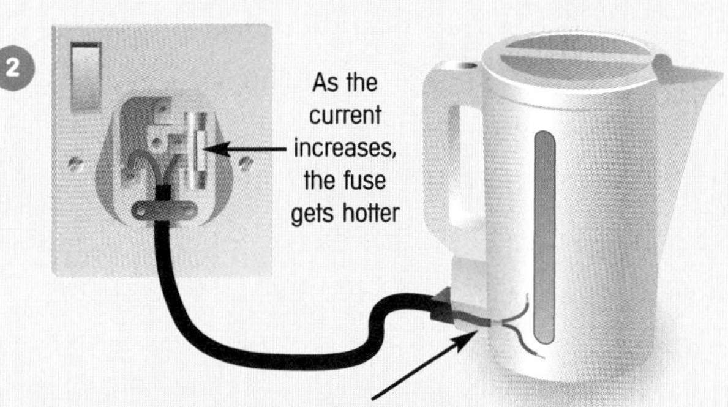

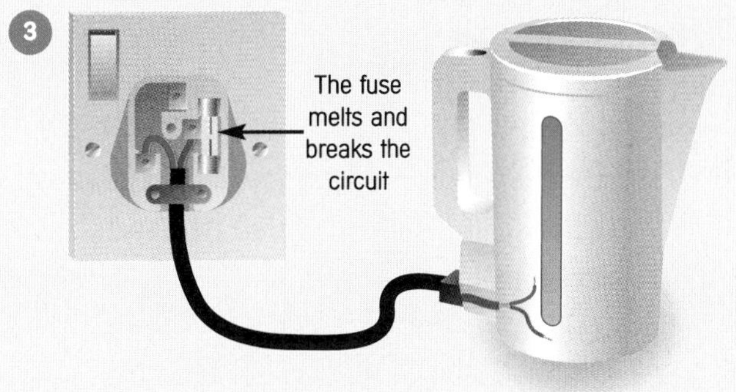

Ultrasound

Ultrasound

Ultrasound is sound waves with frequencies above the upper limit of the human hearing range (i.e. above 20 000 hertz (Hz)).

Ultrasound travels in a **longitudinal wave**. This can be demonstrated using a slinky spring.

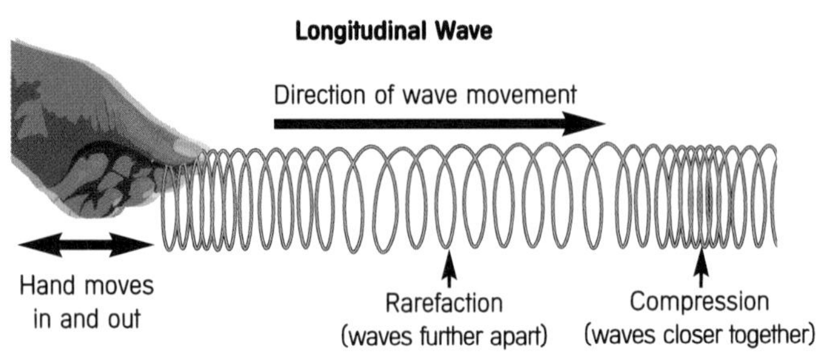

The key features of waves are...

- **amplitude** – the maximum disturbance caused by a wave
- **wavelength** – the distance between corresponding points on two successive disturbances
- **frequency** – the number of waves produced (or that pass a particular point) in 1 second.

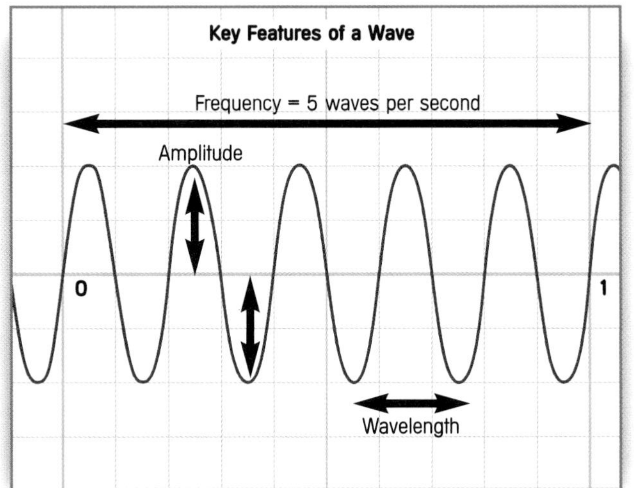

Applications of Ultrasound

Ultrasound can be used in **medicine** to...

- see inside people by scanning the body
- measure the speed of blood flow
- break down stones, e.g. kidney stones.

Ultrasound waves can **break down kidney stones** so they can be removed from the body naturally. This avoids the need for painful surgery.

HT Ultrasonic waves cause the kidney stones to vibrate. The stones break up, are dispersed, and can then be passed out of the body in urine.

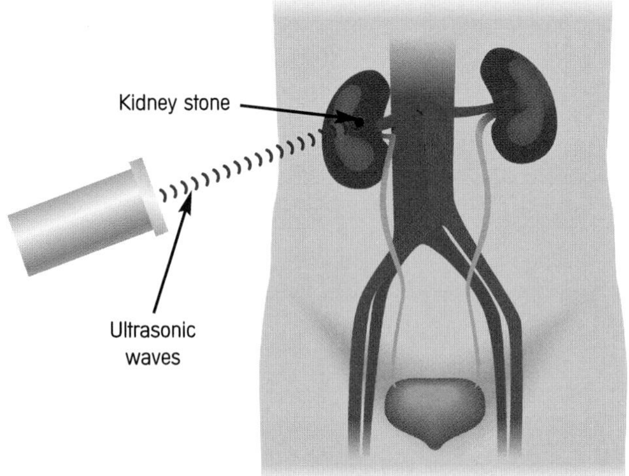

Scanning the body with ultrasound waves can build up a picture of the body's organs, including the heart, lungs and liver. Ultrasound can also be used...

- to detect **gallstones** and **tumours**
- for **pre-natal scanning** because there is no risk to mother or baby.

Key Words

Amplitude • Frequency • Longitudinal wave • Transverse wave • Ultrasound • Wavelength

HT More on Ultrasound

Ultrasound waves are **partially reflected** at a **boundary** as they pass from one medium or substance into another. The **time taken** for these **reflections** to be **detected** can be used to calculate the depth of the reflecting surface. The reflected waves are usually processed to produce a visual image on a screen.

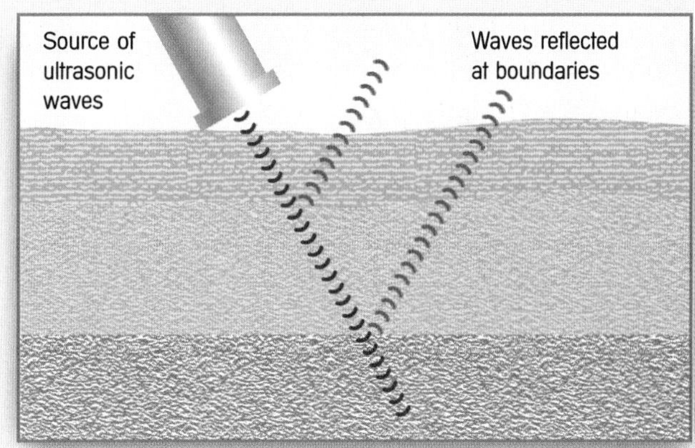

Ultrasound has two main advantages over X-ray imaging:

- It's able to produce images of soft tissue.
- It doesn't damage living cells.

Particle Motion in Waves

All waves **transfer energy** from one point to another **without** transferring any **particles of matter**. In the following diagrams, each coil of the slinky spring represents one particle. There are two types of wave – **longitudinal** and **transverse**.

Longitudinal Waves	Transverse Waves
Each particle moves backwards and forwards about its normal position in the same plane as the direction of wave movement.	Each particle moves up and down about its normal position at 90° to the direction of the wave movement.
Direction of wave movement Hand moves in and out	Direction of wave movement Hand moves up and down

Treatment

Radiation

X-rays and gamma rays are **electromagnetic waves** with similar **wavelengths** although they are produced in different ways.

X-rays and nuclear **radiation** (i.e. gamma and beta radiation) can be used in medicine.

X-rays can be used to build up a picture of the inside of a patient's body. The person in a hospital who takes X-rays and uses radiation is called a **radiographer**.

Nuclear radiation can pass through skin and damage cells:

- Gamma rays damage cells, so they can be used to **treat cancer**.
- Beta and gamma rays pass through skin, so they can be used as medical **tracers** (i.e. to track the progress of a substance through a patient's system).

Gamma rays can also be used to **sterilise medical equipment** because they kill germs and bacteria.

HT X-rays are made by firing high-speed **electrons** at metal targets. X-rays are easier to control than gamma rays.

After alpha or beta decay, a nucleus sometimes contains surplus energy. It emits this as gamma radiation, which is very high frequency electromagnetic radiation.

Treating Cancer

Gamma rays can be used to treat cancer:

1. A wide beam of **gamma rays** from a source outside the body is focused on the tumour.
2. The beam is rotated around the outside of the body with the tumour at the centre.
3. This concentrates the gamma rays on the tumour, but minimises damage to the rest of body.

Gamma radiation treatment can destroy cancer cells without the need for surgery, but it may damage healthy cells and cause sickness.

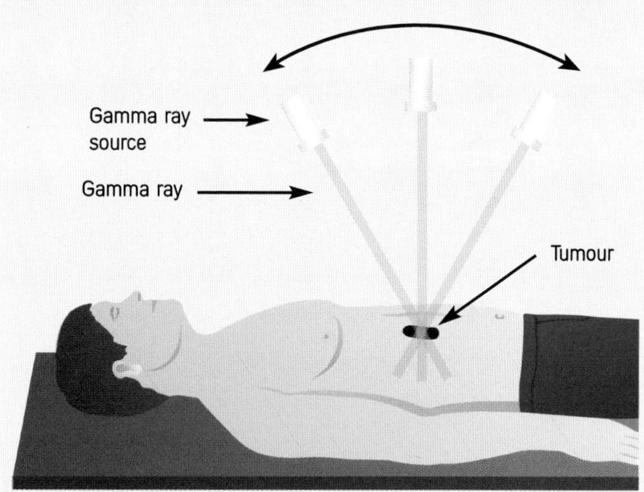

Tracers

Tracers are small amounts of radioactive materials which are swallowed or injected into a patient. The tracer is given time to spread through the body, whilst its progress is followed using an external radiation detector.

For example, the thyroid gland in the neck affects the body's metabolic rate. It absorbs iodine, so a patient can be given a tracer which contains iodine-131. A detector follows the tracer's progress and you can tell how well the gland is working by measuring the amount of iodine it absorbs.

*N.B. The radioactive material **must** emit either gamma or beta radiation, because they both pass through skin so they're able to be detected.*

What is Radioactivity?

Radioactivity

Radioactive materials give out nuclear radiation from the nucleus of their atoms. The atoms are **unstable** and **decay naturally**.

During this decay, radiation can be given out in the form of alpha, beta and gamma rays:

- An **alpha particle** is a **helium** nucleus.
- A **beta particle** is a fast-moving **electron**.

Radiation is measured by the **number of nuclear decays emitted per second**. This number decreases with time.

Key Words

Electromagnetic wave • Electron • Radiation • Tracer • Wavelength

HT Alpha Emission

During alpha emission, the atom decays by ejecting an **alpha particle** (a helium nucleus made up of two protons and two neutrons) from the nucleus.

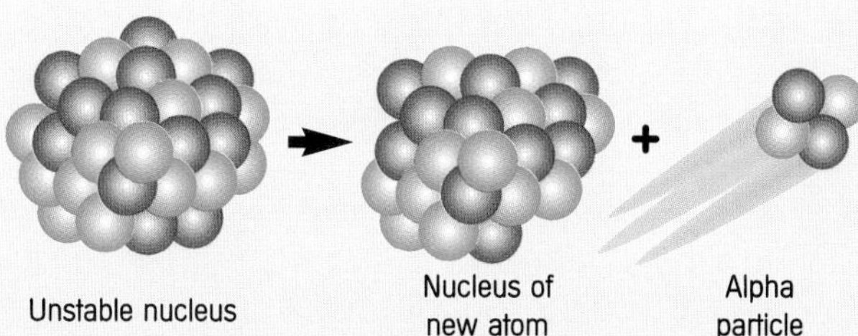

The nucleus of the new atom formed differs from the original one in a number of ways:

- It is a different element.
- It has two fewer protons and two fewer neutrons.
- The atomic number has decreased by two.
- The mass number has decreased by four.

Example – alpha decay of radium-226 into radon-222:

$$ {}^{226}_{88}\text{Ra} \longrightarrow {}^{222}_{86}\text{Rn} + {}^{4}_{2}\alpha $$

N.B. The mass numbers (at the top) and the atomic numbers (at the bottom) balance on both sides.

Beta Emission

During beta emission, the atom decays by changing a neutron into a **proton** and an **electron**. The high-energy electron ejected from the nucleus is a **beta particle**.

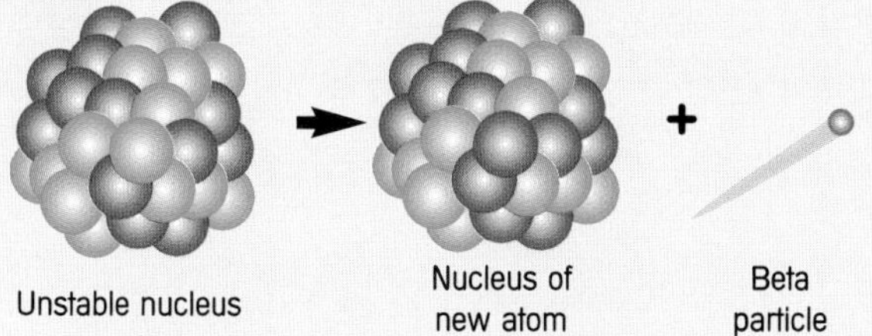

The nucleus of the new atom formed differs from the original one in a number of ways:

- It has one more proton and one less neutron.
- The atomic number has increased by one.
- The mass number remains the same.

Example – beta decay of iodine-131 into xenon-131:

$$ {}^{131}_{53}\text{I} \longrightarrow {}^{131}_{54}\text{Xe} + {}^{0}_{-1}\beta $$

N.B. The mass numbers (at the top) and the atomic numbers (at the bottom) balance on both sides.

What is Radioactivity?

HT Half-Life

Half-life is the time it takes for half the undecayed nuclei in a radioactive substance to decay. If the substance has a very **long half-life** then it remains **active** for a very **long time**.

Igneous rocks can contain uranium atoms which decay to produce stable atoms of lead. It's possible to date rocks by...

- measuring the proportion of uranium and lead in the rock
- knowing the half-life of uranium.

Atoms in a Sample of Radioactive Substance

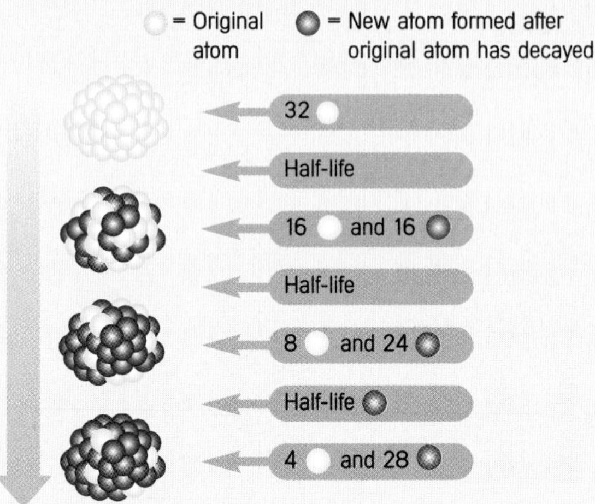

N.B. This is a collection of atoms, not a nucleus.

Calculations Involving Half-Life

Half-life can be calculated using a table or a graph.

Example 1

The table shows the activity of a radioactive substance against time.

Time (min)	0	5	10	15	20	25	30
Activity (Bq)	200	160	124	100	80	62	50

Calculate the half-life of the substance by...

a) using a table

b) drawing a graph.

a) Find an average by choosing three pairs of points between which the activity has halved.

Activity	Time	Half-Life
200 → 100	0 → 15	15 min
160 → 80	5 → 20	15 min
100 → 50	15 → 30	15 min

The half-life is **15 minutes**.

b)

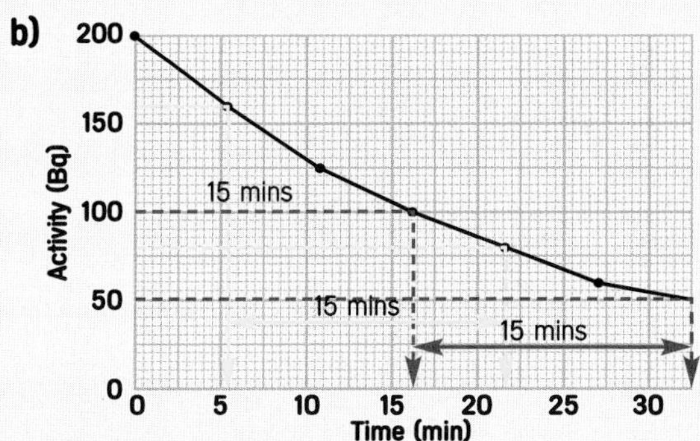

The half-life is **15 minutes**.

Example 2

The half-life of uranium is 700 000 000 years. Uranium forms lead when it decays. A sample is found to contain three times as much lead as uranium. Calculate the age of the sample.

Fraction of lead present is $\frac{3}{4}$. Fraction of uranium present is $\frac{1}{4}$.

Fraction of lead $\left(\frac{3}{4}\right)$ + Fraction of uranium $\left(\frac{1}{4}\right)$ = Original amount of uranium (1).

Work out the number of decays it takes to get $\frac{1}{4}$

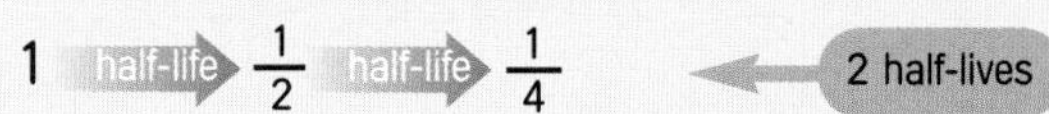

Age of rock = 2 x half-life

= 2 x 700 000 000 years

= 1 400 000 000 years

Uses of Radioisotopes

Background Radiation

Background radiation occurs naturally in our environment and is all around us. Most is released by...

- radioactive substances in soil and rocks
- cosmic rays from outer space.

HT Some background radiation comes from man-made sources and waste products. Industry and hospitals both contribute to background radiation levels.

Tracers

Radioisotopes are used as tracers in industry and hospitals. In industry, tracers are used to...

- track the dispersal of waste
- find leaks and blockages in underground pipes
- find the routes of underground pipes.

HT A radioactive material that emits gamma rays is put into the pipe. (Gamma is used because it can penetrate through to the surface.) The progress of the material is then tracked by a detector above ground. If there is a...

- **leak** – the radioactive material will **escape** and be detected at the surface
- **blockage** – the radioactive material will **stop flowing** so it can't be detected after this point.

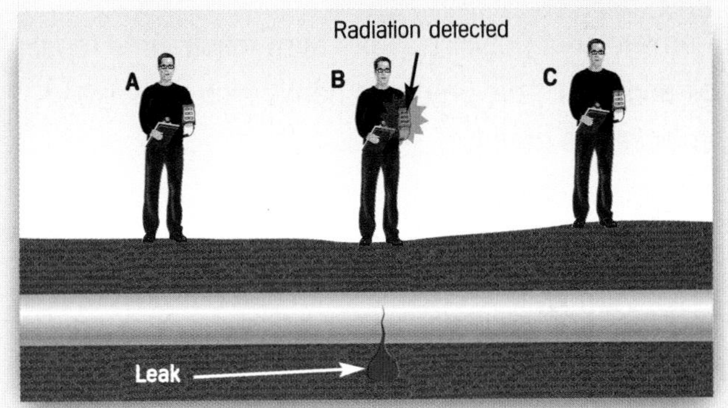

Smoke Detectors

Most smoke detectors contain **americium-241**, an **alpha emitter**. Emitted particles cause air particles to ionise, and the ions formed are attracted to the oppositely charged electrodes. This results in a current flowing.

This is what happens when smoke enters the space between the two electrodes:

1. The alpha particles are absorbed by the smoke particles.
2. Less ionisation takes place.
3. A smaller current than normal now flows, and the alarm sounds.

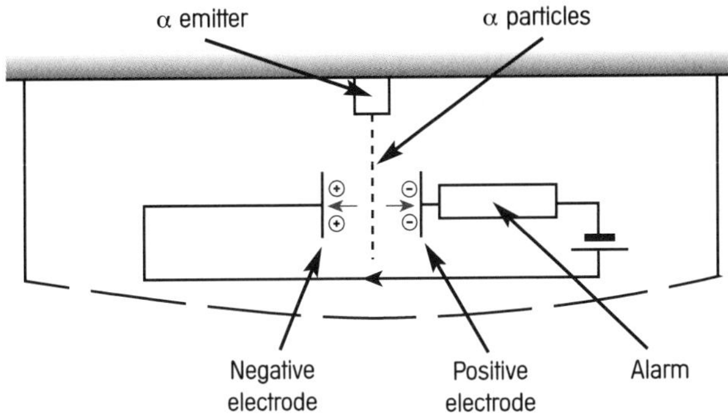

Key Words

Half-life • Radiation • Tracer

Uses of Radioisotopes and Fission

Carbon Dating

A small amount of the carbon in our atmosphere and the bodies of animals and plants is radioactive Carbon-14. **Measurements** from **radioactive carbon** can be used to **date** old materials and rocks.

Key Word

Nuclear Fission

HT The amount of radioactive Carbon-14 in the atmosphere has remained unchanged for thousands of years. A dead object doesn't exchange gases with the air as living matter does. As the Carbon-14 in the dead object **decays**, the radioactivity of the sample **decreases**.

So, the dead object will have a different radioactivity to living matter. The **ratio** of these two activities can be used to find a fairly accurate approximate age for the object.

Producing Electricity

Power stations use **energy sources** to produce electricity.

Conventional power stations **burn fossil fuels** (coal, oil and gas). This produces heat which boils water and creates **steam**.

Nuclear power stations use **uranium**. A nuclear reaction takes place which produces the heat required to make **steam**.

Both power stations then **use the steam** to drive turbines, which turn generators and produce electricity.

Nuclear Reactor

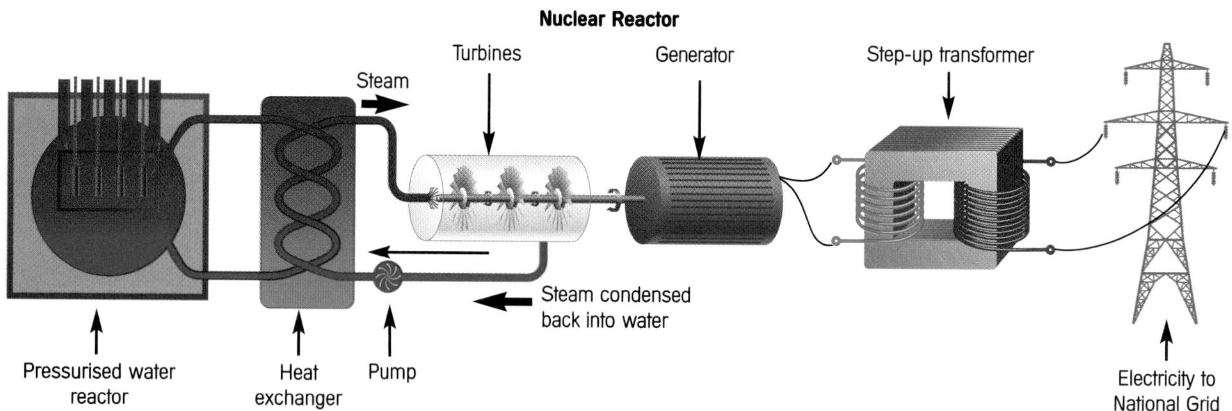

Fission

Nuclear fission is the process by which heat energy (using uranium) is given out in a nuclear reactor. **The decay of uranium** can be a **chain reaction**.

When the uranium nucleus absorbs a single neutron, it becomes radioactive and splits, releasing heat energy and more neutrons. These neutrons cause more uranium nuclei to split and so the **chain reaction** continues.

A nuclear bomb is a chain reaction that has gone out of control. It results in the release of **one powerful burst of energy**.

Nuclear fission produces radioactive waste, which can be very dangerous.

HT Small Scale Nuclear Fission

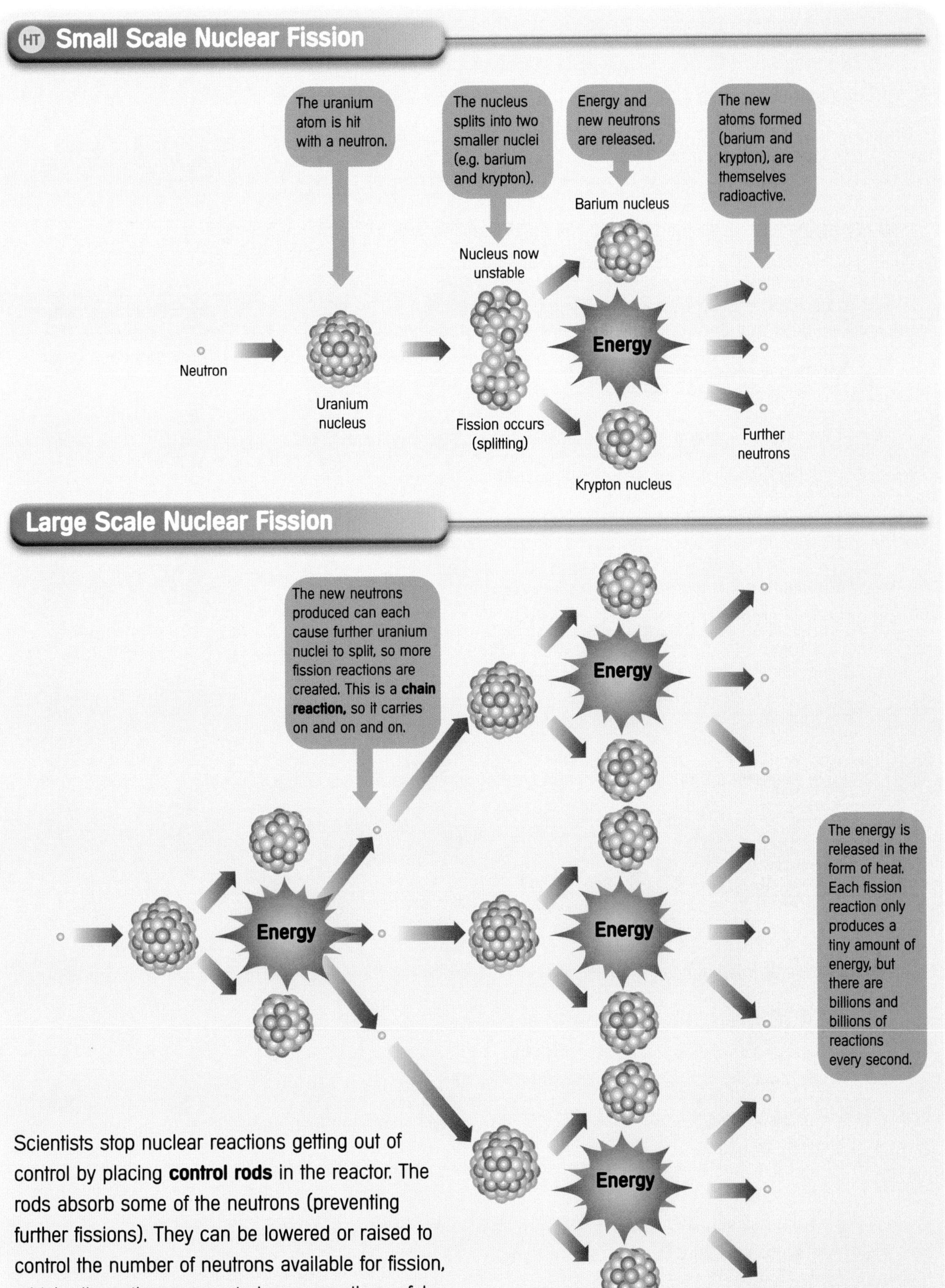

Scientists stop nuclear reactions getting out of control by placing **control rods** in the reactor. The rods absorb some of the neutrons (preventing further fissions). They can be lowered or raised to control the number of neutrons available for fission, which allows the process to keep operating safely.

Module P4 Practice Questions

1 **a)** Fill in the missing words in the following sentence:

An .... material can become electrically .... when rubbed with another .... material.

b) *The build up of charge is due to the transfer of positive electrons.* Is this statement **true** or **false**?

....

c) Draw lines between the boxes to link each situation with its correct outcome.

Two positively charged rods are brought together.	They attract each other.
A positive rod and a negative rod are brought together.	They repel each other.
Two negatively charged rods are brought together.	

d) List two ways in which electrostatics are being used in your school.

i) .... **ii)** ....

2 Put the following sentences into the correct order by numbering them **1** to **4**.

a) The appliance is undamaged. ☐

b) The fuse wire heats up and melts. ☐

c) A fault occurs, causing the current in the appliance to increase. ☐

d) The circuit is broken so the current is unable to flow. ☐

3 Draw lines between the boxes to link each type of wire to its correct colour.

Neutral	Green and yellow
Earth	Brown
Live	Blue

4 *Double insulated appliances require neither a fuse nor an earth wire.* Is this statement **true** or **false**?

Explain your answer. ....

5 **a)** Fill in the missing words in the following sentence.

When using a fixed resister, the .... will increase when the voltage ....

b) i) A 12V supply causes a current of 0.3A to flow through a bulb. Calculate the resistance.

....

HT **ii)** The bulb is replaced by one with a resistance of 80Ω. What is the new current in the circuit?

....

6 What is the frequency range of ultrasound? ....

HT 7 What is the name of the waves which move particles backwards and forwards, about their normal position, in the same direction as the wave movement?

....

8 **a)** Complete the table.

Medical Use	Type of Radiation Used
Tracers	**i)**
Bone imaging	**ii)**
Cancer treatment	**iii)**
Sterilising equipment	**iv)**

b) List three main sources of background radiation.

i) .... **ii)** .... **iii)** ....

HT **c)** What kind of emission leaves behind a new element, with one less neutron but the same mass number?

....

d) If the half-life of a radioactive sample is 8 days, what fraction will be left after 32 days?

....

....

e) *Animals that have been dead for a significant period of time will contain less carbon-14 than living ones.* Is this statement **true** or **false**? Explain your answer.

....

9 The following sentences describe how power stations convert fuel into electricity. Put them into the correct order by numbering them **1** to **4**.

a) The steam turns the turbines. ☐

b) Fuel is burned, generating heat. ☐

c) This movement produces electricity in the generators. ☐

d) The heat is used to boil water. ☐

HT 10 When the uranium nucleus is split during fission, which particles are responsible for the chain reaction that follows?

....

Glossary of Key Words

Acceleration – the rate at which an object increases in speed.

Acid – a substance that has a pH value lower than 7.

Air resistance – the frictional force that acts on a moving object.

Alkali – a substance that has a pH value higher than 7.

Amplitude – the maximum disturbance caused by a wave.

Artery – a type of blood vessel that transports blood away from the heart.

Atom – the smallest part of an element which can enter into chemical reactions.

Atomic number – the number of protons in an atom.

Attraction – the drawing together of materials with different charges.

Auxin – a plant hormone that affects the growth and development of the plant.

Base – a substance that will neutralise an acid.

Batch process – a process where chemicals are added into a container, the reaction takes place, and the products are removed before a new reaction is started.

Biological control – the introduction of a predator to kill pests.

Biomass – the mass of matter in a living organism.

Capillary – a type of blood vessel where the exchange of materials takes place.

Carbon cycle – the constant recycling of carbon by the processes in life, death and decay.

Catalyst – a substance that speeds up a chemical reaction without being changed itself.

Chlorophyll – the green pigment found in most plants, responsible for photosynthesis.

Cholesterol – a type of fat that builds up in the walls of arteries.

Chromosome – a long strand of DNA found in the nucleus.

Clone – a genetically identical copy of a plant or animal.

Compound – a substance consisting of two or more elements chemically combined together.

Consumers – organisms that eat other organisms.

Continuous process – a process that doesn't stop; reactants are fed in at one end and products are removed at the other end at the same time.

Covalent bond – a bond between two atoms in which a pair of electrons is shared.

Current – the rate of flow of an electrical charge, measured in amperes (A).

Cytoplasm – the substance found in living cells (outside the nucleus) where chemical reactions take place.

Denatured – the state of an enzyme that has been destroyed by heat and can no longer work.

Detritivores – organisms that feed on dead organisms and the waste of living organisms.

Detritus – waste material produced by living organisms.

Differentiation – a process by which simple plant or animal cells become specialised to perform a specific function.

Diffusion – the movement of particles from high concentration to low concentration.

Diploid – a cell which has two sets (pairs) of chromosomes.

Distance–Time graph – a graph showing distance travelled against time taken; the gradient of the line represents speed.

DNA (deoxyribonucleic acid) – molecule which contains the genetic information carried by every cell.

DNA fingerprinting – an identification technique using a person's unique DNA.

Earthed – connecting the metal case of an electrical appliance to the earth wire of a plug.

Egestion – the removal of waste products from an animal's body.

Electrode – a piece of metal or carbon (graphite) which allows electric current to enter and leave during electrolysis.

Electrolysis – the process by which an electric current causes a solution to undergo chemical decomposition.

Glossary of Key Words

Electrolyte – a liquid or solution that conducts electricity.

Electromagnetic waves – includes radio waves, visible light and gamma, all of which travel through a vacuum at the speed of light.

Electron – a negatively charged particle that orbits the nucleus of an atom.

Element – a substance made up of one type of atom.

Enzyme – a biological catalyst that speeds up reactions.

Exothermic – a reaction that gives out energy (heat) to its surroundings.

Fertilisation – the fusion of a male gamete with a female gamete.

Force – a push or pull acting on an object.

Frequency – the number of waves produced (or that pass a particular point) in one second.

Friction – the resistive force between two surfaces as they move over each other.

Fuse – a thin piece of metal which overheats and melts to break an electric circuit if it's overloaded.

Gamete – specialised sex cell.

Gene – a small section of DNA in a chromosome which determines a particular characteristic by coding for a particular protein.

Genetic engineering – the alteration of the genetic make-up of an organism.

Gravitational potential energy (GPE) – the energy an object has because of its mass and height above the Earth.

Gravity – a force of attraction between masses.

Group – a vertical column of elements in the periodic table.

Haemoglobin – the red pigment inside red blood cells that carries oxygen.

Half-life – the time taken for half the atoms in radioactive material to decay.

Halide – a compound of a halogen.

Halogens – elements in Group 7 of the periodic table.

Haploid – a cell which has only one set of chromosomes.

Hormone – chemical signal which controls processes inside an animal or plant.

Hydroponics – a method of growing plants without using soil.

Insoluble – a substance that is unable to dissolve in a solvent.

Ion – charged particle formed when an atom or group of atoms gains or loses electrons.

Ionic bond – the process by which two or more atoms lose or gain electrons to become charged ions and are then held together by forces of attraction.

Isotopes – atoms of the same element which contain different numbers of neutrons.

Kinetic energy (KE) – the energy possessed by an object because of its movement.

Longitudinal wave – an energy-carrying wave where the particles move in the direction of energy transfer.

Mass – the quantity of matter in an object.

Mass number – the total number of protons and neutrons in an atom.

Meiosis – cell division that forms daughter cells with half the number of chromosomes as the parent cell.

Mitochondria – the structures in the cytoplasm where energy is produced from respiration reactions.

Mitosis – cell division that forms two daughter cells, each with the same number of chromosomes as the parent cell.

Mutation – a change in the genetic material of a cell.

Nanochemistry – a branch of science that deals with materials at their atomic level.

Neutralisation – a reaction between an acid and a base which forms a neutral solution.

Neutron – a particle found in the nucleus of an atom that has no electrical charge.

Nitrogen cycle – the constant recycling of nitrogen by the processes in life, death and decay.

Nuclear fission – the splitting of atomic nuclei.

Nucleus – the control centre of a cell.

Osmosis – the movement of water through a partially permeable membrane from high to low concentration of water.

Period – a horizontal row of elements in the periodic table.

Glossary of Key Words

Phloem – tissue that carries nutrients around a plant.
Photosynthesis – the chemical process that uses light energy to produce glucose in plants.
Pollutant – a substance that contaminates the environment.
Power – a measure of how quickly work is done.
Precipitate – insoluble solid formed during a reaction involving solutions.
Precipitation – the process of forming a precipitate by mixing solutions.
Producers – organisms that produce biomass when they photosynthesise, i.e. green plants.
Product – a substance produced in a reaction.
Proteins – large organic compounds made of amino acids.
Proton – a positively charged particle found in the nucleus of an atom.
Radiation – electromagnetic waves given out by an object.
Reactant – a starting material in a reaction.
Reduction – a reaction involving the loss of oxygen or the gain of electrons.
Relative atomic mass (A_r) – the average mass of atoms of an element compared with $\frac{1}{12}$ of a carbon atom.
Relative formula mass (M_r) – the sum of the atomic masses of all atoms in a molecule.
Repulsion – the pushing away of materials which have the same charge.
Resistance – the measure of how hard it is to get a current through a component at a particular potential difference.
Respiration – the process of releasing energy from glucose inside cells.
Reversible reaction – a reaction in which products can react to reform the original reactants.
Salt – the product of a chemical reaction between a base and an acid.
Saturated fat – a fat which contains only single carbon–carbon bonds (i.e. no double bonds).
Selective breeding – where animals are deliberately mated to produce offspring with desirable characteristics.
Soluble – a substance that can dissolve in a solvent.
Solution – the mixture formed when a solute dissolves in a solvent.
Solvent – a liquid that can dissolve another substance to produce a solution.
Specialised – developed for a special function.
Speed – how far an object travels in a given time.
Speed–Time graph – a graph showing speed against time; the gradient of the line represents acceleration.
Static electricity – electricity that is produced by friction and doesn't move.
Stem cells – cells from human embryos or adult bone marrow which have yet to differentiate.
Stomata – tiny openings on a plant leaf used for gas exchange.
Terminal speed – a steady falling speed, when the weight of an object is equal and opposite to its air resistance.
Tracer – a radioactive substance which can be followed and detected.
Translocation – the transportation of food through phloem in plants.
Transpiration – the evaporation of water from plants, especially from their leaves.
Ultrasound – sound waves with a frequency above 20 000Hz.
Universal indicator – a mixture of pH indicators, used to measure the pH of a solution.
Vein – a type of blood vessel that transports blood towards the heart.
Voltage (potential difference) – the energy transferred in a circuit by each Coulomb of charge.
Wavelength – the distance between corresponding points on two adjacent disturbances.
Weight – the gravitational force that pulls an object towards the centre of the Earth.
Xylem – tissue that transports water and mineral ions in a plant from the roots to the shoots.
Yield – the amount of a product obtained from a reaction.
Zygote – a cell formed by the fusion of the nuclei of a male sex cell and female sex cell (gametes).

Glossary of Key Words

HT **Active transport** – the movement of substances against a concentration gradient requiring energy.

Allotropes – different forms of the same element with atoms arranged in different molecular structures.

Crenated – the shrivelling up of an animal cell due to lack of water.

Distillation – a process used to separate liquids by evaporation followed by condensation to produce a pure liquid.

Eutrophication – excessive growth of algae due to the enrichment of water with minerals from fertilisers.

Flaccid – a plant cell that isn't rigid.

Hydrophilic – water loving.

Hydrophobic – water hating.

Lysis – the bursting of an animal cell due to too much water being taken in by osmosis.

Oxidation – a reaction involving the gain of oxygen or loss of electrons.

Oxyhaemoglobin – haemoglobin with oxygen bound on.

Plasmolysis – the contraction of the inside of plant cells due to the loss of water.

Saprophytes – bacteria and fungi that feed on dead organic material.

Surface area : volume ratio – the relationship between surface area and volume of a living organism. Small organisms (or cells) have a large SA:V ratio which increases the rate of diffusion.

Synapse – the gap between neurones.

Transverse wave – a wave where the vibrations are at 90° to the direction of energy transfer.

Turgid – a rigid plant cell.

Acknowledgements

The authors and publisher would like to thank everyone who has contributed to this book:

p.20 ©iStockphoto.com / Stas Perov
p.90 ©iStockphoto.com / Dar Yang Yan

ISBN 978-1-905896-29-5

Published by Lonsdale, a division of Huveaux Plc.

Authors: Robert Johnson, Steve Langfield, Jacquie Punter

Project Editor: Charlotte Christensen

Cover Design: Angela English

Concept Design: Sarah Duxbury and Helen Jacobs

Designer: Ian Wrigley

Artwork: Lonsdale and HL Studios

Author information

Robert Johnson (Physics) is a full-time teacher of physics at a respected co-educational public school. He has an innovative approach towards teaching, which makes physics relevant and interesting.

Steve Langfield (Chemistry) has been a science teacher for over 20 years and is an experienced examiner and moderator. He currently works as a science coordinator at a designated Specialist Science School, at the forefront of innovation in science and mathematics.

Jacquie Punter (Biology) has taught biology at Key Stages 4 and 5 for over 17 years. She has also taught health and social care and has an excellent understanding of the practical applications of science and its impact on society.

Answers to Practice Questions

Module B3

1. Mitochondrion — Releases energy from food through respiration
   Nucleus — Contains DNA (genetic information)
   Cell membrane — Controls the movement of substances in and out of the cell
   Cytoplasm — Where chemical reactions happen in the cell
2. **a)** True; **b)** False; **c)** False; **d)** True
3. The sequence of bases dictates the sequence of amino acids in the protein. This is what makes proteins different.
4. **a)** They speed reaction rates up.
   b) Temperature; pH levels.
   c) It is the temperature the enzyme works best at.
   d) The enzyme would be denatured and would be unable to work, so the reaction would slow down.
5. **a)** The movement of molecules from an area of high concentration to an area of low concentration.
   b) Accept any two: Surface area of the cell; Concentration gradient (difference in concentration between high concentration and low concentration); The distance particles have to travel (the shorter the better).
6. Millions of alveoli create large surface area, wall of alveolus only one cell thick, good blood supply to transport substances.
7. Platelets; Plasma; White blood cells; Red blood cells.
8. **a)** Arteries **b)** To cope with high pressure generated by the heart.
9. **Accept any two**: Major, expensive operation; Long waiting time for suitable donor; Patient needs immunosuppressants for rest of life.
10. Single-celled organisms have a small surface area : volume ratio so the rate of diffusion of substances into and out of the cell is slow. Multi-cellular organisms have many smaller cells which increase the surface area for diffusion and speed up reactions inside the cell.
11. The process by which a diploid cell divides to produce two more diploid cells.
12. False
13. GM foods may not be safe to eat in the long term; Genetically modified plants may cross-breed with wild plants and release their new genes into the environment.
14. Embryos used are produced by animal parents with desired characteristics. The embryonic cells are transplanted into the uteruses of surrogate females. The females give birth to clones.

Module C3

1. **a)** Covalent bonding.
   b) One magnesium atom, 2 nitrogen atoms and six oxygen atoms.
   c) $2Na + 2H_2O \rightarrow 2NaOH + H_2$
   d) $AgNO_3$
2. **a)** Positive
   b) Atoms of the same element with different numbers of neutrons.
   c) There are equal numbers of protons and electrons.
3. **a)** A charged atom or group of atoms.
   b) Add 2 electrons.
   c) Accept any two: High melting point; High boiling point; Conducts electricity in solution when molten but not when solid.
   d) $Fe_2(SO_4)_3$
4. **a)** Non metals.
   b) There aren't any charged particles to carry the electricity.
   c) Group 4, Period 3.
5. **a)** They react with air and water.
   b) Lithium + Water → Lithium hydroxide + Hydrogen
   c) Potassium; **d)** $2K + 2H_2O \rightarrow 2KOH + H_2$
6. **a)** Chlorine
   b) Sodium iodide + Chlorine → Sodium chloride + Iodine
   c) $2NaI + Cl_2 \rightarrow 2NaCl + I_2$
   d) $Br_2 \rightarrow 2Br^- + 2e^-$
7. **a)** A liquid or solution that conducts electricity.
   b) Positive
   c) Aluminium oxide → Aluminium + Oxygen
   d) $Al^{3+} + 3e^- \xrightarrow{\text{Reduction}} Al$
8. **a)** Breaking up a substance using heat.
   b) Copper carbonate → Copper oxide + Carbon dioxide
   c) Iron (III)
9. **a)** It is strong.
   b) They have delocalised electrons in the structure which can move and carry the charge.
   c) A material that conducts electricity with very little or no resistance. But, they only work at very low temperatures.
   d) The strong forces holding the closely packed positive metal ions and delocalised electrons together.

Module P3

1. **a)** How much distance is covered every second.
   b) Speed $= \frac{400}{20} = 20m/s$
   c) Time $= \frac{\text{Distance}}{\text{Speed}} = \frac{400}{40} = 10s$
2. **a)** False – it is stationary.
   b) True – as time passes, more distance is being travelled each second.
3. **a) In any order**: Change in speed; Time taken
   b) Straight line with a positive gradient — Acceleration.
   Straight line with a negative gradient — Deceleration.
   Horizontal straight line — Constant speed.
4. **a) In any order**: Gravity; Friction; Air resistance
   b) F = 1500 x 5 = 7500N
5. The road is icy — Only the braking distance is increased.
   The driver is drunk — Only the thinking distance is increased.
   The car is travelling too fast — Both the thinking and breaking distance will be increased.
6. **a) In any order**: Force applied; Distance moved
   b) Time $= \frac{\text{Work done}}{\text{Power}} = \frac{30\,000}{1000} = 30s$
7. **a)** mass; speed
   b) Kinetic energy = $0.5 \times 2000 \times 20^2 = 400\,000J$
8. **Accept any three**: Electric windows; Adjustable seating; Cruise control; Paddle shift controls.
9. **a)** 2; **b)** 4; **c)** 1; **d)** 3
10. **a)** i) A dog sitting by the side of a road.
    b) doubled; quadrupled.
    c) Height $= \frac{\text{Potential energy}}{(\text{mass x g})} = \frac{30}{(0.1 \times 10)} = 30m$
    d) Weight = 0.08 x 10 = 0.8N

Answers to Practice Questions

Module B4

1. **a)** ii) Through the roots.
   b) Diffusion
   c) They have a single layer of cells close to upper surface of the leaf to absorb the maximum amount of sunlight.
2. The diffusion of water from a high to low concentration of water through a partially-permeable membrane.
3. Inelastic; turgor; osmosis; turgid; flaccid; plasmolysis
4. Transpiration is the process by which water travels through plants and eventually evaporates out of stomata on the leaves. The plant uses transpiration to draw water (and dissolved minerals) from the soil to supply the plant's needs.
5. Less water. A humid atmosphere decreases the rate of transpiration, so the plant would have taken in less water to replace water loss.
6. Phosphates
7. The absorption of substance from a low to high concentration, i.e. against a concentration gradient.
8. **a)** Sunlight
   b) Accept any two: Movement; Respiration; Waste materials; Heat
9. The layers of the pyramid represent the mass of living material at each trophic level.
10. c) It decreases
11. **Accept any two**: Fast-growing trees; Manure; Corn or sugar cane; Bio-ethanol
12. False
13. **a)** Temperature; Oxygen; Water
    b) They break waste down into small particles so there is a large surface area for decomposers to feed on.
14. **Accept any two**: Sealing – prevents microorganisms getting air for respiration; Storing at low temperatures – slows down growth of microorganisms; Pickling – destroys microorganisms' enzymes; Storing in salt or sugar – makes conditions too concentrated; Drying – removes moisture.

Module C4

1. **a)** One nitrogen atom and three hydrogen atoms.
   b) Hydrochloric acid – HCl; Nitric acid – HNO_3; Sulfuric acid – H_2SO_4
   c) Ammonium sulfate.
2. **a)** It starts off with a pH greater than 7, falls through to pH7 and then ends up a pH below 7.
   b) i) Sodium nitrate **ii)** Ammonium nitrate **iii)** Copper nitrate
   c) H^+
3. **a) i)** 106 **ii)** 132
   b) 60%
4. **a)** Nitrogen
   b) They use up all the oxygen in the water.
   c) 21.2%
5. **a) In any order**: Nitrogen; Hydrogen
   b) A reversible reaction.
   c) The reaction would be too slow.
6. **a)** To help the water drain off the crockery so it dries quickly.
   b) The hydrophobic end of the washing-up liquid detergent is repelled by water, causing it to stick to the grease droplets. As more and more detergent molecules are absorbed into the grease, it is eventually lifted off the plate. When the molecule is totally surrounded, it can be washed away, leaving the plate clean.
7. **a)** The materials for the new drug could be rare or may require expensive extraction from plants.
   b) Accept any two: You can make a product quickly on demand; You can make a product on a small scale; The equipment can be used to make a variety of products.
8. **a)** Carbon.
   b) It has free (delocalised) electrons.
   c) Diamond is made of carbon atoms bonded to four other carbon atoms by strong covalent bonds. It has a high melting point because of the large number of covalent bonds. It doesn't have any free electrons so it doesn't conduct electricity.
9. **a) In any order**: As a raw material; As a coolant; As a solvent
   b) Add silver nitrate solution, and a white precipitate indicates that chloride ions are present.
   c) $BaCl_2 + K_2SO_4 \rightarrow BaSO_4 + 2KCl$

Module P4

1. **a)** insulating; charged; insulating.
   b) False
   c) Two positively charged rods are brought together – They repel each other.
   A positive rod and a negative rod are brought together – They attract each other.
   Two negatively charged rods are brought together – They repel each other.
   d) Accept any suitable answer, e.g. laser printers; photocopiers
2. **a)** 4; **b)** 2; **c)** 1; **d)** 3
3. Neutral – Blue; Earth – Green and yellow; Live – Brown
4. False. They still require a fuse to protect the appliance.
5. **a)** current; increases.
   b) i) R = V/I = 12/0.3 = 40 ohms
   ii) I = V/R = 12/80 = 0.15A
6. Above 20 000Hz
7. Longitudinal
8. **a) i)** Beta/Gamma; **ii)** X-rays; **iii)** Gamma; **iv)** Gamma
   b) Accept three suitable answers, e.g. soil; rocks; cosmic rays
   c) Beta emission.
   d) $\frac{32}{8} = 4$ half lives. $\frac{1}{2} \times \frac{1}{2} \times \frac{1}{2} \times \frac{1}{2} = \frac{1}{16}$
   e) True. Carbon-14 is radioactive, so decays away. When animals stop breathing they no longer renew carbon-14 in their bodies so their level goes down.
9. **a)** 3; **b)** 1; **c)** 4; **d)** 2
10. Neutrons

Index